Digital
Citizenship

Digital
Citizenship

Promoting Wellness For Thriving in a Connected World

Alfonzo Porter

Vertex Learning, LLC
www.vertexlearning.com

Washington DC ▪ Atlanta ▪ Denver ▪ St. Louis ▪ Dayton-Cincinnati ▪ San Diego

Digital Citizenship: *Promoting Wellness for Thriving in a Connected World*
Vertex Learning, LLC Educational Research, Publishing, and Consulting
Copyright © 2018 by Alfonzo Porter.
All Rights Reserved.

Published by Vertex Learning, LLC, Hyattsville, MD 20875 USA
The rights of Alfonzo Porter to be identified as the author of this work has been asserted in accordance with the U.S.
Copyright Act of 1976, Pub. L. No. 95-533, 90 Stat. 2541, Title 17.
No part of this publication may be reproduced, stored in a retrieval system or transmitted in any form or by any means
electronic, mechanical, photocopying or otherwise without the prior written permission of the author.

For more information on Vertex Learning, LLC Educational Research, Publishing and Consulting
Visit our website at www.vertexlearning.com

ISBN: 978-1-64007-357-9

Editor-In-Chief: Deborah Sherman

Editorial Assistants:

Rachel Oliva
Lucas Cardona
Taylor Oxenfeld
Alaysha Powell
Brennen Sampson
Joshua Graham

Library of Congress Cataloging-in-Publication Data
Porter, Alfonzo
Digital Citizenship: Promoting Wellness for Thriving in a Connected World

ISBN: 978-1-64007-357-9

Printed and bound in the United States of America

Discounts on this title may be available at the author's discretion available in bulk orders:
Contact Vertex Learning at:

www.vertexlearning.com

CONTENTS

———————●———————

INTRODUCTION

DESIGN RATIONALE

This text—Digital Wellness and Citizenship—is designed to be a resource written "for teachers, by a teacher." All told, the author has more than 30 years of classroom experience drawing from a variety of content areas and disciplines. He remains very conscious of the competing demands on teachers' time and developed a text he hopes will provide educators with resources and activities that can be easily customized to meet the specific and unique needs of students enrolled in their classrooms. To this end, the textbook is structured to more closely resemble the organization of a curriculum rather than a resource meant solely to cover and disseminate standardized content. Each chapter has been organized around the most common teenage online behaviors and their relationship to some of society's most pressing issues related to health, wellness, and what it means to be a citizen. Intended to be modular in nature, the resources and activities included in this text have been designed to give teachers the ability to "pick-and-choose" based on their available time, instructional goals, and teaching style. Stated directly, there isn't "one way" for teachers and students to make use of this text—it has been created to serve as a curriculum, a resource guide, or a set of engaging and relevant activities.

While the text is customizable, the author closely followed a curriculum framework created to promote student engagement, understanding, and transfer of what is learned to situations outside of the classroom. This framework—entitled Understanding by Design[1]—was developed by Grant Wiggins and Jay McTighe to help teachers assist students with making sense of essential concepts, enduring understandings, and real-world skills. To implement this approach, curriculum designers are required to "begin with the end in mind"— by first identifying what students are "expected to learn and be able to do" by the end of each instructional unit[2]. This curricular approach differs significantly from other methods that traditionally start the design process chronologically at the beginning of a course or unit. Like Wiggins and McTighe, the author believes working "backward" from what students need to be able to learn, understand, and apply at the end of a unit provides teachers and curriculum designers with a strategic process to improve how we create activities, sequence learning experiences, and develop assessments. Additionally, resources and activities suggested in this text were developed to help teachers foster a student-centered classroom—drawing on learning principles from cognitive and social constructivism[3] –to create classrooms built around students' active discussions, collaborations, and discoveries of knowledge while investigating questions they find personally meaningful.

CHAPTER STRUCTURE

Each chapter can be considered a curriculum unit and has been structured so teenagers can become aware of how some of their most common behaviors are associated with a wide range of unintended physical, mental, and ethical considerations. To promote awareness of these risks, the author has drawn heavily on relevant content standards written by established and respected health and civics professional associations. These standards are listed at the beginning of each recommended learning task and are intended to frame how both teachers and students interact with included resources and activities. Students' framing of the problem is further supported by essential questions written to provoke an open-ended investigation into concepts and themes frequently underlying these common behaviors that are already having a historic impact on their lives.

BEHAVIORS AND THEMES

Following these essential questions, each chapter begins by describing the scale and scope of one common online behavior and the potential impact on teenagers' developing social, mental, and physical lives. In total, the author has condensed his research into five to six topic descriptions to provide teachers and students with a compressed and concise overview. These descriptions, while comprehensive, are not intended to be an exhaustive summary of research, but rather as a launching point for students to begin their own investigations of the online behaviors outlined in each chapter. We have provided teachers with a considerable number of footnotes within each of these topic descriptions to allow for review and evaluation. Additionally, these topic descriptions have been developed so teachers can have their students readily form Jigsaw Expert Groups[4] to collaboratively research and share their understanding of separate but related facets of a behavior. To those unfamiliar with the strategy, Jigsaw Groups are a cooperative learning strategy[5] created to place students in the center of their own learning, increase equity in the classroom while also improving learning and motivational outcomes. Finally, we provide teachers with key concepts to help students evaluate, analyze, and apply underlying mechanisms in relation to these common, but frequently overlooked, online behaviors.

REAL-WORLD SITUATIONS, LEARNING SCENARIOS, TIPS FOR WELLNESS

To anchor students' developing comprehension, the author has provided teachers with real-world situations intended to both extend and personalize students' understanding of how these common actions can have direct, immediate, and even long-standing consequences in their lives. The real-world situations included in this text were curated from an extensive search of emerging resources and include links to the originally sourced material. These situations were selected to provide students with additional context, meaning and relevance as they make sense of these frequently complex and personal issues. Preceding each of the selected real-world situations is a set of guiding questions written to scaffold and support students' reading of the source material. In addition to promoting comprehension, these guiding questions were written to provide teachers with prompts to be used to facilitate both small and whole-group discussions. Following these real-world situations, the author has also provided teachers with three learning scenarios that place students in situations that trigger a first-person perspective to allow for critical rehearsal, practice, and revision in one's decision-making. Finally, at the end of each chapter, the author supplies teachers with three to four tips for wellness that have been collected from existing best practices in the field and can provide students with needed suggestions and strategies.

LEARNING TASKS

The author has concluded each chapter by providing teachers with three kinds of learning tasks designed to help students' make sense of how common online behaviors can significantly impact their lives inside and outside of schools. As mentioned previously, these learning tasks were designed with teachers in mind and created to fit within competing demands on their time. The first suggested learning task in each chapter is a 20-minute discussion of the chapter's essential questions designed specifically to engage as wide an audience of students as possible (by not privileging students with extensive background knowledge). The author highly recommends teachers use a Think-Pair-Share[6] participatory structure to debrief these questions and establish a classroom routine that prioritizes students' questions, beliefs, and assumptions to start their learning experience. To those unfamiliar, Think-Pair-Share is another cooperative learning strategy (like Jigsaw Groups) created to help students individually reflect on their beliefs and assumptions, advance their comprehension with the aid of a small group of classmates, and finally share, justify, and defend (if necessary) this developing understanding within a whole class discussion. Building on this 20-minute discussion, the author provides teachers with a second suggested learning task created to fit one day—either period or block—requiring students to apply what they've learned within the context of a real-world role, like policymaker or public advocate. These daylong activities are designed to provide teachers with the kinds of authentic learning experiences educational researchers have found promote students' transfer of what is learned in the classroom to their lives outside of school[11]. Finally, moving beyond the one-day activity, the author provides teachers with a third suggested learning task designed to fit within the time span of one week. These extended learning experiences—created to be implemented alongside regularly scheduled weekly activities – were created to provide teachers and students with the deepest opportunity to make sense of the resources and activities outlined in each chapter. These one-week tasks are differentiated from their one-day counterparts by requiring students to move into the world outside of the classroom to act as experts, advocates, and responsible citizens.

As mentioned previously, the sections within this text were created to provide teachers with a wide range of instructional choices to best suit their students' needs and interests. If a teacher wanted, these suggested learning tasks could be implemented in the sequence provided or remixed completely to reflect their personal teaching style. However, using backward design, the author created these activities with a specific curriculum sequence in mind—he envisioned teachers beginning each chapter with the suggested 20-minute discussion and concluding with either the one-day or one-week learning tasks if time allowed. To facilitate this flexibility, every activity has links to supporting resources that provide teachers access to a set of pre-approved materials that can be immediately used by students to begin their inquiry. In this way, the author also hoped to provide teachers with a variety of resources to help them better differentiate their instruction to meet their students' range of learning and motivational needs. Finally, the author structured each learning task in a way that readily provides teachers with the design rationale, applicable standards, intended learning outcomes, and sequence of activities needed to justify these topics inclusion and coverage within any mandated curriculum.

DIGITAL LIFE

It is hard to dispute that a majority of teenagers have access to multiple electronic devices and spend a considerable amount of time each day online and in front of screens. In fact, a number of organizations, including the technology education non-profit Common Sense Media, report that many teens are spending, on average, nearly nine hours a day checking social media, watching TV, videos and movies, playing video games, texting, reading, and/or listening to music. Even though widespread access to both digital technology and the Internet make many aspects of day-to-day life more convenient, non-stop media consumption has the potential to impact our personal safety, finances and relationships, school and job performance, and even physical and mental health. With society's rapidly expanding reliance on technology, there is genuine need for engaged conversation with teenagers' about two distinct, but interrelated dynamics that are at the core of this book: online behavior and online decision-making. It is important to be able to identify and examine those online behaviors that have become so commonplace we do not even notice them most of the time. Additionally, because these behaviors are so routine and habitual, the implications, risks, and consequences of these behaviors are not often discussed in ways that can help teenagers develop deeper understanding of how to make responsible and ethical decisions. This text aims to provide a curricular framework for doing just that – facilitating meaningful dialogue and reflection with teenagers about their online behavior as well as how to improve decision-making when utilizing digital technology.

DIGITAL WELL-BEING

Digital Well-Being promotes the development of the knowledge, skills and habits that facilitate a healthy, ethical, and responsible use of digital technology. This concept provides a frame that can be used to engage and support students in examining their online behaviors and decision-making in a society where technology is ever present, always accessible, and highly impactful. While digital technology creates new and unique ways for us to communicate with one another and even provides access to different forms of community, where we may not always see one another but can share our lives, there are definitely concerns that need to be addressed. Moreover, because teenagers spend a great deal of time online without supervision or guidance from a trusted adult, there is a need for individual accountability that requires thoughtful, intentional decision-making. An exploration of digital well-being will also help students understand potential dangers, impact, and challenges that they will most certainly encounter as they navigate the digital landscape and spend more and more time online and engaged with technology. Teenagers, like adults, do not always make the right choices when online or fully understand the effects of how they communicate with others in virtual spaces. Hence, it is imperative that they have meaningful opportunities to reflect on their behaviors when using technology so they can thoughtfully consider the impact within their own lives. This recognition will serve as a foundation in developing productive strategies to improve personal decision-making. Ultimately, we want students to use digital technology to connect, learn, pursue interests, collaborate, and communicate in responsible, ethical, and safe ways.

DIGITAL CITIZENSHIP

The concept of digital citizenship advances the ideals of citizenship in a democratic society to the digital environment. These ideals include respectful, informed communication, tolerance of various voices and opinions, equity for all individuals, and responsibility for one's actions. Technology use has increased among teenagers and the current generation spends more time communicating and engaging in content via the digital world than any previous generation. With this increased use, it has become imperative for teenagers to develop constructive citizenship skills in the technological environment. Without intentional instruction and guidance, teenagers may lack the skills and knowledge necessary to make good decisions in relation to interacting with one another and engaging with content in the digital world. Further, teenagers may unknowingly encounter dangerous individuals or groups online, which can have a devastating impact on their health and well-being for the short and long term. Transferring respect, tolerance, equity and responsibility to the digital environment will allow youth to make healthy choices for themselves and others. The content of this book and thought-provoking interactive activities are designed to facilitate knowledge of digital citizenship and promote the choices and habits needed to engage as skilled and responsible citizens in the digital environment.

DIGITAL HYGIENE

Most of us think about (or are at least aware of) effective hygiene habits such as washing our hands, brushing our teeth before bed, not drinking after someone who is sick, etc. Practicing such habits increase our chances of remaining healthy. Rarely do we apply the concept of health to the digital world. Yet, our digital foot print is just as important to our personal health and well-being. Digital hygiene means practicing healthy routines in the digital environment, such as checking privacy settings, creating secure passwords, protecting our identity, and knowing when to disengage in technology. While it is tempting to identify specific activities that are good for our health and those that are bad for our health in the digital world, this is not feasible and would oversimplify the issue. Digital hygiene is somewhat subjective and healthy practices exist along a continuum in which teenagers must constantly balance the benefits and trade-offs of online activity. Many technological activities in which teenagers partake are healthy and, in fact, beneficial when the requisite habits for a safe and healthy digital footprint are utilized. Developing knowledge is the first step in promoting well-being in an online environment. Establishing the habits and ability to analyze the pros and cons of online activities is complex and requires teenagers to implement thoughtful, informed decision-making skills. The information presented in this book is designed to foster the development of a healthy digital footprint and prompt teenagers to cultivate the requisite decision-making skills for implementing essential, healthy routines online in order to maintain a balanced and safe lifestyle.

---

[1] Wiggins, G., & Tighe, J. M. (2005). *Understanding By Design*. Heatherton: Hawker Brownlow education.

[2] McTighe, J., Seif, E., & Wiggins, G. (2004, September). You Can Teach For Meaning. *Educational Leadership*, 26-31.

[3] Brown, J. S., Collins, A., & Duguid, P. (1989). Situated Cognition and the Culture of Learning. *Educational Researcher, 18*(1), 32.

[4] The Jigsaw Classroom. (2000). Retrieved from https://www.jigsaw.org/

[5] Aronson, E., & Patnoe, S. (1997). The jigsaw classroom: Building cooperation in the classroom. New York: Longman.

[6] Lyman, F. (1981). The Responsive Classroom Discussion: The Inclusion of All Students. Mainstreaming Digest. University of Maryland, College Park, MD.

[7] Bransford, J. D., Brown, A. L., & Cocking, R. R. (Eds.). (2000). Learning and transfer (Chapter 3). In *how people learn: Brain, mind, experience, and school*. Washington, DC: National Academy Press. [Online]. Available: http://books.nap.edu/html/howpeople1.

ABOUT THE AUTHOR

ALFONZO PORTER

ALFONZO PORTER is the Managing Partner of Vertex Learning, LLC, a full service educational publishing and consulting firm with an operational footprint in Washington, DC, Atlanta, GA, St. Louis, MO, Denver, CO, Dayton-Cincinnati, OH, and San Diego, CA. He is past President/CEO of PE&C, Inc., an award winning education consultancy which provided a broad portfolio of services to school systems nationally. It was the recipient of numerous awards and honors including Small Business of the Year, Inc. 5000's Fastest Growing U.S. Companies, Who's Who in Business and MEA Magazine's Fastest Growing Minority Firms, among others. As a journalist, he has written for several publications including the *Washington Post* and *The Examiner*. He has also worked as a public school teacher and administrator across multiple school systems. His undergraduate degree is in Journalism and Public Relations. He completed a graduate program in Educational Policy and Leadership with endorsements as a secondary principal and district level administrator. He holds a graduate certificate in management and his doctoral program focused on the Administration of Teaching and Learning. Porter is also currently an Adjunct Professor in the Department of Journalism and Technical Communications at MSU-Denver.

CHAPTER ONE

———————●———————

Cyber-Bullying

Why can it be so easy to mistreat others?
What does it feel like to be a victim?
Why can it be easier to do-nothing?

BEHAVIORS AND THEMES

SCALE AND SCOPE: Cyberbullying is not a problem that has recently emerged. The Cyberbullying Research Center at Florida Atlantic University has been collecting data from middle and high school students from across the United States since 2002. Surveys of more than 15,000 students, over a number of years, found that one out of every four teens has experienced cyberbullying and about one out of every six teens has cyberbullied others at some point in their lifetime.[1] [2] In 2007, the National Crime Prevention reported 43% of teens reported experiencing cyberbullying.[3] More recently, researchers from the Family Online Safety Institute found, that among the 1,000 teens/pre-teens surveyed, 35% indicate that they have bullied people on social media; this included making fun of other people to someone else, calling someone fat or ugly, making fun of others' physical appearance, and tagging mean pictures or threatening someone.[4] Of those who bullied others, the main reasons for bullying were because the others were mean to them (61%) or they just didn't like the other person (26%).[5] In their biennial survey of students the Centers for Disease Control and Prevention found 15.5% of students reported they were bullied electronically.[6] Findings from a 2015 study of over 450 middle school students between the ages of 11 and 15 provide a nuanced perspective on both cyberbully victimization and offending, and how this violence is typically perpetuated.[7] The findings underscore the reality that cyberbullying is a common occurrence among teenagers.

Cyberbullying has become so widespread that it has grabbed the attention of state lawmakers across the United States. As of 2016, all states and the District of Columbia have bullying laws.[8] While only 24 states have bullying laws that specifically include "cyberbullying," all but one state addresses "electronic harassment" within their bullying laws. Additionally, as of 2016, all states and the District of Columbia require public schools establish school policies addressing bullying and 18 states allow for the criminal prosecution of bullying. Cyberbullying is a fast growing problem among teenagers of all walks of life. A primary reason for this growth is due to the increasingly large numbers of kids who regularly access both personal electronic devices and the Internet and have embraced online interactivity as a normal part of daily life. Online communication is just so easy and because teenagers typically use their laptops, smartphones, tablets, and portable gaming devices out of sight from adult supervision, their activities are not difficult to conceal. It is not surprising some have decided to use technology to be malicious, threatening, and harmful towards others.

PROBLEM DEFINED: As online communication, social networking, and texting have become everyday practices among teens, the prevalence of cyberbullying has become a widespread problem within youth culture. Cyberbullying, which can be defined as "willful and repeated harm inflicted through the use of computers, cell phones, and other electronic devices," has even been labeled as an epidemic.[9] Please remember that one instance of mistreatment online is not the same as cyberbullying, as cyberbullying must involve harmful, intentional actions that are repetitive. For example, suppose someone posts an embarrassing or hateful story about another person on social media so that others can see it, share it, and post comments. While the posting of the message only happens once, the fact that so many other people can see it, share it, and comment on it can result in reoccurring humiliation and embarrassment.

Even with increases in public awareness and the growth of prevention programs in K-12, cyberbullying is still one of the most prevalent dynamics teenagers encounter. Because of its reliance on technology, cyberbullying has far reach and can result in an assortment of tragic consequences; its impact cuts across ethnicity, gender, race, class, sexual preference, and grade level, and does not discriminate whether an individual lives in urban, suburban, or rural communities. Cyberbullying occurs in a variety of ways. While chat rooms were initially the primary venue for this harassment, in recent years social media platforms like Instagram, Twitter, Snapchat, Yik Yak, Secret, and Whisper as well as popular video sharing sites such as YouTube and TinyPic have become environments where cyberbullying has taken hold. Texting, email, and gaming devices are also common tools utilized by cyberbullies.

Typically, victims of cyberbullying have some type of relationship with a bully, which, a lot of times, makes it more difficult to permanently remove oneself from the situation. Additionally, a power imbalance almost always exists in cyberbullying situations. Because the harm associated with this behavior takes place solely online, having power or control over another person does not rely on size, physical strength, or social status. Having the upper hand can simply be the result of possessing certain information that might be embarrassing or harmful to another person or simply just being more tech savvy than others. Anyone that makes the choice to use technology to mistreat others is in a position of power, at least for that moment, in relation to a possible or chosen target.

It is not an understatement to say that a large percentage of adolescents are routinely exposed to interpersonal violence, aggressive behavior, and repetitive harassment while online. This experience has a significant impact on the emotional, social, psychological, and even physical well being of all those involved in cyberbullying. Unfortunately, this impact can go undetected for long periods of time because, many times, it is difficult to identify the necessary support structures to end the behaviors that are causing harm. Although there is some variation in the research examining the extent of cyberbullying among teenagers, there is certainly consensus around the fact that this behavior is a common presence in the lives of many adolescents.

CORE DYNAMICS OF CYBERBULLYING

Electronic devices and social media are the primary tools of a cyberbully. These tools provide distance between victim and perpetrator, and enable the attacks to be seen by large numbers of people with just a few clicks. It is much easier to perpetuate violence online than in person because a cyberbully doesn't have to physically witness the response of their target. Additionally, because adults do not have the ability, time, or access to always keep track of what is happening online, cyberbullying incidents can easily be missed or overlooked.

Methods to cyberbully: sending harmful or threatening messages using electronic devices; posting libelous, harassing, and harmful messages on social media; uploading humiliating images or videos to the internet without permission; sharing personal information about someone electronically; and/or breaking into someone's email or social media account to send vicious or embarrassing material to others. A cyberbully can post messages and images that can be posted anonymously and distributed quickly to a wide audience. Due to the rapidly evolving online environment and easy access to electronic devices, cyberbullies have many ways and opportunities to carry out their violent behavior.

Cyberbullying reflects a pattern of behavior. These are not isolated incidents, but occur over a period of time. Cyberbullying can occur 24 hours a day, 7 days a week, and reach a victim whether he or she is alone or with friends.

Cyberbullying is willful and deliberate. Perpetrators have made a decision to cause harm to others and are taking specific actions to carry out their intentions. Because cyberbullying by definition requires harmful behavior that is repetitive in nature, it cannot occur accidentally or by chance. Victims of cyberbullying are targets and their perpetrators are purposeful with their actions to cause harm.

The roles involved in cyberbullying. While every situation is different, two roles always exist. Cyberbullies perpetuate voluntary and repetitious abuse that is inflicted through electronic devices. Their targets, which are referred to as cybervictims are harmed, victimized, injured, and even killed as a result of cyberbullying. Two other roles can be present in any bullying situation. One role, which is fairly common, is the bystander, and the other, much less common, is the upstander.

WHAT MAKES CYBERBULLYING SO EASY: While traditional bullying and cyberbullying are closely related, they do have distinct characteristics. For example, cyberbullies can easily hide his or her identity behind an electronic device using anonymous identifiers or even fictitious names. Intel Security's 2015 study of teenager's online behavior found 42% of teens use anonymous names or aliases for their social media profiles, with one in three reporting they do so because they simply do not want others knowing they are posting something online. [10] Additionally, the harm caused by cyberbullies goes viral immediately and is on display for all to see, share, and even comment on. It is also easier to cyberbully because it can be done remotely and the perpetrator does not have to witness the in-time response from their target. This distance removes much of the emotional investment typical in traditional bullying.

Those individuals who are bullied at school are frequently bullied online and those who bully at school are common online bullies. Involvement in bullying, particularly as perpetrator, can frequently be the result of other issues present in a child's life. These can include problems at home or in school, anti-social behavior, substance abuse, physical abuse, and delinquent behavior. One other point to emphasize is that many cyberbullies feel as though there are few, if any, consequences for their behavior. Because teenagers engage in an almost parallel online world from adults, it can be hard to identify or "catch" a cyberbully committing harm. Although it is difficult, it is important to pursue efforts to do what ever is possible to stop cyberbullies and hold them accountable.

Possible Signs of Cyberbullying [11]

> **A CHILD MAY BE A VICTIM OF CYBERBULLYING IF HE OR SHE:**
> - Unexpectedly stops using their device(s)
> - Appears nervous or jumpy when using device(s)
> - Appears uneasy about being at school or outside
> - Appears to be angry, depressed, or frustrated after texting, chatting, using social media, or gaming
> - Becomes abnormally withdrawn
> - Avoids discussions about their activities online

BECOMING AN UPSTANDER REQUIRES AN INDIVIDUAL TO:

1. Refuse to be a bystander!
2. Recognize the signs of cyberbullying.
3. Take direct action by demanding a cyberbully to stop.
4. Take direct action by enlisting others to come together to stand up to a cyberbully and demand an end to harmful actions and behaviors
5. Take direct action to help the victim.
6. Take direct action by redirecting the cyberbully away from the victim.
7. Take direct action by telling an adult who can help put an end to cyberbullying

IMPACT ON HEALTH: The effects of cyberbullying have widespread impact and often result in significant consequences. Cyberbullying can affect everyone—those who are bullied, those who bully, and those who witness bullying. Cyberbullying is linked with many consequential outcomes including a negative impact on mental health, drug use, and even suicide. Victims of cyberbullying can experience detrimental physical, mental, and socio-emotional health issues. Individuals preyed on by cyberbullies are likely to experience anxiety, social isolation, embarrassment, unhappiness, changes in behavior, and an unusual distance from activities and relationships that were previously important parts of their lives.[12]

A CHILD MAY BE CYBERBULLYING OTHERS IF HE OR SHE:

- Quickly switches screens or hides their device
- Uses their device(s) at all hours of the night
- Gets unusually upset if they can't use device(s)
- Avoids discussions about what they are doing online
- Seems to be using multiple online accounts, or an account that is not their own.

Victims of cyberbullying also often see adverse effects to their school performance. This can include diminishing grades, GPA, test scores, and participation in school activities. Those experiencing any form of bullying are likely to miss or drop out of school as this behavior helps them to avoid those individuals or groups perpetrating harmful behavior. It is also worthwhile to note that in many of the school shootings in the United States, including high-profile case like Columbine, Sandy Hook, and Virginia Tech, the shooters had a history of or reported being bullied.

There are also negative outcomes for kids who bully others. It is likely that these outcomes can even be sustained into adulthood. Kids who bully are more likely to abuse drugs, alcohol, and other substances during adolescence. These individuals are more likely to engage in violent behavior such as fighting, vandalizing property, and physically assaulting others, and as childhood bully's move into adulthood there is also a tendency to be abusive toward their partners, spouses, or children.[13] Involvement in bullying can lead to a variety of harmful outcomes. This is why it is so important for upstanders to confront cyberbullying and stop it and for adults to help identify the underlying issues at the heart of bullying behavior.

CYBERBULLICIDE: Bullying of all forms has even been linked with suicidal tendencies. Youth who are bullied or who bully others, are at an elevated risk for suicidal thoughts, attempts, and completed suicides. [14] [15] The fact that cyberbullying victims are almost twice as likely to have attempted suicide compared to teenagers who had not experienced cyberbullying is a sobering reality.[16] Researchers at Yale University's School of Medicine's Child

Study Center have also confirmed an association between bullying, being bullied and suicide in children. In recent years, there have been an increasing number of examples of teens taking their own lives as a result cyberbullying. This phenomenon, which has been termed cyberbullicide, can be defined "as suicide indirectly or directly influenced by experiences with online aggression." [18] Cyberbullying victims often have **lower self-esteem, increasing depression and loneliness, and feelings of powerlessness**[19], all of which have been identified as precursors to suicidal thoughts and behavior.

KEY CONCEPTS

Bullying: An unwanted, aggressive behavior that involves a real or perceived power and control imbalance, unwanted negative actions, and a pattern of behavior that is repeated over time.

Victimization: An individual threatened, harmed, injured, or killed as a result of an intentional act by another person.

Bystander: A person who witnesses or has knowledge of an event, action, or correspondence but does not directly participate and does not engage in direct action to stop or prevent a bully's harmful actions and behaviors.

Upstander: Courageous, powerful individuals who stand up for victims when they are bullied, assaulted, or persecuted.

REAL WORLD SITUATIONS

Immigrant Teen Taunted by Cyberbullies Hangs Herself

—Source: By Susan Donaldson James, ABC News, January 26th, 2010 [20]

What makes cyberbullying different from other types of bullying? What should someone do if they are a victim of cyberbullying?

Even in death, Phoebe Prince was bullied. On a memorial page dedicated to the Massachusetts teen who had recently committed suicide, Facebook members left taunting comments that had to be removed. The 15-year-old—a recent immigrant from Ireland with a pretty face and a soft brogue—was found dead in her South Hadley home Jan. 14, according to police. Afterward, her fellow students came forward to tell school officials that Prince had been teased incessantly, taunted by text messages and harassed on social networking sites like Facebook. "It's heart-wrenching," said South Hadley Police Chief David LaBrie. "She had only moved here last summer." "We are looking at all factors," said LaBrie, who was assisting the Northwest District Attorney's office with an investigation into Prince's death.

LaBrie refused to discuss the details of Prince's suicide out of "respect for the family's privacy." It's tremendously emotionally draining on the family and the whole community right now," he told ABCNews.com. "It's such a sad thing." Many in the suburban community of about 17,000 in western Massachusetts was in shock after learning that Prince had reportedly hung herself just days after accepting a date to a high school dance. In a letter to parents, Principal Daniel Smith called Prince "smart, charming, and as is the case with many teenagers, complicated. ... We will never know the specific reasons why she chose to take her life." Prince is not the only case of apparent bullying that has sparked national headlines.

In 2006, Megan Meier killed herself after the mother of a former friend created a fictitious profile to harass the Missouri 13-year-old. Three years earlier, 13-year-old Ryan Patrick Halligan of Vermont hung himself after he'd been bullied online. Just this week in Lewisville, Texas, a 9-year-old boy hung himself in the nurse's bathroom at his elementary school." It's just sad. I can't imagine what would make a 9-year-old boy feel this way," Stephanie Rodriguez, the school's PTA treasurer, told ABC affiliate WFAA television.

This is apparently the second high-profile suicide bullying case in Massachusetts in the past year. In nearby Springfield, 11-year-old Carl Joseph Walker-Hoover hung himself with an extension cord after bullies repeatedly called him gay. In the case of Phoebe Prince, the family recently relocated from a tiny village in the west of Ireland. But she had trouble adjusting to her new school and became the victim of incessant bullying by classmates.

"The real problem now is the texting stuff and the cyberbullying," South Hadley School Superintendent Gus A. Sayer told the Boston Globe." Some kids can be very mean towards one another using that medium."

SUICIDE PROMPTS INVESTIGATION

First Assistant District Attorney Renee Steese said her office is conducting an "open investigation" of the circumstances of Prince's death with local and state police, as well as the medical examiner.

"It's a small community, and obviously for the family a tragic loss," she told ABCNews.com. Bullying has become increasingly common in schools throughout the United States. The National Youth Violence Prevention Resource Center estimated that nearly 30 percent of American youth are either a bully or a target of bullying. In addition, researchers at the Yale School of Medicine, in a new review of studies from 13 countries, found signs of an apparent connection between bullying, being bullied and suicide. "The incidence of bullying is getting more and more frequent and takes lots of forms," said Herbert Nieberg, associate professor of criminal justice at Mitchell College in Connecticut and a psychologist who specializes in adolescents. When the bullying moves to the Internet, the trauma to the victim is "astronomically" escalated, according to Nieberg.

"In the old days kids would threaten to beat someone up, but now it's gone into the cyberworld," he told ABCNews.com. "Kids go on to Facebook because they get a wider audience than in the hallway." Cyberbullying also appeals to the crowd instinct, according to Nieberg. "Everybody likes to watch the action. Why do three girls on Long Island beat up another young woman and put it on YouTube? They vicariously enjoy identifying with the aggressor." Why some teens can survive their tormentors and others cannot depend on their self-image and psychological mood. "Anyone with a mood disorder is at risk," said Nieberg. "The answer is vulnerability versus resiliency," he said. "Some kids are good copers."

But some advocates say Massachusetts, a typically progressive state, falls behind 37 other states that have taken action on school bullying. Several bills before the state legislature address school bullying. House Bill 483, sponsored by the Anti-Defamation League of New England, would require schools to have anti-bullying training and procedures in place. It would also require districts to produce an annual report citing incidents for the state legislature and the department of primary and secondary education "We take no comfort or false security that we grew up with bullying and what's the big deal, we survived," said Derrek Shulman, regional director of the ADL.

"Statistics show in a survey of fourth-and eighth-graders that a large percentage said they had been bullied or were bullied themselves," he told ABCNews.com. "We know that bullies are more likely to get into trouble with narcotics and law enforcement and that the bullied suffer from self-esteem and there are significant repercussions on being productive members of the community," he said.

STUDENTS HOLD VIGIL

Meanwhile, hundreds attended a candlelight vigil organized by students on the South Hadley High School softball field the day after Phoebe Prince died. Parents are also pushing to create an anti-bullying task force at the high school. But the first meeting, scheduled for Tuesday, has been postponed for a month. Prince's death notice in the Springfield Republican newspaper said she left three sisters and a brother. Her family members, who couldn't be reached for comment, wrote that they had moved to South Hadley so the family could experience America. "What her family and friends from both sides of the Atlantic grieve is the loss of the incandescent enthusiasm of a life blossoming," the notice read. "She enjoyed life with an energy only the young possess.

Successful Anti-Bullying Program Identified by UCLA

—Source: By Stuart Wolpert, UCLA News, February 3rd, 2016[21]

What are some ways upstanders can directly respond to cyberbullies?

Why can it be so difficult to talk with others about cyberbullying?

Many programs to reduce bullying in primary and secondary schools have proven ineffective, but a new UCLA-led study finds one that works very well. The study of more than 7,000 students in 77 elementary schools in Finland found that one program greatly benefited the mental health of sixth-graders who experienced the most bullying. It significantly improved their self-esteem and reduced their depression. The research-based anti-bullying program, called KiVa, includes role-playing exercises to increase the empathy of bystanders and computer simulations that encourage students to think about how they would intervene to reduce bullying. ("Kiusaamista vastaan" means "against bullying," in Finnish, while the word "kiva" means "nice."). KiVa is one of the world's most effective anti-bullying programs, said Jaana Juvonen, lead author of the study and professor of psychology at UCLA. "Our findings are the first to show that the most tormented children — those facing bullying several times a week — can be helped by teaching bystanders to be more supportive," Juvonen said.

FIRST PROGRAM FOUND TO HELP REPEATEDLY BULLIED CHILDREN

Thirty-nine of the schools in the study used KiVa; in the other 38 schools, students were given some information about combating bullying, but these efforts were much less comprehensive. Anti-bullying programs are typically evaluated based on whether they decrease the average rates of bullying. Until this study, no school-wide programs have been found to help those who most need help — children who are bullied repeatedly. KiVa significantly reduced the depression of the 4 percent of sixth-graders who were bullied most frequently — on at least a weekly basis. The researchers also found improved self-esteem among the approximately 15 percent of sixth-graders who had been bullied at least a few times per month.

A recent meta-analysis of 53 anti-bullying programs worldwide found the KiVa program to be one of the most effective. The odds that a given student experienced bullying were 1.5 to nearly 2 times higher in control schools than in KiVa schools nine months after KiVa's implementation. "Our analysis shows that KiVa improves students' perceptions of the school environment, especially among those who are bullied. For sixth-graders, it also improves their mental health, which is a big issue," said Juvonen, who has conducted research on bullying for more than 20 years. "Typically we think individuals with mental health needs must be addressed individually. The beauty here is that this school-wide program is very effective for the children who need support the most.

TEACHING STUDENTS KINDNESS

Students in all grade levels studied, 4th-6th, benefited in terms of having significantly more favorable perceptions of the school environment. This was especially true for the students who were most frequently bullied before the intervention. The study is published online in the Journal of Consulting and Clinical Psychology. Juvonen does not advocate zero-tolerance school policies, which she said punish students but do not teach them about bullying. KiVa is much more effective in leading students to be kinder to one another, she said. KiVa is now Finland's national anti-bullying program. It is being tested and used in several other European countries, and it is being evaluated in the United States, Juvonen said. It is based on scholarly research about bullying, including Juvonen's, but she was not involved in developing the program.

Teen Charged in Fatal Cyberbullying Case of Rebecca Sedwick Remains in Jail

—Source: By Alyssa Newcomb, ABC News, January 15th, 2013[22]

Why is it so easy to cyberbully others?
What are appropriate consequences for cyberbullies?

One of two teenage girls arrested in connection with the bullying death of a Florida girl is expected to remain in jail overnight, while a judge released the other suspect into the custody of her parents. The two girls were arrested and charged Monday night with felony aggravated stalking in the death of 12-year-old Rebecca Sedwick who jumped from a concrete silo tower to her death on Sept. 9. Polk County Sheriff, Grady Judd, said today he brought both girls, ages 14 and 12, into custody because he saw a lack of remorse. He pointed to a Facebook post allegedly written over the weekend by the 14-year-old suspect that said, "'Yes, I bullied Rebecca and she killed herself but I don't give a f—.'"

"You can add the last word yourself," Judd said. Police said Rebecca was allegedly tormented by as many as 15 girls. The alleged bullying started in December 2012 when Rebecca and the two suspects were students at Crystal Lake Middle School, according to a statement from the Polk County Sheriff's Office. Judd said the 14-year-old suspect had started dating a boy Rebecca had been seeing, however the girl "didn't like that and began to harass and ultimately torment Rebecca." The girl allegedly sent Rebecca menacing messages on Facebook calling her ugly, telling her to "drink bleach and die," and encouraging her to kill herself, police said.

The alleged bullying soon escalated to confrontations at school, including at least one physical attack, according to police. Police said witnesses, including Rebecca's ex-boyfriend, told them she did not engage her tormentor, leading them to believe she was being bullied. The 14-year-old suspect also allegedly bullied anyone who was friends with Rebecca, according to police, and even encouraged the 12-year-old suspect, who was Rebecca's friend, to turn on her. The girl was suspended for one fight in February 2013, according to police, in which the older suspect encouraged her to "beat up" Rebecca. During a recent interview, police said the girl told them she bullied Rebecca and expressed remorse. The 12-year-old was released into the custody of her parents and has been placed on home detention pending further proceedings. Rebecca tried to get a fresh start at a new school for the 2013-14 school year, authorities said, however the torment continued online. "Rebecca's family is absolutely devastated by this," Judd said. "Quite frankly, we're all devastated by this."

LEARNING SCENARIOS

Scenario #1

You are upset by the comments a group of high school male students are making about your physical appearance and sexuality. You do not really consider these individuals to be friends, but have known them your entire life. This group of students created a phony account to impersonate you on an online dating website. Posing as you and using your personal information and image, the group of students begins sending out suggestive and sexually explicit emails to others on the dating site. When you start receiving correspondence from members of the dating site, you are extremely embarrassed, humiliated, and devastated. Although you have shared the situation with a few of your closest friends, how should you deal with this situation? What can be done? What are some productive ways that you might try to deal with this issue? As an upstander what role can you play in responding to and preventing further harm?

Scenario #2

You are new student that has just moved to town from another state and don't know any students in your new school. You are an excellent student. You are also outgoing, attractive, and immediately liked by teachers. You have attracted the attention of a number of the varsity basketball players. It is very clear that this "attention" is not sitting well with a number of the cheerleaders. One of the senior cheerleaders, Betsy, is overly sensitive to the attention and interest her boyfriend is suddenly showing towards you. With the support of her close friends, Besty creates an anonymous twitter account where other girls can tweet reasons why they dislike you and why she should find another school to attend. After a few weeks, almost the entire school has become aware of the twitter account and the chain of hurtful comments. As a new member of the school community who just wants to fit in, you are crushed. Consequently, you begin to feel isolated and depressed, your academics begin to suffer, and you now hate coming to school. As an upstander who knows this is happening, what action should be taken? As a victim, what steps might you take to deal with the present situation?

Scenario #3

You and another classmate are exchanging mean and inappropriate texts back and forth because of a recent misunderstanding. The texts have escalated from name-calling to dangerous, inflammatory statements, which include threats of physical harm. Both you and your classmate have discussed the situation with a school counselor and are extremely angry, upset, and even a little regretful about the exchange of texts. The situation has gotten so out of hand that other students in the school have learned about it. In fact, others are becoming involved and taking sides. The situation has become disruptive to teachers and has even led to a few minor incidents of physical violence that have occurred on school property. What suggestions do you have for de-escalating the situation? What strategies can be implemented? As an upstander, what steps can be taken?

HELPFUL STRATEGIES

DON'T RETALIATE: Many times some sort of retaliation is exactly what a cyberbully is looking for because it provides them power and control over their victim. Retaliation can result in a dangerous, escalating scenario. Individuals need to remove themselves from the situation and seek out help from trusted friends and adults.

KEEP EVIDENCE: The only good news about cyberbullying is many times incidents can be captured, saved, and shared with someone who can help and offer support. Save that evidence in case things escalate. Become familiar with how to screen shot images on your electronic devices and computer screen.

DEMAND AN END TO BEHAVIOR: Take direct action to stop a bully. While this can be difficult, it is a necessary step in ending a bully's controlling and harmful behavior. Communicate to a bully that their behavior will no longer be tolerated. Victims may need to have a trusted friend or adult by their side when they do this or to practice with.

SEEK OUT SUPPORT: Victims of any form of bullying need and deserve help. Identify a trusted individual who can listen, help process experiences, and identify solutions. This would also be an ideal person to have present when demands are made for a bully to end harmful behavior.

LEARNING TASKS

20-Minute Activity
- Standard:
    - *Standard 1:* Students will comprehend concepts related to health promotion and disease prevention to enhance health.

    - *Standard 5:* Students will demonstrate the ability to use decision-making skills to enhance health

- **Rationale for the Question:** It is important for students to consider the underlying factors related to why it is so easy and acceptable to engage in behaviors that harm others. Examining this reality can provide insights to help students make the decision to become upstanders and stop harmful behaviors when they are observed or experienced.

- **Learning Outcome:** Students will discuss their perspectives about the ease with which we mistreat others so they can become more aware of this dynamic within their lives.

- **Description of Activity:** To start, students can read one of the first-hand student stories cataloged by the Cyberbullying Research Center (see link below under supporting resources). This pre-work can be completed at the start of class as a warm-up or assigned as homework. Students can engage in a think-pair-share with classmates about why it is so easy to mistreat others. Students will talk in small groups and then can become involved in a larger class discussion. It is important for teachers to record student responses and provides opportunities for open discussion of these responses.

- **Supporting Resources:**
    - Cyberbullying Stories, Cyberbullying Research Center, Florida Atlantic University, http://cyberbullying.org/stories/
    - Stopbullying.Gov, U.S. Department of Health & Human Services, https://www.stopbullying.gov/cyberbullying/index.html

ONE-DAY ACTIVITY
- **Standard:**
    - *Standard 3:* Students will demonstrate the ability to access valid information and products and services to enhance health.
    - *Standard 8:* Students will demonstrate the ability to advocate for personal, family, and community health.

- **Rationale:** This assignment will help students increase attention to the presence and impact of cyberbullying within their school community. Students will spend time researching cyberbullying's causes, effects, and impact as well as strategies to curb this dangerous and damaging behavior. This activity will also provide an opportunity for students to take a stance against cyberbullying by advocating for solutions, becoming upstanders, and highlighting actions and behaviors to stop cyberbullying.

- **Learning Outcome:** Students will design anti-cyberbullying advertisements so they can educate peers, teachers, and other school staff about the various issues and outcomes related to cyberbullying.

- **Description of Activity:** Teachers engaging in this activity should inform school leaders of the project and secure public space to post anti-cyberbullying advertisements once they are complete. To begin, it would be useful if students get the opportunity to learn about effective advertising by exploring what characteristics define an effective advertisement? Students should also spend time looking at existing marketing campaigns focusing on cyberbullying (see links below under supporting resources). Students can work individually or be divided into small groups. Students can spend time exploring resources through the Cyberbullying research Center to enhance their understanding of the issues surrounding cyberbullying. Once advertisements are complete, teachers and students in the school as well as other school community members can be asked to vote on the best advertisements. Categories could include most creative, most persuasive, most informative, etc.

- **Supporting Resources:**
  - Ad Council, bullying prevention: adcouncil.org/Our-Campaigns/Safety/Bullying-Prevention
  - Anti-cyberbullying slogans: nobullying.com/our-favorite-anti-cyber-bullying-slogans
  - Cyberbullying slogan images: stopbullying.gov/image-gallery/index.html
  - Cyberbullying Research Center, Florida Atlantic University: http://cyberbullying.org

ONE-WEEK ACTIVITY
- **Standard:**
  - *Standard 2:* Students will analyze the influence of family, peers, culture, media, technology, and other factors on health behaviors.
  - *Standard 4:* Students will demonstrate the ability to use interpersonal communication skills to enhance health and avoid or reduce health risks.

- **Rationale:** It is hard to advocate for meaningful change if there is not a clear understanding about the various dynamics shaping problems. This activity will help students identify specific problems related to cyberbullying that exist within their school community. Additionally, data will also help students utilize important findings to develop recommendations for action to help curb instances of cyberbullying and help educate others about this issue. The opportunity to make a public presentation to peers and others within the school community will allow students to engage in the public policy development process.

- **Learning Outcome:** Students will develop and administer an electronic questionnaire on cyberbullying so they can examine their school culture and advocate for necessary changes and resources.

- **Description of Activity:** Teachers will support students in an authentic research project to collect data on the presence, extent, and impact of cyberbullying within their local school community. It is important to work with school leaders and, if necessary, district staff before beginning this activity to ensure the proper protocol is followed for collecting and reporting anonymous survey data. An ideal first step is to teach students about surveys, why and how they are used, and how to develop effective questions. Next, students should spend time researching major issues related to cyberbullying. This work will support the development of questions that will be included in the questionnaire to be disseminated to students within the school. Students can build on questionnaires that already exist (many online) or develop their own using likert-scale and open-ended questions. Students can work in groups to develop questions and then share as a class to identify the most useful questions. The questionnaire can be disseminated in either paper format or more preferable, via an online survey tool that will more effectively ensure participant anonymity. Students can then analyze findings and develop a set of recommendations for action that can be presented to their peers as well as school and district leaders.

- **Supporting Resources:**
  - Cyberbullying Research Center, Florida Atlantic University, www.cyberbullying.org
  - Harvard University Program on Survey Research, Questionnaire Design Tip Sheet: psr.iq.harvard.edu/book/questionnaire-design-tip-sheet
  - Student Reports of Bullying and Cyber-Bullying: Results From the 2011 School Crime Supplement to the National Crime Victimization Survey, US Department of Education: nces.ed.gov/pubs2013/2013329.pdf

ADDITIONAL RESOURCES:

Cyberbullying Research Center at Florida Atlantic University: http://www.cyberbullying.us/ Megan Meier Foundation: www.meganmeierfoundation.org

State by State Cyberbullying Laws: www.cyberbullying.org/Bullying-and-Cyberbullying-Laws.pdf

National Crime Prevention Council and the Office for Victims of Crime: http://www.ncpc.org/topics/cyberbullying

Olweus Bully Prevention Program: http://www.clemson.edu/olweus

Bullying Beyond the Schoolyard: Preventing and Responding to Cyberbullying, Sameer Hindjuda and Justin W. Patchin

Teen Cyberbullying Investigated, Thomas A. Jacobs

[1] Cyberbullying Research Center. (2017). Cyberbullying Statistics. Retrieved from http://cyberbullying.org/statistics

[2] National Crime Prevention Council, (2007, February 28). Teens and Cyberbullying. Retrieved from http://www.ncpc.org/resources/files/pdf/bullying/Teens%20and%20Cyberbullying%20Research%20Study.pdf

[3] Family Online Safety Institute. (2015, June). The Realities of Cyber Parenting: What Pre-teens and Teens Are Up To Online? Retrieved from https://www.fosi.org/policy-research/realities-cyber-parenting

[4] Family Online Safety Institute. (2015, June). The Realities of Cyber Parenting: What Pre-teens and

[5] Teens Are Up To Online. Retrieved from https://www.fosi.org/policy-research/realities-cyber-parenting

[6] National Bullying Prevention Center. (2016, December 8). Bullying Statistics. Retrieved from http://www.pacer.org/bullying/resources/stats.asp

[7] Cyberbullying Research Center. (2015, October 21). Our latest research on cyberbullying among school students. Retrieved from http://cyberbullying.org/2015-data

[8] Bullying and Cyberbullying Laws across America. (2017) Retrieved from http://cyberbullying.org/bullying-laws

[9] Hinduja, S., & Patchin, J. W. (2009). *Bullying Beyond the Schoolyard: Preventing and Responding to Cyberbullying.* Thousand Oaks, CA: Sage.

[10] Family Online Safety Institute. (2015, June). The Realities of Cyber Parenting: What Pre-teens and Teens Are Up To Online? Retrieved from https://www.fosi.org/policy-research/realities-cyber-parenting

[11] Cyberbullying Fact Sheet: Identification, Prevention, and Response. (2016, October 02). Retrieved from http://cyberbullying.org/cyberbullying-fact-sheet-identification-prevention-and-response

[12] Cyberbullying Research Center. (2017). Cyberbullying Facts. Retrieved from http://cyberbullying.org/facts

[13] Stop Bullying.Gov. (2012, February 29). Effects of Bullying. Retrieved from http://www.stopbullying.gov/at-risk/effects/index.html#bully

[14] Van der Wal, M. F., De Wit, C. A., & Hirasing, R. A. (2003). Psychosocial health among young victims and offenders of direct and indirect bullying. *Pediatrics, 111*(6), 1312-1317.

[15] Rigby, K., & Slee, P. (1999). Suicidal ideation among adolescent school children, involvement in bully—victim problems, and perceived social support. *Suicide and life-threatening behavior, 29*(2), 119-130.

[16] Cyberbullying Research Summary: Cyberbullying and Suicide. (2010). Retrieved from http://www.cyberbullying.org/cyberbullying_and_suicide_research_fact_sheet.pdf

[17] Bullying-Suicide Link Explored in New Study by Researchers at Yale. (2008, July 16). Retrieved from http://news.yale.edu/2008/07/16/bullying-suicide-link-explored-new-study-researchers-yale

[18] Hinduja, S., & Patchin, J. W. (2009). *Bullying Beyond the Schoolyard: Preventing and Responding to Cyberbullying.* Thousand Oaks, CA: Sage.

[19] Anderson, J., Bresnahan, M., & Musatics, C. (2014). Combating weight-based cyberbullying on Facebook with the dissenter effect. *Cyberpsychology, Behavior, and Social Networking, 17*(5), 281-286.

[20] James, S. D. (2010, January 26). Immigrant Teen Taunted by Cyberbullies Hangs Herself. Retrieved from http://abcnews.go.com/Health/cyber-bullying-factor-suicide-massachusetts-teen-irish-immigrant/story?id=9660938

[21] Wolpert, U. S. (2016, February 03). Successful anti-bullying program identified by UCLA. Retrieved May 15, 2017, from http://universityofcalifornia.edu/news/successful-anti-bullying-program-found-ucla

[22] Newcomb, A. (2013, October 15). Teen Charged in Fatal Cyberbullying Case of Rebecca Sedwick to Remain in Jail. Retrieved from http://abcnews.go.com/US/teen-charged-fatal-cyberbullying-case-rebecca-sedwick-remain/story?id=20580689

CHAPTER TWO

———•———

Online Dating

What steps can you take to ensure personal safety when meeting individuals from an online site?

How can you avoid becoming the victim of an emotionally abusive acquaintance?

What are some strategies against being catfished?

BEHAVIORS AND THEMES

SCALE AND SCOPE: Today, there are nearly 60 million Americans in the online dating scene. Globally, online dating grosses nearly $5 billion annually.[1] These days, if you are bored and want to meet someone yet don't know how to go about it, you sign onto an online dating site. You post your photo, write a paragraph or more about yourself, and/or complete their questionnaire. You answer questions such as your age, height, eye color, interests, and personal information about yourself. You have expectations of meeting someone just right for you. It seems quick, easy and painless, and the odds of finding true love are pretty good. As awesome as that is, what happens when something goes wrong, and they aren't your match at all?[2]

The vast majority of teen relationships occur outside the realm of the internet. Nevertheless, the internet is now one of the primary sources for searching for relationships. Teens like to flirt in person but also, "like," "friend," and joke with individuals on whom they might have feelings.[3]

It is a whole new world when it comes to developing relationships; the internet has changed everything. While some teens find success online, there are far too many stories that cause parents considerable concern. Many teens have been drawn into dangerous situations by predators, pedophiles and sex traffickers. The bad news is that these incidents are more common than not. Therefore, the teen who is well versed technologically is a greater target for those who would do them harm.

Because the number of sites dedicated to meeting online has increased over the past few years, the level of concern for teen safety has also increased. Popular sites like Facebook, friendstir.com, and plentyoffish.com offer opportunities for teens to meet new people. Although these are not so-called dating sites, they offer easy sign up and access within minutes. This sometimes seems to serve as a gateway.[4]

You can post personal information and pictures of yourself, as well as, contact information offline. These sites do not have anyone who monitors them on any consistent basis but rather only respond when a complaint is filed. Site administrators only become involved if a parent or other adults lodge a formal complaint. However, the overwhelming majority of profiles is not monitored and only opens the door to predators. This makes teens using these sites primary targets for online criminals.[5]

You can upload pictures and can post any information about yourself that you want including how to reach you in the real world. And while complaints are taken seriously, especially those made by parents, most profiles go unmonitored making these types of websites a prime target for Internet predators.[6] Many times these predators mask themselves as teenaged girls or boys when they are in fact adult men or women posting fictitious pictures and profiles to "catfish" teens. They study your profile and present themselves as the ideal mate based on your information. Once they convince you that they are the guy or girl of your dreams, they move to build and earn your trust.[7]

The goal is for you to develop deep feeling for them. It then seems only logical to make plans to meet. Because most teens use dating sites without the knowledge of parents, these meet-ups with the online individual typically happens without anyone else's knowledge. The stigma regarding online dating and relationships has diminished in recent years, but the level of secrecy among teens dating online has not. The question becomes, how do you stay safe while seeking to date online? Good common sense will prove valuable but here are some essential rules to follow for online relationships.[8]

- Unless you already know the person offline, always assume the person you are dealing with on the Internet is not who they claim to be and conduct yourself accordingly.

- Never give out personal information like last name, addresses, phone numbers, school names or where you work online.

- Never post provocative pictures of yourself or anybody else.

If an online friend starts getting intimate with you or asks you sexually suggestive questions back off and ignore them in the future. If they persist, tell a parent or other trusted real world adult and report them to the site administrator.

BY THE NUMBERS

- 55% of all teens ages 13 to 17 have flirted or talked to someone in person to let them know they are interested.

- 50% of teens have let someone know they were interested in them romantically by friending them on Facebook or another social media site.

- 47% have expressed their attraction by liking, commenting or otherwise interacting with that person on social media.

- 46% have shared something funny or interesting with their romantic interest online

- 31% sent them flirtatious messages.

- 11% have made them a music playlist.

- 10% have sent flirty or sexy pictures or videos of themselves.

- 7% have made a video for them.

- 59% say social media makes them feel more connected to what's happening in their significant other's life; 15% indicate that it makes them feel "a lot" more connected.

- 47% say social media offers a place for them to show how much they care about their significant other; 12% feel this way "a lot."

- 44% say social media helps them feel emotionally closer to their significant other, with 10% feeling that way "a lot."

- 27% say social media makes them feel jealous or unsure about their relationship, with 7% feeling this way "a lot."[1]

Source: Pew Research Center, Teens, Social Media & Technology, 2015

PROBLEM DEFINED: Anyone you meet online is a stranger, and you need to remember that. The potential dangers of online dating have come into sharp focus following the case of Jason Lawrence was found guilty of raping five women and girls and attacked two more after meeting them on an online site. Although presenting himself as a young man, Lawrence was actually 50-years-old. He reportedly made contact with thousands of young females through online sites; including those he was found guilty of raping and assaulting.[9] During the jury trial, it was determined that the website failed in its responsibility to delete Lawrence's profile after multiple complaints. The presiding judge called for greater scrutiny and security on online dating apps.

When you are reduced to a mere few lines in a profile it becomes very hard for people to see you as the full fledged human being you are. Meeting through electronic modalities is impersonal. That tends to even transfer over when you decide to meet in person. You are still viewed as dispensable. Time will undoubtedly tell whether a person is truly interested in you.[10]

In a report by the Child Trends Data Bank (CTBD), over 10 percent of high school students say that they have experienced violent episodes while dating. Although girls are more likely to be victimized by dating violence, boys are also victims of dating violence. Many express surprise to learn that most relationship violence occurs in the home of the victim. CTDB found that there is no statistical difference between girls and boys when it comes to being hurt by a partner; although physical harm is borne more by females.

The internet is responsible for more than 16,000 abductions, thousands of rapes and over 100 murders annually, according to the CTDB. It also revealed that about 10 percent of members of dating websites are scammers with another 10 percent being some form of sex offender.[11] Therefore, your odds of meeting a dishonest individual online are about 20 percent.

Whenever you meet someone online, you should be mindful to keep your communications to a minimum; making certain that you confine discussions to the app or site. You should block people who seem weird or suspicious. Meet them in a public place, if at all, and try to find more information about them online. Be sure to let others know your whereabouts.

POWER AND CONTROL: Teens must be aware of the dynamics involved in dating and relationships; particularly with someone who you have just met. There are several ways that others might attempt to manipulate and control you. Sometimes, your partner may engage in peer pressure by threatening to expose a secret about you or telling a malicious lie about you to your friends. They might begin to put you down and play on your self-esteem by playing mind games and attempting to humiliate you. You should be careful of any attempt to isolate you from friends and loved ones. Other attempts at control involve treating you like a servant and refusing to allow you to make any decisions. He/she might also issue threats to do harm to him/herself to commit suicide. They may also attempt to intimidate you through gestures, looks, and actions.

YOU SHOULD ALWAYS:

- Report any offensive or negative online correspondence to the website's support team and to your parents. There are online bullies who love to taunt teens online. If this happens to you, be sure to report it so that the bully can be stopped.

- Keep private information private. Never give out your social security number and other identifiable information over the internet. Someone could use it to steal your identity.

- Keep your passwords to the various websites in a safe place. The last thing that you would want would be for your annoying little brother or that weird friend from school to hack into your account and start messaging people. Keep your passwords private and in a safe place that only you know about.

- Be real online. Don't try to be someone who you are not. Nobody likes fake people. If you're going to date online, be yourself. The people who you are speaking to will appreciate you more.[1]

Source: Mark Hardcastle, Meeting People Online, 2016[12]

IMPACT ON HEALTH: Dating does not always and need not involve a sexual relationship, but teenagers who are engaging in sex are at risk for sexually transmitted diseases and – if you are a heterosexual couple having intercourse – pregnancy. Sexual harassment, while it may be more often thought of as occurring between people who are not in a relationship, can be by definition as any unwanted sexual approach that makes the recipient uncomfortable or interferes with his or her life – occur within a dating relationship. Teens should both feel empowered to say no within relationships and should understand the difference between the conversation that occurs when two parties have different ideas and are discussing the situation and the pressure and unsuitable advances that are defined as harassment.

There are some obvious steps for physical safety that teens can take when dating someone for the first time or meeting someone who is not previously known. Double-dating or going out in a group is a good choice in this situation. Meeting in a public place during daylight hours is also advisable. Teens should not use any substances that could impair their judgment nor go somewhere – particularly in a vehicle – with someone who has. You should also guard your beverages, as well as personal belongings and have a plan in place for an alternate way home (e.g., transportation by a parent) if you need one for any reason. Particularly when with someone new, being able to contact others is important – and a cell phone is helpful for this. Teens going out should leave a general plan of their itinerary, call if it changes, and have a curfew for their return. [13]

Whether officially dating or simply going out with a group of friends, teens should let your parents know who you will be with, who you are riding with, are parents home, what is cell or home phone number, what activities will you be engaging in, and what time you will be home.

You should also contact your parents if plans change, which they sometime legitimately do. Any particular limits on behavior, including but not limited to sexual behavior and mind-altering substances, should be spelled out. Since teens should not go on trips of any duration without being able to communicate – and though you may not wish your teen to have a cell phone, this is a way of ensuring that they can get in touch; if necessary, you can lend them yours, or have a cell phone that is used only as needed. [14]

These things could be an indication of a genuine love connection. However, the BIGGEST indicator, is if you meet in real life, and they are IDENTICAL to the person that you have talked to online. Normally it isn't like this. Normally people are a bit different to the person that you thought you were talking to online. As the sociopath is deceptive and faking who they are, when you meet, they will be (if their photos are clear), EXACTLY who you thought you were talking to online. This is the biggest tell-tell giveaway. [15]

KEY CONCEPTS

Catfishing—The act of an individual pretending to be someone else online in order to lure someone into a romantic relationship online without having met face to face.

Deception—A plot to get what one desires through a scam or hoax. Attempting to convince someone of something that is false or untrue.

Empathy—Being capable of feeling what another person feels. The ability to relate and understand others and their outlook.

Fraud—The act of intentionally deceiving others through deceit.

Narcissism—Overwhelming selfishness and self absorption. Having an extreme sense of self-importance.

Predation—The act of aggressive and plundering behavior from one person upon another.

REAL WORLD SITUATIONS

Alarming Number of Teen Girls Meeting Strangers
on Internet (. . . Which I Stupidly Did At 15).

—Source: Samantha Escobar, The Gloss, Jan 14, 2013

When is it appropriate to meet a connection from an online site?

How can you ensure personal safety if you decide to meet someone from an online site?

When I was in early high school, I met a friend who was all about MySpace (remember that creepy, glittery, even-more-vain-than-Tumblr beta Facebook?). She had met several guys via the site after exchanging lots of edited, angled photos—thereby making it a little difficult to recognize one another—and had actually seen some success with dating one or two of them. At the time, I was awkward, unhealthily pale and afraid of approaching guys, so her means of acquiring significant others seemed pretty appealing. Of course, teenage online dating via social networking sites is extremely normalized nowadays, but at the time, it was new territory that was sort of seeing its primitive stages.

I started talking to some guy named Matt and we hit it off because, shockingly, bored, single 15-year-olds tend to have a lot in common. For example, we were both bored and single. The friend who had gotten me into the whole MySpace dating thing claimed she had gone out with him at some point (which he later denied when I questioned his introducing himself to her), so at the time, I felt like it was safe to meet him. We wound up seeing a movie, I believe, and then getting to know each other further, culminating a few weeks later into an awkward make out session in my basement wherein we both realized we weren't actually attracted to one another. So it goes.

Granted, at least mostly-stupid 15-year-old me had the sense to meet the guy in the mall and I was lucky that he was just some sophomore Catholic school stoner who was dropped off by his mom just like myself, but this is not the case with everybody. It's eerily easy to lie on the Internet and so many people take advantage of that fact which is pretty unsurprising to most of us who have lived with and been gradually jaded by the web. However, more young girls than ever are meeting strangers from the Internet.

30 percent of surveyed teenage girls reported meeting strangers from the Internet, even when their identities were not yet confirmed. Jennie Noll, a professor of pediatrics at the University of Cincinnati, conducted the study that revealed these alarming results. In it, Noll and her team surveyed more than 250 teenage girls ages 14 to 17, 130 of whom had "experienced a documented form of abuse or maltreatment." They were attempting to see if the girls who had experienced trauma at the hands of others were more likely to engage in risky Internet behavior (like meeting somebody from the Internet or having an explicit profile on a social media site).

The results of the study after about a year to 16 months of observation showed that 30 percent had met a stranger from the Internet in real life, with the young women who had experienced abuse being more likely to do so. Noll said that predators tend to target teens who have more risqué photos than others:

"If someone is looking for a vulnerable teen to start an online sexual discourse, they will more likely target someone who presents herself provocatively. Maltreatment poses a unique risk for online behavior that may set the stage for harm."

Of course, regardless of what a kid has on her Facebook or wherever else, she doesn't deserve to be abused by some e-predator. Nevertheless, it's a lot different than when an adult has explicit photos. For one thing, it's obviously illegal for minors to have highly sexual photos on the Internet, but it's also important to remember that a lot of the creeps on the Internet know how to manipulate young teenagers into feeling safe, comfortable and as though the two are tight friends. Remember how lonely middle and high school were? Sometimes, the Internet is the only place where kids feel like they can make connections — even though those connections are not always safe ones.

In order to combat the potential for kids to engage in such behavior, it's important for parents to take a role in their kids' e-lives. According to the study, those filtering programs that remove sexual content from view don't actually have any impact on the teens' behavior. However, building trust between the parents and kids as well as keeping an eye on what teens are doing can greatly reduce the risk of them winding up in a terrible position like around some predator they thought was their friend. It's also important that parents keep in mind that their daughters and sons can partake in this type of behavior and be in danger even if they're not showing skin in photos and have never experienced trauma before.

Hopefully, this number reduces in the near future, as hypocritical as that sounds since I once engaged in such an idiotic act as meeting somebody from the Internet when I was just a youngish teenager. But until then, it's best to just discuss the importance of being safe online with your younger siblings, cousins, nieces, nephews and kids.

REAL WORLD SITUATIONS

When Teen Dating Violence Goes Online
—Source: Jennifer White, Futures Without Violence, May 4, 2016

What are primary signs that you are in an abusive relationship?

How might you safely end an abusive relationship?

This year, a film named *Audrie and Daisy* was part of the U.S. Documentary Competition at the Sundance Film Festival and will be available on Netflix later this year. The film tells the stories of two high school girls in different parts of the country whose kinship is the result of a common tragedy: both girls were sexually assaulted by boys they thought were friends.

Both girls were tortured by their communities and schools, particularly over social media. Both girls tried to take their own lives. The film highlights our failures as a nation to protect our young people, it illustrates a fundamental misapprehension about gender-based violence, it demonstrates our inclination to blame victims rather than believe them, and it vividly depicts the power and pervasiveness of social media as a weapon.

Forty percent of the world population is connected to the Internet, with more than three billion unique Internet users. According to an annual survey by Cox Communications and the National Center for Missing & Exploited Children:

- On average, teens spend just over five-and-a-half hours online every day.

- 92% are social network users.

- 74% share photos or videos of themselves, friends (58%) or family members (51%) online.

- Survey results show that, during the time teens spent online, one in four teens has been a victim of cyberbullying.

The use of social media as a weapon of choice in abusive dating relationships has made personal pain public, pervasive and perpetual. It has, at best, created suffering for victims on a world stage at a time when social connectedness and identity is most important and vulnerable. At worst, it has led to young people taking their own lives after the dissemination of particularly private and painful acts of violence were captured and spread throughout their digital worlds. The rise and evolution of social media has created a world where connection is immediate, boundless, enduring, and infinitely accessible and has, for victims of dating violence, manifested as a limitless opportunity for victimization and re-victimization.

"Online culture represents the worst forms of gang violence," noted the report *Cyber Violence Against Women and Girls*, by the UN Broadband Commission for Digital Development Working Group on Broadband and Gender.

Digital dating violence tends to manifest in one of three ways against young people: privacy, pressure, and control. Teens may experience invasion of their privacy, such as having social media accounts hacked or surveilled. Young people may experience pressure, such as for nude pictures, or experience coercion to comply with the demands of the abuser in an online capacity. Perpetrators of teen dating violence may also use social media and technology generally to track and monitor victims, to harass and scare victims, to maliciously embarrass and bully victims, to impersonate victims, and in some cases, to recruit or lure victims into dangerous or violent situations. Fifty-two percent of teens who experience digital abuse also experience physical abuse. Only 9% of teens seek help, and rarely from a parent or teacher.

The biggest challenges surrounding digital dating violence are:

(1) The relative ignorance of adult allies as to the seriousness, pervasiveness and potential harm associated with it;

(2) The ease with which perpetrators can reach victims online in a permanent and limitless manner;

(3) The impotence of legal recourse and/or enforcement of laws for victims.

Adult Allies. Futures Without Violence and www.thatsnotcool.com have an online toolkit that helps adults to become allies to teens in order to support them and facilitate conversation around healthy relationships and maintaining digital boundaries and a safe online space. As in all forms of violence against young people, the presence of a loving and supportive adult can make all the difference in a victim's resilience and recovery.

Safe Spaces. One of the most effective methods to help teens to protect themselves from digital abuse is to connect them with each other and with information. The That's Not Cool campaign includes a range of print, television, mobile, radio, and web ads, active engagement on Facebook, Twitter, Instagram, and Tumblr, as well as innovative new apps and games, providing ways for teens to learn and practice healthy relationship skills, and to ultimately "draw their digital line."

Legal Reform and Enforcement. Digital abuse thrives in part because it can be perpetrated with relative impunity and anonymity. The lack of applicable laws and the difficulty obtaining enforcement of existing laws leaves victims especially vulnerable. In fact, in a recent Supreme Court case, the judges decided by a 7-2 margin that online threats to kill, without actual evidence of the specific intent to threaten, do not violate the federal law. In other words, for an online threat — even one to rape, maim, or kill — to be criminal; prosecutors must have evidence to show what the threatening party is *actually* thinking. To quote Michelle Garcia, former director of the Stalking Resource Center, the Internet is "the crime scene of the 21st Century."

SOLUTIONS

The National Council of Juvenile and Family Court Judges works to enhance judicial skills to promote safety and batterer accountability through their program, the National Judicial Institute on Domestic Violence. Despite the sometimes grim legal outlook, court staff and judges can still be part of the solution for young people. They can:

- Check whether applications for protection or restraining orders include questions around the existence of digital abuse.

- Display information in courts about resources for teens that may experience digital abuse.

- In court hearings for physical violence or assault, assess whether the alleged perpetrator has engaged in other bullying behaviors that could be part of a pattern of cyberbullying or digital harassment.

- Provide accountability measures that are age-appropriate and reasonable with respect to the level of harm, if any.

- Mandate counseling and education for teens who are abusing others in the digital sphere.

- Refer teens who have been hurt from digital abuse as part of teen dating violence to specialized services for victims of dating violence.

- Collaborate with prosecutors, defense attorneys, mental health professionals, educators, other service providers, and parents to provide a wider range of effective responses to digital abuse.

- Visit local schools and other community venues to present information to teens and their parents about digital dating violence. Support and assist in (within ethical constraints) community-based efforts to provide teens with age-appropriate information about how to form healthy relationships and avoid abusive behaviors.

Consider providing your opinion to the legislature to support or critique bills, educational programming, or commissions to study the issues around digital abuse.

REAL WORLD SITUATIONS

Teen dating abuse is common and complex, studies say

—Source: Kim Painter, Special for USA TODAY, July 31, 2013

What are some strategies you might use in determining whether a relationship has the potential of becoming abusive?
Who would you inform about troubling developments in your relationship?

More than a third of teen guys and girls say they've been physically, emotionally or sexually abused in their dating relationships, according to new, unpublished data from a nationwide survey. Similar numbers of both sexes say they've been abusers.

Additional new research shows teens who abuse their girlfriends and boyfriends often share a past as middle-school bullies.

These findings, to be presented today in Honolulu at a meeting of the American Psychological Association, are the latest to shed light on a problem that has only come out of the shadows in recent years. Researchers and educators eager to stop violent patterns early—and reduce abuse not only among teens but among the adults they will become—already are testing programs that teach younger children and teens how to have healthier relationships. But as they seek to understand why so many young people hit, demean or force sex on their partners, much remains unclear.

One big question: Are boys and girls really equally at risk to become victims or abusers?

Some studies suggest they are and that girls may even be more likely than boys to lash out physically. In the new nationwide survey, which included 1,058 youths ages 14 to 20, 41% of girls and young women and 37% of boys and young men said they had been victims of dating abuse; 35% of girls and 29% of boys said they had physically, emotionally or sexually abused a partner, according to a news release from the association. Girls were more likely to say they had physically abused their partners; boys were "much more likely" to say they had sexually abused someone, the association says. But it did not provide specific numbers on those differences.

The survey also found that 29% of girls and 24% of guys said they had been both victims and abusers, in the same or different relationships.

Lead author Michele Ybarra, a researcher with the Center for Innovative Public Health Research in San Clemente, Calif., said in an e-mail that she could not discuss the study because it is under review for publication in a scientific journal. In general, data presented at a conference are not considered as authoritative as results reviewed by outside experts and then published.

The survey findings stand in stark contrast to one other set of statistics: In 2012, 94% of abuse victims who contacted the National Dating Abuse Helpline were female and just 6% were male, says Katie Ray Jones, president of the dating abuse helpline and the National Domestic Abuse Hotline. The dating line, which offers 24-hour help by online chat (at loveisrespect.org), text (text "loveis" to

22522) or phone (1-866-331-9474), is aimed at young people of both genders. But abused girls may be more willing to seek help, Jones says: "There's a lot of stigma about boys and men reaching out when they are victims."

The new survey results are in the line with some other findings, says Carlos Cuevas, a researcher from Northeastern University-Boston, who is presenting new data on dating violence among Latino youth at the conference. But he says the details behind the gender findings in various studies are important. When girls are the aggressors, he says, "it tends to be low-level behaviors, light hitting, name calling, things like that. When you look at serious sexual and severe physical assault, we tend to see a bit more from the boys than the girls."

Dorothy Espelage, a researcher at the University of Illinois-Urbana-Champaign, says, "Without measures of fear, severity and injury, we need to be cautious" about interpreting the new nationwide survey results. Espelage worked on the survey with Ybarra and on another study to be presented today which shows links between middle school bullying and teen dating violence. That study followed 625 youths from middle school to high school and found that those who admitted verbally bullying peers as middle-schoolers were seven times more likely than other young people to report physically abusing their dates four years later.

Both behaviors are often "about establishing dominance," she says. The results suggest there is a "violence trajectory" and "if it's not addressed, it will escalate."

While programs at school and elsewhere in communities may help, families can play a central role. In his own survey of 1,525 Latino youths ages 12 to 18, Cuevas says he found that boys with the strong family support "typical in traditional Latino culture" were less likely to psychologically abuse dates.

Teens, like adults, sometimes have trouble recognizing that they are in an abusive relationship, experts say. The website loveisrespect.org says it's a warning sign when a partner: Checks your cell phone or e-mail without permission, constantly puts you down, is extremely jealous or insecure, has an explosive temper, isolates you from family or friends, makes false accusations, physically hurts you in any way, tells you what to do, repeatedly pressures you to have sex.

LEARNING SCENARIOS

Scenario # 1

Manti Te'o's Story
Manti Te'o was a popular college football star who was the victim of catfishing in 2012. It is perhaps the most famous case of catfishing behavior. Te'o was involved in a long-distance online relationship with a woman allegedly by the name of Lennay Kekua. Te'o confessed that both he and his girlfriend were madly in love; despite having never met. Te'o was a football player for Notre Dame and moments before a nationally televised game, he was informed that his grandmother has passed away. The next day, he was told that his girlfriend had also passed away. Despite it all, Te'o went on to prevail in the big game and because of the devastating news, he received wide-spread news coverage.

Upon investigation, it was determined that Lennay Kekua did not exist and the Te'o had been catfished. How could Manti have avoided this situation? How could you determine whether an online profile is real?

Scenario #2

While on an online dating site, you recognized that one of your matches happens to be a guy your mom has dated. Your mom says that he was cute but not really her type—too young and he bored her. It was awkward as he continued to flirt with you, not knowing your real identity. You begin to notice that every time you log onto the site, he is online. He asks you to meet him at the mall for a "first date." He's much younger than your mother and seems to really be your type. Would you tell your mom? Would you meet with him? Why/Why not?

Scenario #3

You start flirting with a girl and really like her. She seems to be a perfect match. You like many of the same activities. You attend high school in different cities only 20 miles apart. You make a date to see a movie. You really seem to hit it off. When you arrive at the movie theatre, you discover that it is your best friend's current girlfriend. He thinks that they are in an exclusive relationship and he has even talked about marriage in the future. Would you continue to date her? Would you tell your best friend?

HELPFUL STRATEGIES

ONLINE DATING IS ONLY A SUPPLEMENT: It is not meant to replace it. Make sure that before you even visit a potential site, you set boundaries. For example: no more than 20 minutes a day using the site. Also, make sure that your in-person interactions far outweigh the amount of time your spend browsing online.

NEVER REVEAL PERSONAL INFORMATION IN YOUR PROFILE: Do not give your name, address, or phone number. Instead, use your non-personal email for communication. Non-personal email accounts are not attached to your work or your internet service provider and do not contain your name in the email address line. You can get a free email account from Gmail, Yahoo, or dozens of other sites. These are easy to use and help you keep your dating mail separate from your other communications.

REMEMBER THAT YOU KNOW NOTHING ABOUT THIS PERSON: The key to staying safe in online dating is staying aware. People who trick others into believing that they are someone else are very good at what they do. They may talk to you for a bit and find out a great deal about what you like or dislike, then model themselves on that information. Be careful about someone who seems, too good to be true. He or she probably is.

ALWAYS MEET IN PRE-ARRANGED PUBLIC PLACES: Tell friends or family where you are going, and call or text when you arrive and leave. It might be a good idea to ask a friend to call you at a pre-arranged time so that you do not lose track of time. You should have a flight plan for the first three dates you have with any individual that you share with someone trustworthy. If there is a problem, your friend will be much more likely to be able to help you if he or she knows where you are, who you are with, and what you are doing.

IF YOU FEEL UNCOMFORTABLE, LEAVE: This is probably the hardest advice to follow in online dating. All of us have been in situations in which we felt somewhat uncomfortable but did not want to be rude. Remember, if someone makes you uncomfortable on a first date, you have no business going out with him or her again, so the best thing to do is end the date quickly and leave.

IF POSSIBLE, HAVE SOMEONE DRIVE YOU TO YOUR DATE AND PICK YOU UP: This means that the person you meet will not have your license plate or a description of your vehicle. This may seem like overkill, but your personal information is available to someone who is dedicated enough to find it, so minimize your information exposure on the first few dates.

USE GOOD JUDGMENT: If someone does not return emails or texts, move on. There are far too many potential dates online for you to worry about someone who seems flaky.

LEARNING TASKS
20-minute Activity
- **Standard:**
    - *Standard 5*: Students will demonstrate the ability to use decision making skills to enhance health.
    - *Standard 7*: Students will demonstrate the ability to use interpersonal skills to enhance health and to avoid or reduce health risks.

- **Rationale:** Students must make decisions regarding online interactions from an informed vantage point. One particular strategy that might aid in this effort is to present real world cases that allow students to discuss consequences of disclosing personal information online. This activity is designed for students to understand the behaviors that may lead to dangerous online dating behavior.

- **Learning Outcome:** Describe the mental, emotional and physical issues related to online dating so that they can analyze the social dynamics surrounding online relationships.

- **Description of Activity:** Students will individually review one of the real world scenarios of this chapter and prepare a paragraph of 4-6 sentences that represent their personal opinions based on the guiding questions at the end of each scenario and share their opinions with the class.

ONE-DAY ACTIVITY

- Standard:
  - *Standard 3:* Students will demonstrate the ability to access valid information and products and services to enhance health.
  - *Standard 6:* Students will demonstrate the ability to use goals setting skills to enhance health.

- **Rationale:** Students need to be able to distinguish between how traditional dating dynamics differ from meeting new people online. This activity is designed to help students comprehend the impact and implications of how the image they present of themselves in online profiles can affect dating outcomes.

- **Learning Outcome:** Students will be able to compare and contrast traditional dating styles and online dating so they can make more informed decisions about how they present themselves online.

- **Description of Activity:** Students will present a self summary of an online profile and discuss the particular aim of the profile; whether it is a casual hook, develop friendships, or establish long term romantic relationships. They will discuss what the profile discloses about an individual and whether the personal information creates the potential for unintended consequences that might endanger the health and security of the individual. The goal is to help students evaluate how and why they assess people: what kinds of snap judgments they make, how they subconsciously make determinations about people without realizing it. It should also spark conversation about sending messages to unintended audiences.

ONE-WEEK ACTIVITY

- Standard:
  - *Standard 2:* Students will analyze the influence of family, peers, culture, media, technology, and other factors of health behaviors.
  - *Standard 8:* Students will demonstrate the ability to advocate for personal, family and community health.

- **Rationale:** The opinion of those close to you has a great deal of influence on how you behave both in real life and online. This lesson is designed to assist in creating awareness of the influence of family, friends and peers upon your personal decisions.

- **Learning Outcomes:** Students will be able to define measures for ensuring appropriate decisions that align with the expectations of family, friends and peers so they can analyze personal behaviors while engaging in online dating scenarios.

- **Description of Activity:** For this exercise, students will analyze an individual's intentions based on the personal summary in the previous activity. Students will have an opportunity to play the role of match maker. You will decide between three different prospective candidates to match with your male or female subject. You will have to justify your decisions based the perceived expectations of family and friends. You will analyze your subject's personal goals and develop a PowerPoint or Prezi presentation designed to address whether their profile is appropriate and aligned with their goals for finding a date online. You will make an argument as to why they "fit" with one of the matches provided - again, based shared values of family and friends. You might consider the following questions: What are the stated dating goals? What makes this person a good dating choice for your subject? Can you determine their true character based on the profile? Provide specific evidence as to whether the candidate is a good match.

ADDITIONAL RESOURCES:

Teens Are Actually More Old-Fashioned Than Adults When It Comes To Online Dating: http://www.techinsider.io/teens-dont-use-dating-apps-start-relationships-2015-10

6 Facts About Teen Romance In The Digital Age: http://www.pewresearch.org/fact-tank/2015/10/01/6-facts-about-teen-romance-in-the-digital-age/

Pros and Cons of Teens Using Online Dating Sites: http://mydatinghacks.com/should-teens-use-online-dating-websites/

Swipe Right For Prom: How Teens Are Using Tinder: https://www.theguardian.com/lifeandstyle/2016/mar/03/swipe-right-teenagers-dating-on-tinder-prom

What Is Teen Dating Violence: http://www.safv.org/teen-dating-violence

Tinder and 5 More Adult Dating Apps Teens Are Using, Too: https://www.commonsensemedia.org/blog/tinder-and-5-more-adult-dating-apps-teens-are-using-too

Is Your Teen on Tinder? https://www.teenlife.com/blogs/your-teen-tinder

---

[1] Looking For Love Online: TODAY Explores The World Of Digital Dating:http://www.today.com/health/looking-love-online-today-explores-world-digital-dating-t71731

2 How Has Social Media, Mobile Technology Affected Teens' Dating Lives?http://www.adweek.com/socialtimes/pew-social-media-mobile-teens-dating/627581

3 Should Your Teen Be Involved in Online Dating?http://www.teensafe.com/blog/should-your-teen-be-involved-in-online-dating/

4 Facebook's 'Teen Dating' Groups Are Every Parent's Nightmare Come To Life:http://www.washingtonpost.com/news/the-intersect/wp/2016.0201/facebooks-teen-dating-groups-are-every-parents-nightmare-come-to-life/

5 Online Dating Abuse Can Lead to Risky Behaviors in Teen Girls:http://loveaddictionnews/online-dating-abuse-can-lead-to-risky-behaviors-in-teen-girls/

6 Online Dating Abuse Can Lead to Risky Behaviors in Teen Girls:http://www.loveaddictiontreatment.com/loveaddictionnews/online-dating-abuse-can-lead-to-risky-behaviors-in-teen-girls/

7 Teenage Dating Apps Are Hunting Ground for Adult Abusers:http//:www.independent.co.uk/life-style/gadgets-and-tech/news/teenage-dating-apps-are-hunting-groound-for-adult-abusers-9662817.html

8 Teens, Technology and Romantic Relationships:http://www.pewinternet.org/2015/10/01/teens-technology-and-romantic-relationships/

9 Online Dating Dangers For Teens:http://www.wxyz.com/news/online-dating-dangers-for-teens

10 Rise In First Date Rape Claims Linked To Online Dating:http://www.bbc.com/news/uk-35513-52?utm_medium=email&utm_source=flipboard

11 Teen Dating Safety: https://www.teenhelp.com/dating-relationships/teen-dating-safety/

12 Mark Hardcastle, (2016). Meeting People Online: Online Safety Tips for Teens. The do's and don'ts of online relationships for teenshttp://teenadvice.about/od/streetsmarts/a/onlinefriends.htm

13 Teen Dating Trends 2015: Technology Can Make Relationships Closer But Facilitate Abuse, Report Finds:http://www.ibtimes.com/teen-dating-trends-2015-technology-can-make-relationships-closer-facilitate-abuse-2122731

14 Fun Activities For Talking About Dating, http://esl.yourdictionary.com/lesson-plans/esl-fun-activities-for-talking-about-dating.html

15 Dating Is More Awkward For Teens Addicted To Snapchat:http://northdallasgazette.com/2016/06/30/dating-awkward-teens-addicted-snapchat/

CHAPTER THREE

---•---

Sexting

What do you do when something private becomes public?

Who do you trust?

How should you respond to peer pressure?
How do you respond/deal with unwanted/unanticipated (sexual) advances/attention?

BEHAVIORS AND THEMES

SCALE AND SCOPE: You may have participated in sexting with a boyfriend or girlfriend. If you have, you are not alone. Some studies suggest that close to 40% of teenagers have been involved in sexting by receiving evocative pictures of someone else[1]. While this is an alarmingly high number, the number of teens who reported sending evocative pictures may be much smaller. Another 2009 survey by LG Mobile Phones found that 43% of teens claim to have sexted. In that same survey, 22% reported receiving a naked photo and 12% of those forwarded the message to others[2].

PROBLEM DEFINED: Sexting is the sending of provocative content (pictures and words) through the use of an electronic device[3]. Messages may be sent via photos, text messages, voicemails, IMs, videos through a phone, computer, tablet or any other electronic device. The concept behind sexting, sending sexually explicit content to a significant other (other hopeful significant other), has existed in our world for hundreds of years. The idea itself has not changed but the tool used to communicate the messages, technology, has drastically changed and, as a result, the consequences of sexting have changed as well.

Sexting in and of itself is not necessarily bad. It may be viewed as a way for individuals who are not physically in the same geographic location with one another to develop a closer relationship and/or maintain a close relationship during times of physical separation. A clinical psychology doctoral student and her colleagues at Drexel University studied the topic of sexting by surveying 870 individuals between the ages of 18 – 82.[4] The survey asked if the survey respondents had ever participated in sexting, if so with whom, and had they ever consented to participate in sexting without really wanting to do so. Survey results indicated that 82% of respondents had participated in sexting. Respondents who reported sexting because he or she wanted to do so reported higher levels of satisfaction with their

relationship. Sasko stated, "We don't know if sexting promotes intimacy or if people who are in satisfied relationship feel more intimate and that lead to sexting." What is apparent from this study is the situation matters. Sexting has a negative impact when an individual participates but does not really want to do so.

Sending and receiving texts and pictures from friends and classmates is easy with the technology we have around us every day. According to the 2015 Pew Research Center's Teens, Social Media and Technology Report, young adults in the US send an average of 30 text messages a day[5]. While no one knows exactly how many of those texts may contain sexually explicit content, whether using words or pictures, recent studies suggest that sexting is quickly becoming part of the typical teenage developmental experience[6]. According to Temple (2014), "We now know that teen sexting is fairly common. For instance, sexting may be associated with other typical adolescent behaviors such as substance use. Sexting is not associated with either good or poor mental well being." [7]

Sexting, like many other activities associated with the developmental experience during the teenage years, can result in serious, harmful consequences. How do you know if the pictures you are sending and receiving are okay? How do you when pictures cross a line and may result in negative consequences for yourself or those around you? The electronic world in which we live has abbreviated the line between private and public information. The line has been abbreviated so much that there may often be no line between them at all any more. This is the crux of the problem with sexting; the time and ease with which sexually explicit pictures and content that was intended to be private and shared with a special individual becomes public. In fact, 40% of teenagers have had a sexually explicit photo forwarded to them or shown to them.[8] (find my citation for this). Additionally, sexting among teenagers has been linked to drug and alcohol abuse, early sexual activity, and higher rates of sexually transmitted diseases.[9]

BIOLOGICAL TRIGGERS FOR SEXTING: Exploring sexuality is a normal and healthy part of adolescent development. In fact the term "adolescence" can be traced back to the Latin word "adolescere" meaning "to grow up". Obviously, this phase in the human development is a crucial time of development as young adults mature into adults. During this developmental time, our thinking shifts as adolescents begin to develop a sexual interest largely due to the change in hormones. This developmental period is marked by exploration and curiosity as new emotions and feelings are encountered and discovered.

The digital environment can provide a safe avenue for young adults who are looking for information related to sexual health and development. Teens may find it easier to look for information digitally than to ask an adult. This is a benefit of the technological world in which we live. It is natural that sexual exploration during adolescence turns to the digital world, and specifically, to the easy sharing of sexually explicit pictures.

LEGAL RAMIFICATIONS: A unique consideration when discussing sexting is the potential for serious legal consequences that could result from sexting. Participating in sexting could result in jail, fines, life-time of placement on the registered sex offender list or required diversion programs intended to educate the offended about sexting. Some states have specific laws about sexting and revenge porn.

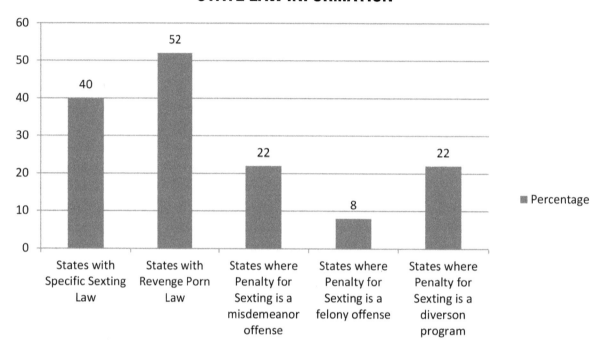

STATE LAW INFORMATION[10]

State Laws for Sexting

IMPACT ON HEALTH: While sexting can be part of a healthy romantic relationship, it can have serious, life altering consequences as well. A picture that is sent electronically can easily be posted online. Once online, the picture will never disappear. The picture will exist online forever. The photo may reappear years after it was first taken and shared. A future boyfriend or girlfriend may see the picture online. How do you think he or she will feel about seeing a photo you sent to someone else? What about a future employer seeing that picture? What about your grandfather seeing that picture?

In addition to the potential embarrassment, some young adults have experienced harassment and bullying and revenge porn. In one recent study of 1,015 teenagers aged 11 to 19, over 300 had experienced online sexual harassment within the previous six months. [11] One young adult, Jane, who had a sexually explicit photo of herself posted online, shared she was terrified to go out in public for fear someone would tell her they saw the pictures. She reported feeling distrustful of everyone, including her closest friends. [12]

The bullying and harassment can be severe enough that young adults develop grave mental and emotional health issues and social isolation, including thoughts of suicide.[13] In 2008, Jessica Logan, took a photo of herself naked while on spring break with her friends. Jessica shared her photo with her boyfriend who forwarded the picture to his friends. Upon returning to school, she was sexually harassed on a regular basis. Despite frequently skipping school, she managed to graduate from high school. One month later, she killed herself. [14] This is just one of many cases where sexting was the impetus for bullying and harassment that resulted in suicide.

In some cases, the harassment became so severe that it led to the development of a new concept known as sextortion.[15] This is the combination of sex and extortion. While those who are extortionists have always held power over their victims, those who are sextortionist hold particular power as the victim becomes desperate to maintain their privacy. The sextortionist, many of whom are registered sex offenders, may use their power for their own financial gain but most often they use their power to further their own sexual desires. Typically a sextortionist captures a photo that was sexted and then contacts the individual threatening to publicly expose the initial photo and embarrass the individual unless more photos are sent.

KEY CONCEPTS

Consent: Giving permission to another individual so that individual can do something or see something personal.

Harassment: Applying aggressive pressure or intimidation to another individual.

Sexting: The sending and receiving of sexually provocative messages and/or photographs via electronic devices.

Extortion: The combination of sex and extortion. This is a form of sexual exploitation that includes using force to obtain money or sexual favors from someone in exchange for keeping their sexting material private.

REAL WORLD SITUATIONS

"Girl, 15, commits suicide after friends share nude Snapchat video taken without permission" [16]

—*Source WFLA.com*

Why do you think students joined in the social media name calling of Tovonna?

What are other ways Tovonna might have handled the situation?

Levon Holton-Teamer sent her 15-year-old to clean her room Sunday afternoon, not knowing that would be the last time she would see her alive. Minutes later, the mom went to look for her daughter, Tovonna.

"I go to the bathroom; I couldn't get in the bathroom. The bathroom light was off so I tried to get in and I looked down and I saw the puddle of blood. I tried to apply the pressure, the pressure to her head. I tried to save her," Holton-Teamer said Wednesday.

Tovonna was a freshman at Wiregrass Ranch High School in Wesley Chapel. The teen had taken the gun from her mother's purse. Just hours before Tovonna had expressed concern over a nude picture her friends had taken of her without her permission.

"Tovonna would say, 'Mommy, I owe them; I owe them'. I said, 'What do you mean you owe them?' I couldn't understand what was wrong," Holton-Teamer said.

Hours after Tovonna's death, the girl's aunt took to Facebook in search of answers.

"I just said, 'If anybody knows anything, what happened? Have you heard of anything? Do you know who these kids are who have the pictures?' I thought it was just pictures and then the kids started inboxing me," said Angel Scott, Tovonna's aunt. Scott learned it was actually a nude video of the girl, taken while she was in the shower.

"Everybody was out there talking about her and calling her names and they said it went up on social media, Snapchat. I'd never heard of that before about 3 something that afternoon," she said.

Tovonna was dead three hours later.

The Pasco County School District heard the bullying complaints and turned the investigation over to the Pasco County Sheriff's Office. Detectives continue to investigate. The school provided a crisis team for students Monday and Tuesday of this week.

Tovonna's picture had been shared thousands of times on social media with the #stopbullying. The teen's family is now calling for justice.

"I want them to pay, to feel what we feeling, even if their child is convicted or in trouble they can go visit their child," Scott said.

"Newtown High School students charged in 'sexting' ring"

—Source: ww.cnn.com[17]

What are the pros and cons of sexting being classified as a misdemeanor offense? A felon? Should this be a criminal offense at all?

What is a reasonable way to addressing the negative impact of sexting?

Three Newtown High School students have been arrested and accused of involvement in a "sexting" ring that circulated sexually explicit images and videos of other students, sometimes for money, police in Connecticut said Wednesday.

Last May, students began transmitting sexually explicit images and videos on cell-phone text messaging apps such as Snapchat, Facetime, iMessage, KiK and others, according to a press release from the Newtown Police Department.

Three male juveniles were arrested Tuesday night and charged with obscenity, transmitting or possession of child pornography by a minor as well as felony counts of possession of child pornography and obscenities as to minors, according to Sgt. Aaron Bahamonde of the Newtown Police Department. It's unclear whether the juveniles have attorneys.

Another 20 students have been referred to a community-based Juvenile Review Board, which delivers a "consequence on the juvenile-aged offender, yet keeps the juvenile offender out of the State of Connecticut Criminal Justice System," according to the press release.

The charges were brought after a six-month investigation that included dozens of interviews with students and parents, as well as executions of search and seizure warrants, the press release says.

Authorities were alerted after the incident was brought to the attention of school officials.

It was their "quick action" that contained the spread of explicit media to 50 students in a school of roughly 1,800, a difficult feat in a digital world known for elements spreading rapidly on the Internet, Bahamonde said.

Some of the students who received copies of the images tried to profit by selling the pictures and videos for $10-$20 apiece, Bahamonde said.

The students whose images were shared were also "held accountable for their action in taking the pictures and forwarding them," but Bahamonde said they are also victims who never intended the images to go beyond the person to whom they were sent.

"There are victims here, real victims. You can imagine, as a student, going to school knowing others might possess pictures of you when you only intended one person to have them," Bahamonde said. "It can be devastating on your psyche and you don't know what can happen afterward. Peer pressure is hard enough in high school."

The names and ages of the three teens that are facing charges have been withheld because they are minors, Bahamonde said.

No court date has been set for them, but they are expected to appear in Danbury Juvenile Court in the "next couple of weeks," according to Bahamonde.

In Colorado last month, high school and middle school students accused of exchanging hundreds of naked photos were spared criminal charges but a district attorney warned of more severe consequences if it happened again.

Thom LeDoux, the district attorney for the state's 11th Judicial District, said investigators did not find aggravating factors like adult involvement, the posting of graphic images to the Internet, coercion and related unlawful sexual contact.

He added that while the "decision does not condone or excuse the behavior of the individuals involved," authorities wanted to avoid "the inequities in punishing just those that have come forward, have been identified, or have cooperated with the authorities."

Colorado is one of 30 states without modern sexting laws, which often provide leniency to adolescents as long as the sexting is consensual and is considered a misdemeanor mistake in exploring sexuality.

Of 20 states with sexting laws -- including Connecticut -- 11 of them classify the offense as a misdemeanor, prescribing out-of-court "diversion" remedies or informal sanctions such as counseling, according to the Cyberbullying Research Center run by Dr. Sameer Hinduja and criminal justice professor Justin W. Patchin of University of Wisconsin-Eau Claire.

Four of the 20 states, however, also allow for felony charges.

Florida and Utah, for example, allow for a felony charge for repeat offenders. Georgia law says the charge depends on the facts of the case.

The fourth state, Nebraska, is the only state among the 20 that makes all sexting offenses a felony, but grants an affirmative defense to those age 18 and younger if the sexting was with another minor at least age 15 and was consensual, without distribution to another person.

Even with all the new laws, most of the country remains far behind the fast-moving pace of teens and technology, analysts say.

Twenty states have modern sexting laws; among them are--Arizona, Arkansas, Connecticut, Florida, Georgia, Hawaii, Illinois, Louisiana, Nebraska, Nevada, New Jersey, and New York.

Think Twice Before you Type: Real Life Sexting Stories
—Written by an anonymous teenage girl[18]

How might one cope with the betrayal of a trusted friend?

What are ways friends can provide support to one another in the midst of sexting betrayal that leads to bullying?

I was a normal 13 year old teenage girl, but one day everything changed for the worse. What happened to me I will never forget and will be imprinted on me for the rest of my life. There was this perfect boy in my life at the time. In the end he was one of the worst things that could have happened to me. I thought he was the one for me; we'd be together for a very long time. I was so happy when I was around him; he told me I was beautiful. All the right things a girl wants to hear, he told me and I believed him. After he had told me he loved me, one night he asked me if I would send a photo of my breasts. I took the photo that night, something I regret even now when I'm past that chapter in my life.

I didn't send the photo to him, the next day I asked my best friend if I should or not. She said the best thing a best friend could say to me that day, no. She told me I was better than that and that I shouldn't have to send a photo for him to like me. Which is what I want you girls to know, even if a boy tells you that he loves you and that he won't show anyone, still don't do it. If he gets angry at you for saying no, in the end, he was really not worth your time. He should love you for who you are and not what your body looks like.

The day I asked my best friend if I should send it, I did a silly mistake and left the photo on my phone. I will never know why I didn't just delete the photo right then and there, that is something I will never be able to tell you. That day, mistakes just kept on coming. I was in class chatting with my friends and not worrying about anything but myself, when someone who I thought was my friend stole my phone out of where I placed it in my pencil case, and found the photo amongst other photos in my phone. They sent it to their phone without me realizing and before I knew it, the whole school had a photo of my breasts on their phone.

Unlike all the other girls that sent a photo to a guy around the time that I did, mine wasn't taken lightly. I was called names, people came up in my face and yelled at me, over five people tried to bash me. I didn't tell anyone because I thought it would get better, but it kept getting worse. I didn't know what to do or who to tell so I lived with being bullied for at least two months. I had no friends; everyone hated me for something I didn't do. The feeling of being hated so much is hard to explain.

You were once the popular girl and you had a lot of friends and then one day everything changes. I became depressed and I hated my body from then on. I still have trouble trusting boys to this day. If I had the chance to go back and change everything I would. I never would have even considered taking the photo. Today I still have to live with the feeling that everyone knows what my body looks like, sometimes, even someone brings up what happened to me. I still feel disgusted with myself and ashamed of what I did.

I felt alone and not wanted at the time and it becomes even worse when you take a photo and what happened to me, happens to you, your parents find out. The way my mum looked at me made me feel like I was disowned. She was ashamed to call me her daughter. My dad on the other hand still to this day, we are and will never be as close as we used to be. This is nothing anyone would want to experience.

The best friend's point of view:

The day I found out what my friend had done. It was the when everything changed; I had found out that my best friend had taken a photo of her breasts and it had gotten around the whole school. Before all of it had happened she was a loud and fun person to be around but when it got sent around she was not herself, she would cry all the time but at the same time acted like everything was okay. She'd put on a smile just so everyone would leave her alone and wouldn't stare at her.

When I saw her she seemed to be becoming more unlike herself it scared me because I didn't know what to do, or how to take her pain away. The humiliation she was feeling was getting too hard for her even to be at school. She even pretended she was sick so she didn't have to go to school and face everyone and their opinions. I was there by her side through this whole experience. We have been through so much in the past five years and this just made us even closer than we already were.

I saw everything that happened to her. When she wasn't even around I heard people talking about it and how much they hated her. They didn't even know her and that hurt me a lot. I can't imagine what she felt and I would never like to either. Watching my best friend go through this made me realize what can really happen if you attempt to send this to a boy you think you love and he loves you, or even a guy who tells you you're beautiful.

The joke about this all is that we thought this guy who sent the picture around was our best friend. Our friendship wasn't the same after this happened, and never will be. Sometimes the people you think you can trust let you down. She got through all of this eventually with me by her side, acting like we did at the start, before all of it happened. True friends will stick by you no matter what. Just think before you send that picture of your body; do you really trust him?

LEARNING SCENARIOS

Scenario #1

Your girlfriend just broke up with you. You are furious after all the time you spent together, not to mention all the money you spent taking her out and buying her gifts. Only a week has passed and she is already dating someone else. In a moment of resentment and anger, you decide to forward a text you had received from her to a couple of classmates, including her new boyfriend. The text contains a picture of her topless. She will regret ever breaking up with you and hurting you. What potential outcomes might occur as a result of your actions for you? What outcomes might occur as a result of your actions for her? How might this make you feel better or worse?

Scenario #2

You have always been athletic and enjoy gym class. The locker room and showers are not your favorite part of the day but you can suffer through that without too much problem. Some of your classmates are bullied and made fun of in the locker room and you are just happy not to be those folks. Then, one afternoon, you realize it could be worse. Someone took pictures in the locker room of students changing clothes and texted them to their friends. The pictures were forwarded and now the pictures are all over the school. How do you show your face in school or anywhere else after those pictures have gone around? Why would someone do this? What might the consequences be for those students who sent the initial pictures? What about consequences for those who looked at and forwarded the pictures?

Scenario #3

You have been dating your girlfriend for four months now. You are having a good time together and things are going well. You decide you want to heat things up a bit so you send her a sexy text of what you want her to do to you. You are hoping she will respond with something equally hot. You are not really intending to act on the text, these are just words. She does not respond and you are annoyed. The next time you see her you want to give her a hard time for not reciprocating. Would it be a good idea to pressure her about the text? Why or why not? What are reasons she might be hesitant to participate in sexting with you? What are potential outcomes for each of you in this scenario?

HELPFUL STRATEGIES

Respect Yourself: Remember the first person you owe respect to is yourself. You should never do something you do not want to do or do something just because some else wants you to. Anyone pressuring you to do something against your will is not a friend.

Respect Everyone: All individuals deserve to have their privacy respected. Taking their pictures and/or sending pictures without their consent is an invasion of privacy. The "Golden Rule" really does apply here: treat others they way you wish to be treated yourself.

Permanence of digital content: Always remember everything posted on the web lives there for eternity. Do not post anything on the internet that you would not want a future employer and future son or daughter to see.

Ask for Advice: When in doubt about looking at something someone sent you, sending a message of your own, or looking at something on the web asks a trusted adult for advice. This adult could be a parent, teacher, older sibling or doctor. Those individuals can help you determine what is a safe activity in which to participate and what is a potentially harmful (illegal even) activity.

Be Supportive: Remember if someone is experiencing unwanted sexting or pressure to participate in sexting, what they need most is a trusted and supportive friend. Be there for that person, do not participate in applying pressure or making fun of that individual, and seek help from a trusted adult.

LEARNING TASKS

20-Minute Activity:

- **Standards**
  - Standard 4: Students will demonstrate the ability to use interpersonal communication skills to enhance health and avoid or reduce health risks.

  - Standard 7: Students will demonstrate the ability to practice health-enhancing behaviors and avoid or reduce health risks.

  - **Rationale:** The pressure to sext from a loved one or a peer can be intense, especially during the teenage years as you are developing into an adult. Many teenagers are unready to respond to this pressure, leading them to make decisions they later may regret. You need to learn ways to make informed, thoughtful decisions about your choices and be prepared to handle this pressure.

- **Learning Outcomes:** Students will learn to identify multiple ways to respond to the pressure to text so they can make thoughtful decisions.

- **Description of Activity:** Teachers will facilitate a discussion of the pressures students may feel to participate in sexting as teenagers. Students should identify ways in which peers apply pressure to one another and discuss ways to mediate this pressure.

- **Supporting Resources**
  - http://www.connectsafely.org/tips-for-dealing-with-teen-sexting/
  - https://www.verywell.com/what-is-sexting-and-how-it-leads-to-bullying-460560

      o   https://www.edutopia.org/discussion/facilitating-meaningful-class-discussions

ONE-DAY ACTIVITY

- **Standards**
  - o Standard 1: Students will comprehend concepts related to health promotion and disease prevention to enhance health.

  - o Standard 5: Students will demonstrate the ability to use decision-making skills to enhance health.

- **Rationale:** This activity prompts you to consider an instance of sexting gone badly from various viewpoints. It is far too easy to jump to conclusions about individuals involved in sexting, including the target, the instigator, and those associated (family and friends) with the target and the instigator. This case will allow you the opportunity to consider multiple viewpoints, empathize with each participant, and develop mechanisms (both the emotional maturity and physical well-being) to handle situations similar to the case study.

- **Learning Outcomes:** Students will develop empathy for all involved in a sexting situation and will share specific ways to be an advocate for themselves and others so they can promote their mental, physical and emotional health when confronted with sexting.

- **Description of Activity:** Teachers will review the case description below with the students and assign students to work in cooperative groups to discuss the case through a role play activity. Students will read the case, work cooperatively with classmates to consider the scenario from various viewpoints and develop possible ways to tackle the situation.

Case Description

You are a sophomore who has been dating the Nick for 4 months. Recently, Nick has been asking you to text him a photo of yourself. You do not want to but fear he will break up if you do not. Nick is a senior and every girl in school wants to date him. After weeks of pressure, you decide to go for it. What can it hurt after all? You are only sending the picture to him and he really cares about you. Over the next month, you text several pictures to him. Each picture is more and more sexy than the last one. He is so happy; you can't believe how lucky you are to be with him. You are positive you will get to go to prom with him. Nick is hanging out with the guys one day and texts them the pictures that they do not believe Carmen is really sending. One of the guys posts some of the pictures online with the caption, "High School Hottie or Sophomore Slut?" just for fun. By the next school day, hundreds of students have seen the picture and are weighing in.

ONE WEEK ACTIVITY

- **Standards**
  - Standard 3: Students will demonstrate the ability to access valid information and products and service to enhance health.
  - Standard 8: Students will demonstrate the ability to advocate for personal, family, and community health.

- Rationale: This activity requires students to research policies from other schools, learn how to write basic policy, delve more deeply in the legal aspects of sexting as teenagers, and communicate expectations concisely and clearly. Students will gain an understanding of the intricacies of policies around sexting and implications of those policies. The activity will also provide students the opportunity to proactively address the issue of sexting in their school.

- **Learning Outcomes:** Students will write expectations for appropriate behavior clearly and succinctly write a usable school policy so they can make informed decisions about sexting.

- **Description of Activity:** Teachers will introduce the idea of policy writing to students. Examples of current school/school district policy may be reviewed to assist students in understanding the format of a typical school policy. Students will research policy writing, current school policies in other school districts around the issue of sexting, and write a proposed policy for their school. Ideally, students should present their policy to the school principal for possible adoption by the school.

- **Supporting Resources**
  - Policy Writing Framework: https://www.eduweb.vic.gov.au/edulibrary/public/schacc/tmpltpolicywriting.pdf
  - Sexting, The School Superintendents Association, http://www.aasa.org/content.aspx?id=3390
  - Addressing Sexting in Your School District, The School Superintendents Association: http://www.aasa.org/content.aspx?id=7672

---

[1] 11 Facts about Sexting | DoSomething.org | Volunteer for ... (n.d.). Retrieved June 6, 2017, from https://www.bing.com/cr?IG=6DB0511E30AD40088C515A99B3C5EBE6&CID=2EA422C441F96E5B165D28 5D40FF6FCC&rd=1&h=ygMzactRADHYxWgLHmeLoPdYlfK6atu-IjV-GtjBvU0&v=1&r=https%3a%2f%2fwww.dosomething.org%2fus%2ffacts%2f11-facts-about-sexting&p=DevEx,5063.1

[2] Toppo, G. (2009, June 17). Retrieved June 06, 2017, from https://usatoday30.usatoday.com/news/education/2009-06-17-cellphones-in-class_N.htm

[3] Lohman, R. C. (2011, March 30). Sexting Teens. Retrieved June 06, 2017, from https://www.psychologytoday.com/blog/teen-angst/201103/sexting-teens

[4] Whitehead, N. (2015, August 08). Could Sexting Help Your Relationship? Retrieved June 06, 2017, from http://www.npr.org/sections/health-shots/2015/08/08/430322824/could-sexting-help-your-relationship

[5] Lenhart, A. (2015, April 08). Teens, Social Media & Technology Overview 2015. Retrieved June 06, 2017, from http://www.pewinternet.org/2015/04/09/teens-social-media-technology-2015/

[6] Sexting may be the new normal for many teens, researchers say. (n.d.). Retrieved June 06, 2017, from http://www.latimes.com/science/la-sci-sn-sexting-teens-risky-sex-20141006-story.html

[7] Hays, B. (2014, October 07). Study: Sexting is the new normal for teens. Retrieved June 06, 2017, from http://www.upi.com/Health_News/2014/10/07/Study-Sexting-is-the-new-normal-for-teens/3341412696568/

[8] 11 Facts about Sexting | DoSomething.org | Volunteer for ... (n.d.). Retrieved June 6, 2017, from https://www.bing.com/cr?IG=6DB0511E30AD40088C515A99B3C5EBE6&CID=2EA422C441F96E5B165D28 5D40FF6FCC&rd=1&h=ygMzactRADHYxWgLHmeLoPdYlfK6atu-IjV-GtjBvU0&v=1&r=https%3a%2f%2fwww.dosomething.org%2fus%2ffacts%2f11-facts-about-sexting&p=DevEx,5063.1

[9] Sexting, Substance Use and Sexual Risk Behavior in Young ... (n.d.). Retrieved June 6, 2017, from http://www.bing.com/cr?IG=66E7B930B185417E8E2B352653B52E1B&CID=2206684B8B016A9F29BD62D28 A076B7E&rd=1&h=GwZ4do9NdbXyjQSFO4WmvHqIwcB9eF-7llQXabTBZwA&v=1&r=http%3a%2f%2fwww.sciencedirect.com%2fscience%2farticle%2fpii%2fS1054139X1200 2327&p=DevEx,5064.1

[10] State Sexting Laws - Cyberbullying Research Center. (n.d.). Retrieved June 6, 2017, from http://www.bing.com/cr?IG=E062EAAFBA71400FAFF67D490B7E29A4&CID=172ED0D256516B361F54DA4 B57576A6A&rd=1&h=4q1Rm_tN-dWEsamJzPRN6YkvWB0ehCFRDh6sq3K2l5c&v=1&r=http%3a%2f%2fcyberbullying.org%2fstate-sexting-laws.pdf&p=DevEx,5062.1

[11] Scheff, S. (2016, February 24). Teens, Cyberbullying, Sexual Harassment and Social Media: The New Normal? Retrieved June 06, 2017, from http://www.huffingtonpost.com/sue-scheff/teens-sexual-harassment-a_b_9310060.html

[12] Cooper, G. (2012, April 12). Sexting: a new teen cyber-bullying 'epidemic' Retrieved June 06, 2017, from http://www.telegraph.co.uk/technology/facebook/9199126/Sexting-a-new-teen-cyber-bullying-epidemic.html

[13] N. (n.d.). Facts and statistics. Retrieved June 06, 2017, from https://www.nspcc.org.uk/preventing-abuse/child-abuse-and-neglect/bullying-and-cyberbullying/bullying-cyberbullying-statistics/

[14] Meyer, E. (2009, December 16). Sexting and Suicide. Retrieved June 06, 2017, from https://www.psychologytoday.com/blog/gender-and-schooling/200912/sexting-and-suicide

[15] (n.d.). Retrieved June 06, 2017, from http://www.wiredsafety.com/sexting-sextortion-and-revenge-porn

[16] McCowan, C. (2016, June 10). Girl, 15, commits suicide after friends share nude Snapchat video taken without permission. Retrieved June 06, 2017, from http://wfla.com/2016/06/08/girl-15-commits-suicide-after-friends-share-nude-snapchat-video/

[17] Ferrigno, L. (2016, January 27). Newtown High School students charged in 'sexting' ring. Retrieved June 06, 2017,

from http://www.cnn.com/2016/01/27/us/connecticut-high-school-sexting-ring/index.html

[18] Real Life Sexting Stories. (n.d.). Retrieved June 06, 2017, from http://think-twice-before-you-type.weebly.com/real-life-sexting-stories.html

ADDITIONAL RESOURCES:

http://childrefuge.org/child-pornography/what-is-sextortion.html

http://cyberbullying.org/state-sexting-laws.pdf

http://www.huffingtonpost.com/2013/05/24/evanston-baseball-sexting_n_3332752.html

http://kidshealth.org/parent/firstaid_safe/home/2011_sexting.html

Lenhart A. Teens and Sexting. 2009, Dec 15

Mitchell KJ, Finkelhor D, Jones LM, et al. Prevalence and characteristics of youth sexting: A national study. Pediatrics 2012;129:13e20.(link is external)

http://www.ncpc.org/programs/living-safer-being-smarter/surfing-safer/cyberbullying-and-sexting-on-social-media.

https://www.nspcc.org.uk/preventing-abuse/keeping-children-safe/sexting/

http://www.pewinternet.org/2015/04/09/teens-social-media-technology-2015/

https://www.psychologytoday.com/blog/gender-and-schooling/200912/sexting-and-suicide

http://www.telegraph.co.uk/technology/facebook/9199126/Sexting-a-new-teen-cyber-bullying-epidemic.html

http://www.utmb.edu/newsroom/article9957.aspx

https://www.verywell.com/what-is-sexting-and-how-it-leads-to-bullying-460560

http://wellconnectedmom.com/blog/2010/09/10/teens-cellphones-sexting-a-primer-part-iv/

Ybarra ML, Mitchell KJ. "Sexting" and its relation to sexual activity and sexual risk behavior in a national survey of adolescents. J Adolescent Health 2014:1-8.(link is external)

CHAPTER FOUR

Hate Speech and Advocacy

Why can it be so easy to say and write mean,
hateful things to each other?

How has technology influenced hate speech and advocacy in the global setting?

What motivates us to hate?

BEHAVIORS AND THEMES

SCALE AND SCOPE: Young adults are among the most active participants in online environments; much of this time is unsupervised by older adults. This usage combined with the still developing teenage brain, particularly in terms of developing critical thinking skills, makes hate speech online especially toxic. A typical component of development during the teenage years includes actively seeking out groups to join either to become part of a social group or to join a cause and movement to further assist in developing an identity separate from your family. Groups who foster hate speech often target young adults for this reason. [1]

PROBLEM DEFINED: Hate speech is any discourse that affronts, threatens, or promotes hatred toward groups or individuals based on race, gender, sexual orientation, religion, national original, disability or other characteristics. In general, hate speech relies on stereotypes about insular groups to try to influence hostile behavior towards that group. While intimidating hate speech does not always result in the commission of discriminatory violence, it can establish a rationale for attacking particular groups."[2]

Hate speech has always existed in our society. The addition of online communications has altered the impact of hate speech. Social media tools such as Twitter, Facebook, Snapchat have provided new outlets for communication. Online newspapers and blogs allow readers to post comments after articles providing additional forums for communication.

PERCENTAGE OF RESPONDENTS WHO HAVE ENCOUNTERED FORMS OF HATE AND HARASSMENT ONLINE

Pew Center http://www.pewinternet.org/2014/10/22/online-harassment/

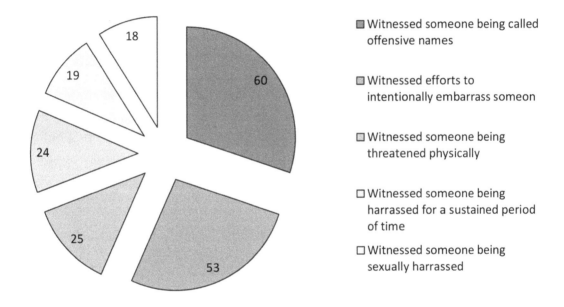

- Witnessed someone being called offensive names
- Witnessed efforts to intentionally embarrass someon
- Witnessed someone being threatened physically
- Witnessed someone being harrassed for a sustained period of time
- Witnessed someone being sexually harrassed

Online Harassment, Pew Research Center [3]

The ease, with which mass communication can occur, often anonymously, leads to more hateful comments shared through social media accounts such as Facebook and Twitter. The anonymity provided by the digital environment allows individuals to share detrimental thoughts and attitudes with little accountability or consequence. The internet also allows individuals to spread hate-filled comments with ease. The Human Rights First organization reported that comments were shared[4]. Those who wish to spread hate are also using the comment section often available at the end of online articles to share racist, sexist, and discriminatory comments. In one example, The Palm Beach Post, a Florida-based newspaper, had to disable the comments section after an article detailing the Bernard Madoff financial scandal due to the torrent of anti-Semitic comments.[5]

The more and more time we spend online, the more accustomed we get to instant gratification. This encourages us to feel we must share our thoughts and opinions immediately regardless of how hurtful or insulting they may be. A recent study by the Pew Center revealed significant percentages of individuals have observed hate speech and hate-filled content online. Social media is now the most likely way in which teenagers will encounter hate.[6]

Individuals are not the only ones participating in hate speech online. The Leadership Conference on Civil Rights reported in 2009 that extremist groups had begun using mainstream social networking sites as well as extremist sites to spread their messages of hate since the mid-2000s.[9] The internet allowed those groups to more quickly and easily connect with other individuals and further spread hate messages.

Teenagers may be prime targets for groups looking to spread hate and grow their membership[9]. Prior to the teenage years, children's lives and social circles primarily revolve around family members and those individual's sanctioned by family members. As teenagers develop they begin to broaden their social lives to include more individuals and begin to seek approval from friends as those relationships become increasingly more important.[10] Additionally, teenagers may begin to feel a strong urge to join activist groups as they are developing into active citizens. These non-familial entities provide connection, a sense of belonging and ways for teenagers to be active in an organized group. The internet provides the perfect marketing tool for hate propaganda and recruitment. Partners Against Hate noted that some groups specifically target youth for recruiting online by developing seemingly historical websites.[11] These websites appear to contain accurate information and the unsuspecting teenager may delve deeply into the website not realizing the information is inaccurate and just a ploy to attract new recruits.

IMPACT ON HEALTH: Psychologist Albert Bandura (1961) conducted experiments to determine if social behaviors, in particular, aggression, could be learned through observation.[12] In the study, 72 children (36 boys and 36 girls) were assessed to determine their levels of aggressive behavior using a rating scale. The children were then assigned to groups so they displayed similar levels of aggression. The groups were subdivided again into three groups with one group being exposed to an aggressive situation, one being exposed to a non-aggressive situation, and serving as a control group. The children exposed to aggressive modeling demonstrated significantly more aggressive behaviors than those in the control group or those exposed to non-aggressive modeling. These results supported Bandura's Social Learning Theory, meaning that aggressive behavior is learned through observation of aggressive behavior by another individual. This has important implications for the rise and spread of hate speech through our digital world.

ADVOCACY AGAINST HATE: Advocacy is the willful and intentional practice of prompting positive and appropriate behavior. In the case of online hate speech, advocacy means encouraging others to refrain from participating in hate-filled speech and rhetoric online.

This type of advocacy includes individuals abstaining from posting comments that are mean and hurtful and targeted at specific groups of individuals. A second aspect to advocacy is recognizing hate speech and acting to stop that speech. Most websites have readily accessible links to report inappropriate content. This is an easy way to advocate for tolerance and acceptance. That really is the easy part.

The more difficult aspect to advocacy is recognizing websites that appear to be reputable websites but are really run by hate groups. These groups are using the internet to develop seemingly accurate websites but are really presenting and promulgating inaccurate information as a way to entice young adults into the world of bigotry, intolerance, hate and, often, violence. As consumers of internet information, it is imperative teenagers develop and utilize skills to determine reputable versus non-reputable websites.

KEY CONCEPTS

Doxxing: Having your personal information shared on the internet as a way of coercing you to refrain from stating your opinion or as retaliation for stating your opinion. Doxxing is most often used against specific groups based on sexual orientation, disability, gender, race, religion, or ethnic origin.

Hate Speech: Any form of speech (oral or written) that attacks a person or group on the basis of characteristic such as sexual orientation, disability, gender, race, religion, or ethnic origin.

Social Learning Theory: The view that individuals learn by observing the behavior and actions of others.

Upstander: Courageous, powerful individuals who stand up for victims when they are bullied, assaulted, or persecuted.

REAL WORLD SITUATIONS

Internet Hate Speech Can Lead To Acts Of Violence
—*Source: By Omar Sacirbey, Religion News Service, May 6, 2014*[14]

What are some ramifications of hate speech online?
What are steps one can take to combat hate speech online?

Anti-Muslim hate speech on the Internet is commonplace and can motivate some people to commit acts of violence against Muslims, according to a report released Tuesday (May 6) by Muslim Advocates, a legal and advocacy group in San Francisco.

"When you have threatening comments online and they go unchecked, people start thinking it's acceptable," said Madihha Ahussain, an attorney and the report's lead author. "And it doesn't take long to figure out that what becomes acceptable online becomes acceptable in the real world."

The report contains examples of hate speech and how it can lead to violence, as well as how victims of online hate speech can report it and counter it. The report aims to help educate parents, students, youth, community leaders, Internet companies and policymakers on how to counter online hate speech.

Ahussain said that anti-Muslim websites give like-minded people a place to gather and at the same time win new supporters through their posts. As an example, Ahussain cited the Facebook page of anti-Muslim blogger Pamela Geller, which she said grew from roughly 19,000 followers in July 2013 to some 78,000 people as of late April.

The report also cites the example of Robert James Talbot Jr., a Texas man who created a Facebook page for the American Insurgent Movement, whose stated aim was to start a revolution and overthrow the U.S. government. Talbot was a regular reader of Geller's Atlas Shrugs blog.

FBI agents arrested Talbot on March 27 on allegations that he plotted to blow up mosques and other buildings.

The report said most social media platforms include features where people can report what they perceive to be violations of speech guidelines.

"I believe they take this very seriously because they want to have a place where people don't feel threatened by others," Ahussain said.

Felicia Day's Public Details Put Online After She Described Gamergate Fears

—*Source: The Guardian*[15]

What are different ways individuals encounter hate online?
How are various groups more or less targeted by online hatred?

Gamer and actor Felicia Day has had her personal details posted online just minutes after making her first public statement about Gamergate – in which she expressed fear about saying anything at all, in case she was targeted as a result.

The publicizing of her details was fiercely criticized by a former American football star Chris Kluwe who also criticized the group in the strongest possible terms this week, who pointed out the gender imbalance among those targeted.

The publication of Day's details is being seen as further strengthening the criticism that Gamergate's participants are pursuing an anti-woman agenda, which has seen female game developers and journalists harassed and threatened, while male critics have been almost untouched.

Day, who appeared in the TV series Buffy the Vampire Slayer and Supernatural, and rose to fame as the writer and lead of online gaming sitcom The Guild, had previously said little about the grassroots campaign against feminism in gaming, "aside from a few replies on Twitter that journalists have decided to use in their articles, siding me against the hashtag".

But, says Day, who has 2.3 million followers on Twitter, "I realized my silence on the issue was not motivated by some grand strategy, but out of fear that the issue has created about speaking out."

She explained that her major fear was being "doxxed" – having her personal information disseminated over the internet. "I have tried to retweet a few of the articles I've seen dissecting the issue in support, but personally I am terrified to be doxxed for even typing the words 'gamer gate'. I have had stalkers and restraining orders issued in the past, I have had people show up on my doorstep when my personal information was hard to get."

But just minutes after her post was made, a commenter with the username "gaimerg8" posted what they claimed was her address and personal email in the comment section below the post. The comment and the entire comment section have since been removed.

Many have pointed to the immediate doxxing received by Day to underscore the differing treatment experienced by men and women who speak out against gamergate. The former NFL star Chris Kluwe, whose own post against Gamergate went viral after he called members of the group "slackjawedpickletits", "slopebrowedweaseldicks" and a "basement-dwelling, cheetos-huffing, poopsock-sniffing douchepistol", made the point himself.

"None of you fucking #gamergate tools tried to dox me, even after I tore you a new one. I'm not even a tough target," he tweeted. "Instead, you go after a woman who wrote why your movement concerns her."

Software firm Adobe also waded into the gamergate controversy on Wednesday, distancing itself from US blog network Gawker over mocking tweets sent by a writer for the site.

The writer, Sam Biddle, had sparked the ire of the movement with a series of tongue-in-cheek tweets which his editor later described as "the tactical mistake of publicly treating gamergate with the contempt and flippancy that it deserves".

Interviews with the trolls: 'We go after women because they are easier to hurt'

Ginger Gorman, News.com.au[16]

What leads people to intentionally hurt others?
What are ways upstanders can address hate online?

The internet can be a frightening place with hidden crevices and dark bridges for trolls to hide under. But who are the anonymous people that provoke and hound others online, sometimes with devastating consequences?

When he was 14-years-old, Mark, who spoke on condition of anonymity, started trolling memorial Facebook pages of public figures who had died. He says it gave him "a feeling of enjoyment and power over causing their family members distress and pain and anger." Among Mark's counterparts this is known as "RIP trolling." "For example if a girl killed herself I would just say something like 'RIP. Couldn't handle the guilt of being an immense s**t any longer.' You don't need much to set their family members off," says Mark. Mark volunteers that the pleasure he derives from trolling isn't "normal." Reflecting on it further, he later adds: "I definitely have psychopathic tendencies."

Other internet trolls found him wreaking havoc on social media and invited him to join their ranks. That was eight years ago.

These days, Mark trolls social media with accomplices from around the globe, spending about 14 hours a week baiting others online. The comments he posts are frequently violent, racist, misogynist and threatening.

Despite being kicked off Facebook more than 260 times and Twitter about 40 times to date, he has no remorse or guilt about his actions. "When you first start ... you feel bad about it sometimes. But once you've been doing it for years, you don't think about it at all," Mark says. To press him on this, I pull out a specific example of one of his Tweets. It says: "Rape is always OK." "That is not an acceptable thing to say in public life," I say to Mark. "Yep, well that was because the discussion that was happening [online] was about defending rape victims and then someone actually said: 'Rape is never OK' so then I replied to that with 'Rape is always OK,' just to get a reaction," he responds. Me: "But why? If you are someone who has suffered sexual assault, that is such a wounding thing to say. It's horrendous." Mark: "Because if you are a victim of sexual assault, you are open to it. You've already got a weakness to that kind of stuff." Me: "So you are targeting a person at their weakest point?" Mark: "Yeah, pretty much."

This meticulous hunt for a stranger's wounds is astounding. Why can't he even attempt to put himself in the victim's shoes? "Oh yeah sure but if I was to think of that, I'd just think: 'Well, I haven't been raped so I don't care'," he says.

I'm then forced to ask: "Do you believe what you are saying?" "Generally not," he says.

This is the point of the conversation at which gender is unavoidable. Not always, but often it is women that are under attack. "Well yeah it is because women are generally weaker," Mark says, "they are more easily offended and easier to anger and stuff like that." Me: "You're not choosing them because of misogyny, you're choosing them because they are an easy target?" Mark: "Yeah generally you can say something about their kids which is gonna set them off pretty quickly. Like you could post what school they go to and stuff like that. That's gonna get them really angry." "I don't actually have any problem with them being a woman. I'm doing it because at that moment it time, I'm going to get a better reaction out of them."

Craig, 26, is another young, fully employed male who spends hours each week trolling others. In theory a troll could be anyone but both Craig and Mark agree that most of their cohorts are just like them — young, white males. Like Mark, Craig also started this pastime in high school and usually trolls in a group. Unlike Mark, he believes deeply in many of his online comments and doesn't take part in or agree with gender-based, racist or violent trolling. You could view him as a political troll who enjoys the "adrenalin rush" and the "intellectual exercise."

Describing himself as "extremely left wing," Craig frequently sets out to wind up public figures who he believes are centre-left or so-called 'new atheists.'

"One of the biggest things I draw out of trolling public figures is that they are just as dumb and stupid as the rest of us. There's nothing special about them," he says.

It might seem odd that he's trolling other people on the same side of politics as him, but Craig claims "they are not far enough left." "The people who really actually annoy me are what you'd call 'keyboard activists' or 'slacktivists,' the ones who sit there on Facebook and Twitter and all they do is post internet memes and images and engage in really soft political discourse. "Their political commitment basically extends to what they can operate from their computer," he says.

Craig goes on to say the centre left is "easy to troll because they are incredibly earnest in their views." A fascinating Canadian study, 'Trolls just want to have fun', published last year found that internet trolling correlates strongly with the so-called dark tetrad of personality traits: psychopathy, Machiavellianism, narcissism and sadism. But in its everyday form, sadism has the strongest link. One of the authors of that paper is Professor Del Paulhus from the University of British Columbia. He says the internet has given the sadist, who delights in hurting others, the perfect platform to consummate this dark desire. "You now have the opportunity to be anonymous and hurt people that can't hurt you back," Professor Paulhus says.

Not only this, he says, but "the entire world can see what you've said."

"This appetite is the precise core of the sadist and it makes them different from the other dark personalities. "Signs of suffering are what bring joy to them, as opposed to the psychopath who simply doesn't care. It's not that they seek out people to hurt. They just don't care when people are hurt. To us that's a key difference," he says. In this context, I put to Craig that he might be a sadist himself. Even though Craig works in the non-profit sector and does plenty of volunteer work, he concedes that perhaps he is a sadist.

"But I guess maybe this comes from a sense of self-righteousness that what I'm doing is good and right. I have no problem with upsetting racists, and homophobes and sexists," he says.

The conversation moves on but after a few minutes Craig deliberately comes back to sadism, stating that he does "enjoy inflicting that sort of suffering on someone who I think is a bad person." Professor Marilyn Campbell from the Queensland University of Technology is one of Australia's foremost experts in cyber bullying and is in the unenviable position of having been bullied herself because of her work.

She says the potential to experience psychological trauma because of online abuse is extremely real. "This is not something to be taken lightly. There's strong evidence to show that if you are the subject of online bullying or trolling, it can cause you significant ongoing distress including anxiety and depression and suicidal thoughts."

When I remark to Canadian Professor Paulhus that some trolls show a noticeable lack of empathy towards others, he agrees wholeheartedly. "Yes indeed. We think empathy is the key to all of the dark tetrad. It's the single variable that ties together the willingness to hurt other people," he says. Mark doesn't just hurt other people, he goes so far as to blame them for becoming a victim.

"You are not just going to go after a random person. You are going to go after a person you already know has a weakness. So people kind of, in some way, make themselves victims," he says.

Craig, on the other hand, appears somewhat empathetic to the victim's position.

"I don't want to do anything to anyone where it's going to pose a credible risk to their employment, their reputation or their feeling of personal safety," he says. And in this game safety is a key consideration; it's a mistake to think that trolling is just a few mean-spirited larrikins saying nasty things on the internet.

"Oh it can get really real-life. It can go pretty far," Mark says to me at one point.

And then later adds: "It's really easy for it to go from just playing around to destroying people's lives. That actually happens really quickly."

To pay back a vendetta, Mark claims to have recently taken part in "swatting" someone based in the U.S. This is an increasingly common practice among trolls where a hoax call is made to law enforcement authorities, usually claiming there is life threatening hostage situation or bomb threat at play. If the prank works, armored personnel arrive at the location in full force: guns, screaming, sirens.

Under section 474.17 of the Criminal Code Act, it's illegal to use a carriage service to menace, harass or cause offence to another person in Australia.

However Mark couldn't care less about the prospect of being arrested for his behavior. "They are bringing in new laws all the time so I know I'm going to get in sh*t for it but I'm just gonna keep on doing it," he says. To Mark, the notoriety he gets from peers is worth it. He uses the word "respect" a couple of times and explains that trolling gives him more status than he has in real life.

"I guess it means a lot to me," he says.

As my talk with Professor Paulhus draws to a close, I'm still searching for some kind of reasonable explanation as to why some people can get such joy out of anonymously hurting others. "I'm afraid to say, it seems to be part of the human condition," he says in a pessimistic tone. "An unfortunate side effect of the free speech permitted by the internet."

LEARNING SCENARIOS

Scenario #1

You are home alone again on a Saturday night bored and looking for something to do. You decide to peruse the web for fun. As you maneuver around various websites, you come along an interesting historical website. You begin reading some articles and find one particularly interesting about the Holocaust. According to what you are reading, very few Jewish individuals were killed during World War II and the Holocaust claims have been grossly overstated. You are intrigued since this is not what you have learned in school. You want to keep reading to learn more. Should you continue reading? What will you do with the information you read? What steps can you take to determine if what you are reading is accurate?

Scenario #2

Your phone buzzes and you see the yellow light blinking. Another Snap Chat has arrived and you are anxious to view it and see what hilarious chat your friend has sent you. You sneak a peek at your phone and see it is not a funny message at all. You have received a message filled with hatred and mean comments from a classmate. Your eyes start to water and you fight back tears at receiving yet another message like this. What do you do with the message that will disappear soon? How should you react to this classmate when you see them in the hall after class? Will you send your own hateful message back in retaliation? What might you do to try to stop this from happening again?

Scenario #3

You've done it again! You have texted an ugly picture and hate filled message to the class nerd. You feel a slight tinge of guilt but that is overwhelmed by the rush you feel at getting to them and knowing you have hurt them. They should stop being such a nerd and get their head out of the book. The next day you arrive at school to learn they killed themselves last night. What do you do now? Do you tell anyone about the messages you sent? Will their parents see the messages and will you get into trouble? Why is it so hard to stop myself from behaving this way? What can I do to stop hurting other people?

HELPFUL STRATEGIES

AVOID REACTING: We are all human and can have powerful reactions to statements other individuals post online. That said, it is important to remember we can only control ourselves and our reactions to others. Reacting to something we dislike with a quick, snarky comment will only further escalate the other individual. It is always better to wait, perhaps count to 10, before responding. This will allow you time to calm down and write a more thoughtful response. Better yet, do not respond at all.

REMEMBER YOUR TIME IS IMPORTANT: You want to think about where you spend your time. Choose to spend your time with friends, doing things you enjoy like sports or music. Do not waste your time reading and responding to hate-filled messages online, doing so will only make you feel bad and take time away from things you like.

INFORM YOURSLEF: Those who wish to spread hate are cunning and clever. Be a smart consumer of knowledge by being an informed consumer. Read to see who is sponsoring the websites you use. Research those sponsors to determine if they reputable.

LEARNING TASKS

20-Minute Activity
- **Standards:**
  - **Standard 2:** Students will analyze the influence of family, peers, culture, media,

technology, and other factors on health behaviors.

- o **Standard 4:** Students will demonstrate the ability to use interpersonal communication skills to enhance health and avoid or reduce health risks

- **Rationale:** Students need time, space, and guidance to share and debrief the information in this chapter. This activity provides the opportunity share their experiences, perspectives, and knowledge about hate speech online.

- **Learning Outcomes:** Students will discuss reasons people utilize the digital environment for hate speech so they can develop a broader understanding of the impact this behavior may have on themselves and others.

- **Description of Activity:** The teachers will engage students in a think-pair-share about why people may engage in hate speech and the implications of this behavior? The students should consider what they have learned in this chapter as they discuss the topic.

- **Supporting Resources:**
  - o Responding to Hate Online, Media Smarts, http://mediasmarts.ca/sites/mediasmarts/files/pdfs/Responding_Online_Hate_Guide.pdf

  - o Anit-defamation League, https://www.adl.org/education/resources/tools-and-strategies/confronting-hate-speech-online

ONE-DAY ACTIVITY
- **Standards:**
  - o **Standard 3:** Students will demonstrate the ability to access valid information and products and services to enhance health.

  - o **Standard 5:** Students will demonstrate the ability to use decision-making skills to enhance health.

- **Rationale:** Students need to develop necessary skills and habits for distinguishing reputable websites from those sponsored by hate groups. This activity prompts students to analyze websites of their choosing to begin to develop these skills and habits.

- **Learning Outcomes:** Students will identify hate speech in the digital environment so they can be informed consumers of information and apply critical thinking skills to the analysis of digital content.

- **Description of Activity:** The teachers will have students select 2-3 websites to examine and provide students with the "Website Evaluation form" provided in the online resource book, Hate on the Internet: A Response Guide for Educators and Families(http://www.partnersagainsthate.org/publications/hoi_full.pdf). Students will review the websites and complete the information sheets. After information is collected the students and teacher should discuss the findings and make determinations about the reviewed websites.

- **Supporting Resources**
  - Hate on the Internet, A Response Guide for Educators and Families, Partners Against Hate Organization, A Collaboration of the Anit-Defamation League, The Leadership Conference on Civil Rights Education, and the Center for the Prevention of Hate Violence, http://www.partnersagainsthate.org/publications/hoi_full.pdf

  - Confronting Hate Speech Online, Anti-Defamation League, https://www.adl.org/education/resources/tools-and-strategies/confronting-hate-speech-online

ONE-WEEK ACTIVITY

- **Standards:**
  - **Standard 7:** Students will demonstrate the ability to practice health-enhancing behaviors and avoid or reduce health risks.

  - **Standard 8:** Students will demonstrate the ability to advocate for personal, family, and community health.

- **Rationale:** Students need to learn how to advocate against hate speech and how to constructively make their voices heard as upstanders. This activity challenges students to create and document some activity and share this activity on the https://www.nohatespeechmovement.org/ website. This website is an international movement designed to put an end to hatred online.

- **Learning Outcomes:** Students will create personal principles for communication in the digital environment so they can become advocates against hate speech online.

- **Description of Activity:** The teachers will have students work as a whole class or in smaller groups to review the types of activities shared by others around the world on the No Hate Speech Movement website. The students will work together to decide their own activity to post on the website. The teacher will need to work closely with administrators and parents to get appropriate permissions for the posting of web material.

- **Supporting Resources**
  - o   No Hate Speech Movement, Youth Department of the Council of Europe – European Youth Centre,https://www.nohatespeechmovement.org/join-the-movement-chain

  - o   How to Create Awesome Online Videos: Tools and Software to Make it Easy, Social Media Examiner, http://www.socialmediaexaminer.com/tools-to-create-online-videos/

ADDITIONAL RESOURCES

Alexander Tsesis, Dignity and Speech: The Regulation of Hate Speech in a Democracy: http://lawreview.law.wfu.edu/documents/issue.44.497.pdf

Fisch, W. (2002). Hate Speech in the Constitutional Law of the United States. The American Journal of Comparative Law: http://www.jstor.org/stable/840886 doi:1 Responding to Hate Online in Diversity and Media Toolbox, Media Awareness, Ottawa, ON Canada: http://www.civilrights.org/publications/hatecrimes/exploiting-internet.html?referrer=https://www.google.com

No, there's no hate speech exception in the First Amendment: https://www.washingtonpost.com/news/volokh-conspiracy/wp/2015/05/07/no-theres-no-hate-speech-exception-to-the-first-amendment/?utm_term=.c4a0431de548

Sorry, kids, the first amendment does protect 'hate speech': http://www.latimes.com/opinion/opinion-la/la-ol-colleges-hate-speech-1st-amendment-20151030-story.html

Online Hate: http://mediasmarts.ca/online-hate/online-hate-introduction

- **Supporting Resources**
  - o   No Hate Speech Movement, Youth Department of the Council of Europe – European Youth Centre,https://www.nohatespeechmovement.org/join-the-movement-chain

  - o   How to Create Awesome Online Videos: Tools and Software to Make it Easy, Social Media Examiner, http://www.socialmediaexaminer.com/tools-to-create-online-videos/

[1] RESPONDING - mediasmarts.ca. (n.d.). Retrieved June 6, 2017, from http://www.bing.com/cr?IG=398D0091887F4C748B8CEC6A22A5FF3D&CID=027E161BAC6C676B2D3C1C82AD6A66DC&rd=1&h=C_muSrjq8qcKOg7NHjQ1hZTTHJDn_6592bNtinWZvsQ&v=1&r=http%3a%2f%2fmediasmarts.ca%2fsites%2fmediasmarts%2ffiles%2fpdfs%2fResponding_Online_Hate_Guide.pdf&p=DevEx,5060.1

[2] Alexander Tsesis. (n.d.). Retrieved June 06, 2017, from https://papers.ssrn.com/sol3/cf_dev/AbsByAuth.cfm?per_id=885226

[3] Duggan, M. (2014, October 22). Online Harassment. Retrieved June 06, 2017, from http://www.pewinternet.org/2014/10/22/online-harassment/

[4] Asgeirsson, S. C. (n.d.). Hate Speech Online: 2016 in Review. Retrieved June 06, 2017, from http://www.humanrightsfirst.org/blog/hate-speech-online-2016-review

[5] The State of Hate: Exploiting the Internet to Promote Hatred - Confronting the New Faces of Hate. (n.d.). Retrieved June 06, 2017, from http://www.civilrights.org/publications/hatecrimes/exploiting-internet.html?referrer=https%3A%2F%2Fwww.google.com%2F

[6] MediaSmarts. (n.d.). Retrieved June 06, 2017, from http://mediasmarts.ca/online-hate/impact-online-hate

[7] Asgeirsson, S. C. (n.d.). Hate Speech Online: 2016 in Review. Retrieved June 06, 2017, from http://www.humanrightsfirst.org/blog/hate-speech-online-2016-review

[8] The State of Hate: Exploiting the Internet to Promote Hatred - Confronting the New Faces of Hate. (n.d.). Retrieved June 06, 2017, from http://www.civilrights.org/publications/hatecrimes/exploiting-internet.html?referrer=https%3A%2F%2Fwww.google.com%2F

[9] Welcome to CDC Stacks | The teen years explained; a guide ... (n.d.). Retrieved June 6, 2017, from https://www.bing.com/cr?IG=2BD29B21B84141BAAFAD1C93F5415840&CID=20D79BF172446FC20AAA916873426E7E&rd=1&h=AxrVWN32jRlkAqM9K3O9b2CxRDItCtigtJAttDzbgHk&v=1&r=https%3a%2f%2fstacks.cdc.gov%2fview%2fcdc%2f12277&p=DevEx,5365.1

[10] II. Defining the Problem: The Internet as a Tool for Hate. (n.d.). Retrieved June 6, 2017, from http://www.bing.com/cr?IG=123E6E175CD94A9EA48E6D57E005E573&CID=0C100C1ADC266CE912970683DD206D00&rd=1&h=kcsNoJufKnZIA82hLrvvJSjPgdY2_RTe17sMhWhuwTY&v=1&r=http%3a%2f%2fwww.partnersagainsthate.org%2fpublications%2fhoi_defining_problem.pdf&p=DevEx,5062.1

[11] McLeod, S. (1970, January 01). Saul McLeod. Retrieved June 06, 2017, from https://simplypsychology.org/bobo-doll.html

[12] 1999, by Jo Monahan, used with permission.

[13] Internet Hate Speech Can Lead To Acts Of Violence 1.—Source: By Omar Sacirbey, Religion News Service, May 6, 201414

[14] Hern, A. (2014, October 23). Felicia Day's public details put online after she described Gamergate fears. Retrieved June 06, 2017, from https://www.theguardian.com/technology/2014/oct/23/felicia-days-public-details-online-gamergate

[15] Trolls go after women because they are 'easier to hurt'. (n.d.). Retrieved June 6, 2017, from http://www.bing.com/cr?IG=BA30A9AB57E64ABF8D547212713A2FA5&CID=08475B040A986C091778519D0B9E6DC7&rd=1&h=FonBIdyUDRcisQFl1hpK1kvUB6ZXYjWsHiwhMos0avQ&v=1&r=http%3a%2f%2fwww.news.com.au%2ftechnology%2fonline%2fsocial%2finterviews-with-the-trolls-we-go-after-women-because-they-are-easier-to-hurt%2fnews-story%2fc02bb2a5f8d7247d3fdd9aabe0f3ad26&p=DevEx,5062.1

CHAPTER FIVE

Binge Watching & Screen Time

Why do people binge?

How does the technology provide an escape?

How do we change behaviors and habits that are so common and widespread?

BEHAVIORS AND THEMES

SCALE AND SCOPE: The rapid growth of on-demand digital streaming as well as user-generated video sites has transformed media consumption patterns. Online video streaming has quickly become a multi-billion dollar industry with companies like Amazon, Hulu, Facebook, YouTube, and Netflix, which valued at $42 billion in 2015, generating large quarterly profits.[1] This entertainment landscape not only provides an endless buffet of choices that are instantly accessible at the touch of a screen or remote control, but it has also contributed to the prevalence of binge watching. A 2015 survey conducted by TiVo revealed, that among its subscribers, 9 out of 10 people regularly engage in "binge viewing".[2] Deloitte's 10th annual Digital Democracy Survey identified binge watching as a common habit, with 70% of respondents binge watching an average of five episodes at a time, and almost 31 percent binging on a weekly basis.[3] Binge watching has quietly become a common and widely accepted part of life. A 2013 survey by Netflix revealed that a majority of respondents considered binge watching a socially acceptable behavior. Additionally, in 2015, Collins English Dictionary selected "binge-watch" as its Word of the Year and both Target and Office Depot glorified binge watching as a traditional summer activity in 2016 advertising campaigns.

TV AND VIDEO WATCHING AMONG TEENS, BY PLATFORM

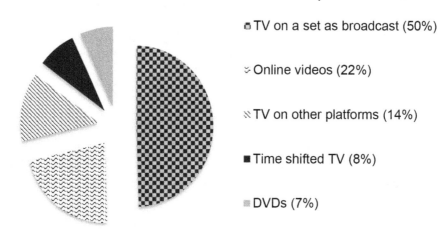

- TV on a set as broadcast (50%)
- Online videos (22%)
- TV on other platforms (14%)
- Time shifted TV (8%)
- DVDs (7%)

Source: Common Sense Media, Common Sense Census (2015)

Media Use by Teens and Tweens[5]

While the American Academy of Pediatrics' recommends that screen time should be limited to two hours per day, teenagers are definitely surpassing this guidance, with many spending large portions of their day binge watching television. These days "watching television" can mean various things and be accomplished through multiple mediums. These mediums include: (1) watching on a television set through real-time broadcast media; (2) time shifted viewing which includes TV shows or movies watched "on demand" or recorded on a DVR; (3) watching TV shows or movies that are downloaded or streamed to an electronic device; (4) TV shows or movies watched on DVD; (5) and watching online videos, which often includes podcasts, webisodes, how-to and music videos, and other user generated content.[4] It is interesting to note that while watching television, movies, videos via electronic devices is popular, watching TV in real-time on a traditional television set is still popular.

What is staggering to realize is just how much time each day teenagers spend in front of a screen watching television, movies, or and online videos. American teenagers average around six and a half hours of screen time a day, excluding time on computers at school; 1 out of every 4 teenagers spends more than eight hours in front of a screen. [6] Findings from a 2015 study conducted by Common Media reveal that on any given day 71% of teens watch TV (either on a TV set or online), while 30% watch for 2 hours or more and 11% for four hours or more.[7] Despite the diversity of available media activities, when asked which activities they enjoy "a lot" and which they "do everyday," teenagers identified watching TV as an overwhelming preference.[8] Many teenagers also regularly watch online videos on sites like YouTube, Facebook, and Vevo. Just under half of all teens (45 percent) report they enjoy watching online videos and a third (34 percent) watch online videos every day; among those teens that watch online videos everyday, they spend, on average, over an hour online engaged in this activity.[9]

PROBLEM DEFINED: Binge watching, which is often defined differently, can be generalized as the act of watching consecutive hours of media, such as TV shows, movies, or online videos, in a single sitting. Binge watching is a passive consumption activity as it revolves around watching, listening, and reading rather than engagement in interactive activities like online gaming, social networking, or developing content through coding or creating digital art or music. Although binge watching has yet to be identified as an official diagnosis or disorder, many consider this excessive use to be a form of addiction or escape, and some have even categorized this behavior as symptomatic of electronic screen syndrome. The portability of electronic devices helps facilitate binge watching as it increases availability and daily use, and is key in displacing other developmentally appropriate activities and interactions.

Although binge watching, especially among teenagers, may seem harmless because common behaviors are often mistaken for healthy behaviors, research demonstrates this habit should be a major concern because it can negatively impact our health and wellness. Researchers have found that physical fatigue, isolation, and loneliness as well as problems like obesity are related to binge watching. [1] Additionally, when this behavior becomes excessive, individuals may neglect their day-today responsibilities and relationships with family and friends. Binge watching can also be considered a way for teenagers to escape. This escapism can be the result of problems at home or school and can even be related to depression, feelings of isolation, and loneliness, or being overwhelmed and over-extended. At the American Public Health Association's 143rd Annual meeting, researchers presented evidence supporting a link between binge watching and an increase in feelings of loneliness and isolation, and higher rates of anxiety and depression.[11]

What makes binge watching even more challenging to address is the fact that many parents set few or no rules about screen time and as a result, provide little guidance to help their kids moderate habits and behaviors. In fact, because many adults have few boundaries with screens and electronic devices, setting acceptable TV watching parameters for their children can be difficult. A 2016 report issued by Common Sense Media found that one out of every two teenagers feels addicted to screens, 28 percent believe their parents are addicted, more than half of adults think their kids are addicted, and a third of parents and teenagers say they have arguments about screen time on a daily basis.[12] The sheer volume of media that is instantly available combined with the extensive time teenagers spend each day watching TV, movies, and online video is creating life-long habits that, ultimately, have the potential to cause serious long-term problems.

IMPACT ON PHYSICAL: *Researchers have been studying both the use and impact of television since the 1980s, when links were made between excessive TV watching and obesity. Because binge watching is now a common behavior among teenagers*, the evidence documenting just how excessive screen time impacts health is expanding. The American Academy of Pediatrics advocates that too much screen time is one of the primary drivers of childhood obesity. Excessive use results in sedentary habits, increased inactivity and isolation, and too much sit-time – all negative outcomes of binge watching. A number of other dynamics related to binge watching contribute to obesity. These include frequent exposure to junk food advertisements, snacking while watching, and unhealthy sleep habits.

The Center for Disease Control (CDC) also advocates that excessive television watching contributes to obesity. In 2014, the CDC issued a statement that cutting screen time is the most important factor in curbing teen obesity. [13] During that same year, The National Center for Health Statistics released a brief summarizing findings from the National Health and Nutrition Survey. One key finding of the survey was overweight or obese adolescents were less able to meet recommended screen time limits. [14] A number of other studies have also confirmed the link between excessive television watching and screen time with childhood obesity and high levels of inactivity. [15] [16] [17] [18] Unless a concerted effort is made to alter habits, these outcomes are unlikely to change, as teenagers continue to be immersed in digital technologies that make binge watching easy.

DESIRE TO ESCAPE: On the face of it binge watching may seem like a common behavior that is harmless. This is, however, not the case and it is important to consider what drives people to binge watch. Why does it happen? What underlies the desire or need to binge watch TV, movies, and online videos? While some enjoy the immersion, engagement, and even the intellectual stimulation of binging on Netflix, Hulu, or HBO for hours at a time, the need to escape from something is a common characteristic typically associated with many binge watchers.

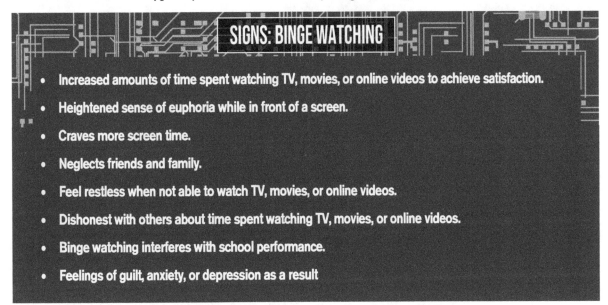

SIGNS: BINGE WATCHING

- Increased amounts of time spent watching TV, movies, or online videos to achieve satisfaction.
- Heightened sense of euphoria while in front of a screen.
- Craves more screen time.
- Neglects friends and family.
- Feel restless when not able to watch TV, movies, or online videos.
- Dishonest with others about time spent watching TV, movies, or online videos.
- Binge watching interferes with school performance.
- Feelings of guilt, anxiety, or depression as a result

Dynamics like loneliness, isolation, depression, and the inability to self-regulate are already well-established signs of general binging behavior. In a 2014 study examining TV watching patterns, researchers found that the more lonely and depressed study participants were, the more likely they were to report binge watching, using this behavior to try and distance themselves from negative feelings and experiences.[19] Another study of self-identified binge watchers revealed those engaging in this behavior were likely to report higher stress, anxiety, and depression.[20] It is relevant to point out that binge watching also takes place in social situations when a group of friends get together to watch multiple episodes of a program. This type of binging is less likely to be associated with depression, isolation, and loneliness. While there is not yet enough research to conclude whether binge watching is used to alleviate pre-existing feelings or this behavior actually causes symptoms, binge watching is often used as an escape mechanism for those struggling with personal, school, or relationship issues. It makes sense – lonely, sad, or depressed individuals can turn to binge watching to escape and get their mind off negative feelings or circumstances. Unfortunately, binge watching is only a temporary fix that ignores underlying problems and can create a sense of isolation that only increases as more time is spent in front of a screen.

IMPACT ON SLEEP: Binge watching also impacts the maintenance of healthy sleep habits. In 2012, researchers examining television watching, screen time, electronic device preferences, and sleep patterns among 10,000 adolescents aged 16 to 19 found those who reported four hours or more of screen time per day were much more likely to sleep less than five hours at night, and were more likely to need 60 minutes or more to fall asleep. [21]

Documentaries like Web Junkie and Screenagers demonstrate the disastrous impact of binging behaviors on teenagers' sleep habits. *Increasing numbers of teenagers also have televisions in their bedrooms and sleep with electronic devices in their bedrooms, many times in close proximity to their beds. This access creates temptation, opportunity, and makes changing detrimental behaviors difficult. Use of any screens, even traditional TV's,* before bedtime can seriously impact both the onset and duration of sleep. Michael Decker, a sleep specialist and associate professor at Case Western School of Nursing, points out late night screen use is problematic because the bright lights that glow from screens often disrupt sleep and "wake up the brain," which makes teenagers, "want to go to bed later and want to sleep later."[22] There is even evidence that high doses of caffeine may have less effect on a teenager's ability to sleep than the bright light emanating from the screens they are using to watch television, movies, and online videos.[23] Ultimately, consistently poor sleep habits can have detrimental effects on day-to-day life and can result in poor job performance, unhealthy relationships, and the inability to fulfill responsibilities.

The lack of sleep resulting from binge watching *can also impact academic performance w*hen it interferes with and takes priority over schoolwork. If the average teenager is spending multiple hours a day binging television, movies, or online videos (excluding time spent for school or work), less time is going to be devoted to academic performance. A 2014 study conducted by researchers at Iowa State University confirmed what many already know - children perform better academically, sleep more, and are at a reduced risk for obesity when all screen time, including traditional televisions, is limited. [24] *It makes sense – the lack of sleep resulting from* continuously staying up late into the night binge watching can negatively impact academics and lead to difficulties in school.

RECOGNIZING SIGNS OF BINGE WATCHING: Because television, electronic devices, and the Internet are so accessible, binge watching can be difficult to identify in friends, family, and even our selves. As the influence of technology continues to grow, there is no doubt that binge watching will continue to become increasingly prevalent. Bingers, as they are often called, can demonstrate a wide-range of characteristics. Dr. Hilarie Cash, founding partner of reSTART, one the United States' first residential programs for Internet and screen addiction, provides helpful insights about the specific behaviors that are symptomatic of binge watching. Isolated from one another, many of these behaviors may seem normal within a society so dependent on digital media and technology. That said, individuals displaying a combination of these behaviors should raise a red flag of concern and signal a need for help.

KEY CONCEPTS:

Binging: A period of habitual, excessive, and often uncontrolled indulgence.

Escapism: The tendency for individuals to seek distraction and relief from unpleasant realities, most frequently by seeking diversion in entertainment or engaging fantasy.

Addiction: A state of physical or psychological dependence on a behavior or substance, particularly compulsive dependence, to the extent that this dependence leads to harm to oneself and/or those around them.

Passive Consumption: Behaviors revolving around watching, listening, and reading rather than engagement in interactive activities like online gaming, social networking, or developing content through coding or creating digital art or music.

REAL WORLD SITUATIONS

Netflix And Chew: How Binge Watching Affects Our Eating Habits
—Source: By Susmita Baral, National Public Radio, December 31st, 2015[25]

How do habits and routines contribute to binge watching?

When watching for extended periods of time, what strategies can help with moderating eating habits?

Binging has become many people's favorite way to consume television. But marathon viewing doesn't just change how we watch, it also affects how we eat. While the culture of the Netflix all-nighter is relatively recent, researchers have been studying the links between TV viewing and mindless eating for years. And the news isn't good for our waistlines. "There's convincing evidence in adults that the more television they watch, the more likely they are to gain weight or become overweight or obese," says Lilian Cheung, director of health promotion and communication at Harvard School of Public Health and author of *Savor: Mindful Eating, Mindful Life*. She says the sedentary nature of prolonged viewing is just one contributing factor: "TV viewing may also promote poor dietary behavior due to frequent exposure to unhealthy food and beverage marketing, as well as providing more opportunities for unhealthy snacking, and interfering with adequate sleep."

Preliminary research has also suggested a connection between binge viewing and higher rates of depression and increased risk of developing type 2 diabetes, among other concerns. University of Houston associate professor Temple Northup has looked at the relationship between food consumption and the number of hours spent in front of the television. Northup's study, published in the January 2015 issue of The International Journal of Communication and Health, surveyed 591 undergraduate students on their viewing, eating and drinking habits. Consistent with past studies, he found that the more people watched TV, the more they engaged in unhealthy eating. "The explanation is relatively straightforward — the act of watching TV is a sedentary activity that encourages snacking," says Northup, the interim director of the university's Jack J. Valenti School of Communication. Lots of research shows mindless eating plays a prominent role in how much we ingest while distracted with what is happening on screen. "Watching TV while eating is also common behavior," says Cheung. "When we are distracted while eating, or eating mindlessly, we are not paying full attention to the food in front of us, and miss the satiety cues letting us know that we are full."

Overall viewing time is certainly a key factor. But the genre of what you are watching may also influence how much you munch. Researchers from Cornell University's Food and Brand Lab have found that action content (say, *The Walking Dead*) made subjects eat twice as much — 98 percent more, to be exact — than their counterparts who watched a talk show. And sad content (like the sci-fi drama Solaris) made participants eat 55 percent more than those who watched more upbeat content, like the romantic comedy My Big Fat Greek Wedding.

Researchers speculate that action and adventure shows may promote mindless eating because people consume more to keep up with the pace of the content. "It might be the level of distraction — how engaging the content is," says Aner Tal, a research associate at Cornell's Food and Brand Lab. "Another possibility is that it's the feelings associated with what you are watching. Specifically, anything that involves a stress reaction enhances people's levels of cortisol — and we know that leads to overeating."

With tearjerkers, the increase in snacking can be credited to stress responses but also to emotional eating, which compensates for sadness. "It makes you feel temporarily better," says Tal. Less obvious cues may also modify eating habits. A separate study from Cornell's Food and Brand Lab found that food-related content on television makes those who are watching their diet ("restrained eaters") eat more. Led by Food and Brand Lab Director Brian Wansink, the study found that, when subjects watched episodes of SpongeBob SquarePants in which the protagonist was selling chocolate bars, they ate more than their counterparts who watched an episode unrelated to food.

But you don't have to cancel Netflix and Hulu subscriptions to save your waistline. Cheung recommends separating food and television by unplugging while eating.

"To reduce mindless eating, one can practice mindful eating for more control over their relationship with food," says Cheung. "When eating, only eat. Turn off the television [and] computer, and put the cell phone away to refrain from checking messages. By removing these distractions, you can bring your full attention to the food in front of you, going beyond just taste and engaging all senses — including sight, smell, texture and the sound your food makes." Tal, on the other hand, suggests you don't have to banish snacking while viewing. He says just be aware how television influences what you put in your mouth, and plan accordingly. "Monitor ahead of time what is there for you to eat. Put out healthier snacks on the table or not have snacks available," says Tal.

Addicted to Netflix: Teen-Soap-Opera Binge As Psychosis
—*Source: By Elissa Bassist, New York Magazine, February 27th, 2013*[26]

Why can it be so easy to become a binge watcher?
How can TV watching be integrated into day-to-day life to create a healthy lifestyle balance?

"I swore to myself I wasn't going to talk to you about *Dance Academy*," I tell my psychologist. Luckily or prophetically, my Master of Fine Arts graduate program provided free therapy to talk about how pursuing a career in the arts is a huge mistake.

"What's *Dance Academy*?" she asks. *Dance Academy* is an Australian teen drama about "making it" at Sydney's top ballet school. Netflix recommended it based on my interests in *quirky independent high-school dance dramedies featuring a strong female lead*. Seasons one and two are available on Netflix Instant, and season three will air in Australia mid-2013 on ABC3. One week prior, I sat in my one-bedroom Brooklyn apartment and clicked "play," my only motivation being distraction — to watch something frivolous and chill out, to think tiny nothing thoughts and mentally exit my body, to tune in and tune out. In the next seven days, I would watch 52 episodes of *Dance Academy*.

I was an undiagnosed addict with a modern addiction, one that might fall under an umbrella epidemic of loneliness in the digital age.

For me, massive television consumption coincided with moving to New York in 2010 and subscribing to Netflix. I could stream media instantly on my laptop for unlimited hours. When I first moved — from San Francisco, where I had three roommates, one boyfriend, and innumerable outdoor adventure opportunities — I'd look in people's windows and notice each had a continuous blue glow. What was the deal? Soon I'd be attached to the same invisible tether, using TV as a substitute for living. Streaming the first few episodes of *Dance Academy* after dinner one night, I listened to freckled protagonist and narrator Tara Webster, age 15, talk about dancing the way I thought of grad school: each required sacrifice, hard work, disappointment, pain, passion, exaltation, and obsession. This was like life, like my life, like a superior version of my life. I watched as Tara meets Ethan Karamakov, who moves in slow motion whenever she looks at him. I knew, from life, that anyone you see in slow motion goes on a pedestal so lofty that you've immunized yourself from reciprocal affection — his position forms the distance between you two, and you're the one who put him there, and then defined him by his distance. Tara says Ethan smells like Christmas. The first boy I saw in slow-mo smelled like Matzo ball soup. I knew, from life, Tara would love Ethan forever. Meanwhile, he — the popular, older boy narcissist — would love *her love* but not *her*. Her obsession would be an aphrodisiac and a repellent. He would never date her, so far asunder is he in their respective cool. "So you see *Dance Academy* as a reflection of your past relationships?" my gratis therapist asks. We both laugh.

On Thursday, I played some more episodes before bed. On Friday, knee-deep in a binge, I began episode eleven, "One Perfect Day," while eating breakfast. Tara performs a sexy contemporary dance, and I zeroed in on Ethan's eyes — from my kitchen table I could see him see her differently — and when he extends his hand and when she takes it and when he twirls her on the floor and then lifts her up, draping her arm around his shoulders, and when they're *this* close and when they kiss — my God!, what a kiss — I'm telling you, you've never seen someone so happy as *this girl,* me, as if I were Tara, as if it were my first kiss. As if eating breakfast had taken on an emotional weight unforeseen in the history of human experience.

I decided I didn't need to work that day anyway. Auto-play seamlessly transitioned to episode twelve, to Tara saying to her friend, "I think I have a boyfriend," and my first reaction was, "You dumb idiot, of course you don't," because I knew, from life, a kiss does not mean a relationship. Wrong! In the next episode, she introduces Ethan to her parents as her "boyfriend," and he doesn't flinch. For the next three episodes — while I ate lunch — they are a couple, and he's *perfect* and she's *perfect* and they are *perfect* and at peace, and for the first time in a long time, I felt perfect and at peace, like I had love in my world. Watching television reminded me that living could be more exciting, more interesting than watching television. I had a lightness and a thrill in me as I waltzed around my apartment, washing my dishes. Of course I had to remind myself these feelings came from the Australian teen dance dramedy *Dance Academy.* My happiness was absolute and tangible and transformative, but it wasn't *real.* I spent enough time absorbing this show that the way I understood myself shifted. The bendy, dewy ballet dancers' desire was my desire; their triumphs, my triumphs; their work ethic, so clearly not my work ethic.

In episode sixteen, Tara cheats on Ethan with her *pas de deux* partner Christian. Immediately I canceled my dinner plans with a friend. What was life? I made some pasta and checked *Dance Academy* message boards and online forums. What did everyone else think of this bullshit? "Everyone else" consisted of prepubescent girls who used so many acronyms, abbreviations, and emoticons it seemed I was reading hieroglyphics. But I needed confirmation and community: Ethan was adoring and affectionate, and he knew Tara, really knew her, you know? He had done nothing wrong, right? The message boards offered no solace, no answers; we were all just a bunch of confused young girls. I viewed each new episode now with a manic hope Tara would beg forgiveness and they'd get back together. This hope has never left me.

On Saturday, around 4 a.m., I finished season one. In one day, I went from beatitude to heartbreak in twenty episodes, favoring the drama of fiction over the dullness of everyday existence. On Saturday afternoon, I extricated myself from my TV-induced emotional prison to meet a friend for lunch. She was going through a real-life breakup.

"Janine, I swore to myself I wasn't going to talk to you about *Dance Academy.*" Then I told her what Tara did to Ethan. "Relationships change so fast. So fast." I sighed profoundly. "Everything you think you have can be lost in five episodes. Everything." I was crying like a dumb idiot in full café view.

I knew I could not endure season two. I didn't think things would be the same for Tara and *Christian.* Like Burt Bacharach and Hal David classic "I'll Never Fall in Love Again" — and like what I faced after my first relationship — Tara falling in love again seemed outside the bounds of rational thought. Everything would be a shadow of the first time, an episode already seen. Lacking promise and hope, full instead of muscle memory of love's letdowns, I couldn't watch Tara go through this — I couldn't go through it — so I read each episode synopsis of season two on IMDb, sure if I knew what happened without having to pseudo-experience it, my *Dance Academy* obsession would be quelled by absence, faded by degrees, etc. No dice. Knowing more only stroked my need to know even more. I closed IMDb, got into bed late Saturday night, reopened Netflix, fell sharply off the wagon, and clicked "play" on episode one of season two. Systematically spoiling every episode quelled zilch.

The phenomenon of Netflix had trained my viewership, ensuring I keep watching: the unlimited access, the 52 episodes available for on-demand viewing, auto-play — features exploiting my dependence on fantasy and on the technology that enables my fantasy 24/7. Also: I couldn't risk being bored, sitting alone in echoing silence. Netflix knows it invites obsession and dependence; why else introduce all thirteen episodes of House of Cards at once? Netflix knows us. On Tuesday, I finished the second season. I went to yoga that evening and moved the way the characters in *Dance Academy* moved, manipulating my body so powerfully I thought I must be sending signals not just to Tara and Ethan but to all of the ballet world. In the shower after class, I ruminated on the finale — specifically the final dance solos at the *Prix de Fonteyn* international dance competition — and stood dead-faced under the water, my chest a tight fist of emotion, until I cried out, actually cried out, because maybe doing so would relieve some internal pressure. I got out of the shower to put on a shirt just so I could rend it. A television show is missing for you, and the whole world is gone. Growing up, I was an indoor kid and only child. I've fallen in love with five men and only two knew about it. I've been emotionally invested in TV shows before: In seventh grade, I locked myself in the bathroom after watching the *Buffy the Vampire Slayer* episode wherein Angel loses his soul. My mom knocked on the door and asked if I'd broken up with my boyfriend. What boyfriend?

Last summer Netflix recommended *Friday Night Lights* based on my preference for "emotional football dramas." (You watch *Rudy* once, and suddenly you have a "preference." With Internet-streaming media, we're overwhelmed by choice and robbed of choice at the same time.) In the fourth season finale, it's time for the game-winning 45-yard field goal, and the announcer says, "Six seconds left ... I hope you're on your knees, because we are going to need a miracle." I pushed back my desk chair, got down on my knees, reached my arms heavenward, and prayed to God

At therapy, post-one-week Netflix spiral, I can't not talk about *Dance Academy*, my recent raison d'être. It doesn't escape my attention that I started Netflixing to divert my mind from the very troubles for which I was in therapy. But I knew it offered way more than distraction. "Have you noticed my outfit?" I ask, with a hint of an Australian accent and my hair in a ballerina bun. Black dance pants and a flowy baby pink tank top with a built-in bra — I am wearing what is essentially a dance leotard, a combo I bought for nearly $180 on Monday at Lululemon Athletica (this store sees my type coming a mile away). In the *Dance Academy* pilot, Abigail Armstrong wears a pink leotard as "her thing." I wanted her thing to be my thing. The grad school psychologist laughs so hard at me she's wiping tears away, and then I start laughing, and next we're both laugh-crying and having a difficult time breathing. "Have you thought about taking ballet classes?" she asks, recovered. No. *Dance Academy* made me feel without requiring me to act. Watching temporarily relieved any external responsibility while deluding me that I had a lot going on. I achieved true *Weltschmerz* — the melancholic understanding that actual physical reality will never compare to the idealized demands of the mind. "Not everyone is born a dancer," I say. That's a line from *Dance Academy*.

How to Overcome a Binge-Watching Addiction: Understanding How TV Scripts and Your Willpower Work

—Source: By Michael Hsu, Wall Street Journal, September 26th, 2014[27]

What other activities can replace binge watching?
What specific guidelines can be implemented to help reduce binge watching?

Binge watching television shows—viewing episodes back-to-back for hours on end—may be America's new favorite pastime, but it's brought me to some pretty dark places. At 3 a.m., bleary-eyed and faced with the choice of watching another episode or going to bed so I could be ready for work and family the next day, I've often found myself opting for "just one more" hit. I've struggled with this habit intermittently for more than a decade (my first all-nighter was season 1 of "24" on DVD). I would hit the Netflix hard and reach rock bottom, then go cold turkey by canceling my membership—only to start the cycle again when I thought I had the wherewithal to watch responsibly. But it wasn't until recently—when my compulsive late-night viewing of "Extant" was making me so tired that it was undermining my ability to be a good father, husband and friend—that I sought a viable long-term cure. I scoured self-help blogs, researched parental Internet controls that would limit my access to streaming video. Ultimately, I discovered that freedom from TV might be hidden in the structure of the episodes themselves.

One trick: Don't watch an episode to the end, because at that point, it's almost impossible to resist continuing to the next one. Instead, stop about three-quarters of the way in. The next time you watch, pick up from that point until most of the way into the following episode. I know this sounds illogical. After all, how can it be easier to stop mid-show than at the end? But there's usually a lull in the narrative arc, when story lines get wrapped up and the pacing slows down. The show actually gets pretty boring. "People unconsciously write this way," said Charlie Rubin, area head of television writing at the Tisch School of the Arts and a former writer for "Seinfeld" and "Law & Order: Criminal Intent." "It's inhale and exhale. There's always a dramatic moment, and then you pull back from it."

What's more, each episode weaves together multiple story lines, Mr. Rubin explained. The "A" story—the one involving the star—is what keeps you watching episode after episode (even the ones that don't end with obvious cliffhangers). The "B" and "C" stories involve the supporting characters. "The usual rule of the universe is that you end your stories in order of their importance," with the minor ones wrapping first, Mr. Rubin said. "The order of finish is C-B-A." Recovering binge-watchers can use this knowledge to their advantage. Although each show has its own template, you should try to quit at the end of the B or C story, said Mr. Rubin. "Once you cycle back to that A story, you want to see what's going to happen to Tina Fey or Tony Soprano."

Colleagues who helped me test the theory (using "Scandal" and "Dr. Who") found that the sweet spot varies by series—but you can intuit it after watching a few episodes. In a roughly 45-minute episode (without commercials), it'll usually fall somewhere around 30 minutes in. Technology simplifies this offset-viewing process, too: Netflix, Hulu, Amazon Instant Video and other streaming services automatically start an episode wherever you leave off. If this approach is too esoteric for you—or if you get too absorbed in watching to track the story lines—there are other strategies to try. An essential one: disabling auto-play, a feature found on services like Netflix and Hulu that automatically starts the next episode in a series when the one you're watching ends. (In Netflix, check "Playback Settings" on the "Your Account" page. With Hulu, the option is located within the playback-control area). According to Roy Baumeister, a psychologist at Florida State University and author of the best-selling book "Willpower," auto-play can be particularly perilous because "it takes more self control to interrupt the sequence of behavior than to simply continue doing whatever you're doing."

What's more, exercising self-restraint gets more difficult when our energy levels drop (as is the case late at night). Eating or drinking might help. "A lot of evidence has shown that getting some food into you can restore your self-control when you're depleted," Dr. Baumeister said. In his experiments, subjects were given lemonade. "I hesitate to recommend sugar to anyone," he said, but it might work "if you want to get a burst of energy" to bolster your willpower late at night. You can also strike the problem at the source: your Wi-Fi router. Many models allow you to shut down access to the Internet on a set schedule; Netgear routers can target specific websites at certain times—for example, Hulu and Netflix between 1 a.m. and 6 p.m. The advantage of this approach is that all of your Internet-connected devices—whether an iPad, Roku or your Wi-Fi-enabled television—will be locked down. And at that point what else is there to do but go to bed?

LEARNING SCENARIOS

Scenario #1

One of your closest friends, Issac, does not seem the same lately. He is withdrawn, irritable, and has completely stopped participating in the usual after school activities. You know his parents just went through a difficult divorce and his older brother recently moved out the house. One of your other close friends has told you that Issac has started spending an increased amount of time watching movies. At school you have noticed Issac is often distracted by whatever he is watching on his tablet.

At first, it did not seem out of the ordinary because so many of your friends always have their electronic devices in hand. The last time you stopped by Issac's house to hang out, he barely noticed you were present as he was fully engrossed in a recently released series on Netflix. You are also aware that Issac is not doing well in classes, which is definitely abnormal, and has started missing a noticeable amount of school. You know there is a problem. What are the red flags? How and to whom should concerns be communicated? How should the situation be handled?

Scenario #2

It's Saturday and you are headed to the movies for some fun with friends. The older sister of one of your close friends is going to pick you up, drop everyone off at the theater, and bring you home later in the evening. On the way to the movies, you notice that the driver, Annemarie, constantly checks her smartphone every time the car stops at a light or stop sign. You do not say anything, but the situation makes you extremely nervous and uncomfortable. Annemarie was waiting in the parking lot when the movie let out. To kill time while waiting, she was streaming a movie on one of her electronic devices. As you begin the 15-minute journey home, you notice the movie is still playing on a tablet that she placed upright on the front seat passenger seat. When you asked her about it, she replied that it was just a short drive home and she was really good at multi-tasking. Since it is just a short drive, should this behavior ignored? What would you say to communicate your concerns? How might you influence this situation to get a safe and reasonable outcome?

Scenario #3

Everyone in your house, including yourself, has access to multiple personal electronic devices and televisions. Additionally, your parents have never established any ground rules or expectations about daily screen time use. While you enjoy this freedom, you have also noticed that your parents always seem to be using one of their electronic devices to email and watch videos. Additionally, when you are at home, multiple televisions are always on. This has really started to bother you, especially when you have a question, need something, or just want to spend time with them. When you wake up in the morning, your parents seem to always be on their phones or tablets or watching TV and they even continue this use at the table during meals. They are constantly on one device or another. In the past, you have made sporadic comments about their behavior, but unfortunately, your parents do not recognize their own behaviors. It has gotten to the point that you want to remedy the situation. How should you start this conversation? What ground rules might you suggest establishing?

HELPFUL STRATEGIES

ESTABLISH INTENTIONALITY, GUIDELINES, AND BOUNDARIES: There's no use in pretending televisions, laptops, smartphones, and tablets aren't an integral part of modern life. That said, it is important to embrace a balanced approach to media and technology. Time spent watching TV, movies, and online videos should be intentional, have definitive start and end times, and should not interfere with school, work, or other important responsibilities.

EMBRACE QUALITY MEDIA USAGE: It is important to understand that television, movies, and online videos are not all equal when it comes to quality. It is important to select media that is age relevant and appropriate and makes sense to familial and cultural contexts.

ESTABLISH TECH FREE ZONES: Establish physical boundaries within the house to reduce screen time. To do this, pick a convenient area that can serve as a tech free zone, establish rules for this tech-free space, and identify alternative activities to engage in when unplugging from technology.

MODIFY ROUTINES: Do something different - change habits. For example, if watching TV is a common after school activity, replace it with a different activity. If watching videos online typically occurs right before bed or first thing in the morning, leave devices in the kitchen at bedtime and identify different routines.

ASK FOR HELP: Binge watching can be a serious issue that causes significant harm to health, wellness, and personal relationships. Sometimes excessive use is the result of other problems (school, home, friends, etc.). Talk with parents or trusted adults, and if necessary, the school's mental health professional about support options.

LEARNING TASKS

20-Minute Activity

- **Standard:**
  - *Standard 1:* Students will comprehend concepts related to health promotion and disease prevention to enhance health.

  - *Standard 2:* Students will analyze the influence of family, peers, culture, media, technology, and other factors on health behaviors.

- **Rationale:** It is important for students to consider the underlying factors related to why it is so easy for people to engage in binging behaviors. Examining this everyday occurrence can provide perspectives to help students reflect on their own media usage behaviors and patterns.

- **Learning Outcomes:** Students will be able to discuss the reason people binge so they can develop a broader understanding the impact of this behavior.

- **Description of Activity:** Students can engage in a think-pair-share with classmates about why people binge. Students will talk in small groups and then can become involved in a larger class discussion. It is important for teachers to record student responses and provide opportunities for open discussion of these responses.

- **Supporting Resources:**
  - The Science Behind Why We Binge (And What To Do About It), http://www.huffingtonpost.com/2013/10/17/why-we-binge-science_n_4102184.html

  - Deloitte's 10th Digital Democracy Survey, http://www2.deloitte.com/us/en/pages/about-deloitte/articles/press-releases/digital-democracy-survey-tenth-edition.html

  - PEW Research Center, Teens, Social Media & Technology 2015 Overview: http://www.pewinternet.org/2015/04/09/teens-social-media-technology-2015

ONE-DAY ACTIVITY

- **Standard:**
  - *Standard 5:* Students will demonstrate the ability to use decision-making skills to enhance health.

  - *Standard 7:* Students will demonstrate the ability to practice health-enhancing behaviors and avoid or reduce health risks.

- **Rationale:** Teenagers need opportunities to become aware of and reflect on their personal habits and the impact these habits have on daily life. Self-awareness and reflection are difficult skills to teach. One strategy for supporting this process as it relates to binge watching is to provide teenagers with the opportunity to provide specific guidance to one another that may lead to a shift in behavior. This assignment will also enable students to make decisions about strategies that can help to curb binging behaviors and enhance personal health.

- **Learning Outcome:** Students will be able to develop guidelines so they can make informed decisions about how to effectively reduce binge watching.

- **Description of Activity:** Working in groups, students will design "one pagers" that provide guidelines for watching TV, movies, and online videos. In addition, to the guidelines, the one-page will include a clear problem statement outlining the issues that make binge watching a widespread problem. Students will start by identifying the major issues related to binge watching and why they think these issues exist. Next, students can use these issues to target their recommendations for effectively reducing binge watching.

- **Supporting Resources:**
  o Let's Move, http://www.letsmove.gov/reduce-screen-time-and-get-active

  o Technology Addiction: Concern, Controversy, and Finding Balance, https://www.commonsensemedia.org/research/technology-addiction-concern-controversy-and-finding-balance

ONE-WEEK ACTIVITY
- **Standards:**
  o *Standard 3:* Students will demonstrate the ability to access valid information and products and services to enhance health.

  o *Standard 8:* Students will demonstrate the ability to advocate for personal, family, and community health.

- **Rationale:** While it is essential that teenagers understand the various issues related to binge watching, it is also important to engage in meaningful conversation with one another about these issues and advocate concerns to the broader public to promote meaningful change. This experience will allow students to participate in a process within society to communicate concerns and solutions to local politicians and advocate for change.

- **Learning Outcome:**
  - Students will be able to develop letters to send local politicians so they can address concerns about the impact and prevalence of binge watching as well as possible solutions.

- **Description of Activity:** Students will need to first identify which concerns about binge watching they would like to address as well as decide which politician(s) they would like to email and/or mail their letter. It would also be helpful if the teacher provides students with a quick lesson on the structure and typical voice of business letters. Once draft letters are complete, the teacher should facilitate a peer review process to enable students to gather formative feedback and reflect on their work. Once students develop final letters they can make presentations to classmates or others in the school, and the letters can even be shared to local media outlets. The compilation letters can even be uploaded online so that they can be viewed more widely. It is suggested that final letters are both mailed and emailed to local politicians.

- **Supporting Resources:**
  - Writing basic business letters, https://owl.english.purdue.edu/owl/resource/653/ 01/

  - The Common Sense Census: Media Use by Tweens and Teens: https://www. commonsensemedia.org/research/the-common-sense-census-media-use-by-tweens-and-teens

ADDITIONAL RESOURCES

reSTART Center: http://www.netaddictionrecovery.com/

Caught in the Net: How to Recognize the Signs of Internet Addiction--and a Winning Strategy for Recovery, Kimberly S. Young

Screenagers: Growing up in the Digital Age: http://www.screenagersmovie.com/

Web Junkie: http://www.pbs.org/pov/webjunkie/

Go Screen Free: http://www.screenfree.org

Internet Addiction Test and Manual, http://netaddiction.com/internet-addiction-test

Center for Internet and Technology Addiction: http://virtual-addiction.com

[1] Levine-Weinberg, A. (2015, September 30). How Netflix Really Creates Value. Retrieved from http://www.fool.com/investing/general/2015/09/30/how-netflix-inc-really-creates-value.aspx BLACK TEXT,

[2] Huddleston, J. T. (2015, June 30). TiVo Study: 92% of People are 'Binge Viewing' Television. Retrieved from http://fortune.com/2015/06/30/binge-viewing-study/

[3] 70 percent of US consumers binge watch TV, bingers average five episodes per sitting, Deloitte US, Press release. (2016, May 04). Retrieved from http://www2.deloitte.com/us/en/pages/about-deloitte/articles/press-releases/digital-democracy-survey-tenth-edition.html

[4] The Common Sense Census: Media Use by Tweens and Teens: Infographic. (2015). Retrieved from https://www.commonsensemedia.org/the-common-sense-census-media-use-by-tweens-and-teens-infographic

[5] The Common Sense Census: Media Use by Tweens and Teens. (2015, November 03). Retrieved from https://www.commonsensemedia.org/research/the-common-sense-census-media-use-by-tweens-and-teens

[6] The Common Sense Census: Media Use by Tweens and Teens: Infographic. (2015, November 03). Retrieved from https://www.commonsensemedia.org/the-common-sense-census-media-use-by-tweens-and-teens-infographic

[7] The Common Sense Census: Media Use by Tweens and Teens. (2015, November 03). Retrieved from https://www.commonsensemedia.org/research/the-common-sense-census-media-use-by-tweens-and-teens

[8] The Common Sense Census: Media Use by Tweens and Teens. (2015, November 03). Retrieved from https://www.commonsensemedia.org/research/the-common-sense-census-media-use-by-tweens-and-teens

[9] The Common Sense Census: Media Use by Tweens and Teens. (2015, November 03). Retrieved from https://www.commonsensemedia.org/research/the-common-sense-census-media-use-by-tweens-and-teens

[10] International Communication Association. (2015, January 29). Feelings of loneliness, depression linked to binge-watching television. *ScienceDaily*. Retrieved from www.sciencedaily.com/releases/2015/01/150129094341.htm

[11] Olson, S., (2015, November 08). Is All That Netflix Why You're Feeling Depressed? Retrieved from http://www.medicaldaily.com/binge-watching-tv-linked-higher-rates-depression-and-anxiety-360776

[12] Technology Addiction: Concern, Controversy, and Finding Balance. (2016, May 03). Retrieved from https://www.commonsensemedia.org/research/technology-addiction-concern-controversy-and-finding-balance

[13] Times, T. (2014, July 11). Obesity, sleep loss associated with teens' excessive 'screen-time', CDC says. Retrieved from http://www.techtimes.com/articles/10165/20140711/obesity-sleep-loss-associated-with-teens-excessive-screen-time-cdc-says.htm

[14] National Health and Nutrition Examination Survey. (2017, April 26). Retrieved from http://www.cdc.gov/nchs/nhanes/

[15] Wijga, A. H., Scholtens, S., Bemelmans, W. J., Kerkhof, M., Koppelman, G. H., Brunekreef, B., & Smit, H. A. (2010). Diet, screen time, physical activity, and childhood overweight in the general population and in high risk subgroups: prospective analyses in the PIAMA Birth Cohort. *Journal of obesity, 2010*.

[16] Tremblay, M. S., & Willms, J. D. (2003). Is the Canadian childhood obesity epidemic related to physical inactivity?. *International journal of obesity, 27*(9), 1100-1105.

[17] Chaput, J. P., Visby, T., Nyby, S., Klingenberg, L., Gregersen, N. T., Tremblay, A., & Sjödin, A. (2011). Video game playing increases food intake in adolescents: a randomized crossover study. *The American journal of clinical nutrition, 93*(6), 1196-1203.

[18] Adachi-Mejia, A. M., Longacre, M. R., Gibson, J. J., Beach, M. L., Titus-Ernstoff, L. T., & Dalton, M. A. (2007). Children with a TV in their bedroom at higher risk for being overweight. *International journal of obesity, 31*(4), 644-651.

[19] International Communication Association. (2015, January 29). Feelings of loneliness and depression linked to binge-watching television. Retrieved from https://www.eurekalert.org/pub_releases/2015-01/ica-fol012615.php

[20] Karmakar, M., & Kruger, J. S. (2016, March 04). Is binge-watching bad for your mental health? Retrieved May 15, 2017, from https://amp.theguardian.com/commentisfree/2016/mar/04/binge-watching-mental-health-effects-research

[21] France-Presse, A. (2015, February 02). Teenagers sleep less when they have more computer screen time says study. Retrieved from https://www.theguardian.com/technology/2015/feb/03/teenagers-sleep-less-when-they-have-more-computer-screen-time-says-study

[22] Samakow, J., & Leibovich, L. (2013, October 17). Here's What A Constantly Plugged-In Life Is Doing To Kids' Bodies. Retrieved May 15, 2017, from http://www.huffingtonpost.com/2013/10/17/teens-on-screens_n_4101758.html

[23] Burke, T. M., Markwald, R. R., McHill, A. W., Chinoy, E. D., Snider, J. A., Bessman, S. C., & Wright, K. P. (2015). Effects of caffeine on the human circadian clock in vivo and in vitro. *Science translational medicine*, *7*(305), 305ra146-305ra146.

[24] Gentile, D. A., Reimer, R. A., Nathanson, A. I., Walsh, D. A., & Eisenmann, J. C. (2014). Protective effects of parental monitoring of children's media use: a prospective study. JAMA pediatrics, 168(5), 479-484.

[25] Baral, S. (2015, December 31). Netflix And Chew: How Binge Watching Affects Our Eating Habits. Retrieved from http://www.npr.org/sections/thesalt/2015/12/31/461594989/netflix-and-chew-how-binge-watching-affects-our-eating-habits

[26] Bassist, E. (2013, February 27). Addicted to Netflix: Teen-Soap-Opera Binge As Psychosis. Retrieved from http://nymag.com/thecut/2013/02/addicted-to-netflix-teen-tv-binge-as-psychosis.html

[27] Hsu, M. (2014, September 26). How to Overcome a Binge-Watching Addiction. Retrieved from http://www.wsj.com/articles/how-to-overcome-a-binge-watching-addiction-1411748602

CHAPTER SIX

———•———

Social Media and the F.O.M.O.

Are all new technologies beneficial?

When can new technologies be healthy and when can they be harmful?

What happens when the costs associated with using new technologies begin to outweigh the benefits?

BEHAVIORS AND THEMES

SCALE & SCOPE: People today are connected to each other in ways that have never been possible in the history of the world. The United Nations estimates over 3 billion people are online using the Internet[1]. In the United States alone, over 225 million people (68% of the population) are connected through their mobile devices[2]. Researchers have found Americans check their cell phones more than 8 million times a day, with some individuals checking their phones on average as much as 150 times a day[3]. Much of this online activity is connected to individuals choosing to participate within a variety of social media platforms throughout the day. For example, more than 1.5 billion people log onto Facebook every day. The second largest network, Instagram (also owned by Facebook), has over 400 million members log on every month, with Snapchat adding another 100 million to this worldwide network[4]. This rapidly growing trend is particularly true of young adults, with 90% of individuals from the ages of 18 to 29 reporting membership in at least one social networking site[5]. Overwhelmingly, individuals report using these social media platforms to help maintain, strengthen, and even rejuvenate relationships with family, friends, coworkers, and even strangers[6]. Supporting this perspective, social media researchers have found members of online communities have more friends, closer relationships, and more diverse connections than individuals who choose to remain offline[7]. Additionally, users of social media have been found to be more trusting, more likely to consider multiple perspectives, and feel more supported by their community[8].

MOST POPULAR SOCIAL MEDIA PLATFORMS AMONG TEENS

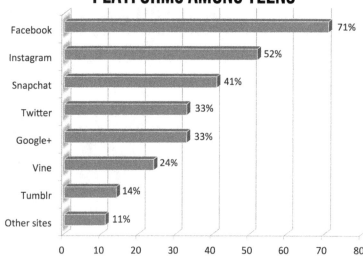

Platform	Percentage
Facebook	71%
Instagram	52%
Snapchat	41%
Twitter	33%
Google+	33%
Vine	24%
Tumblr	14%
Other sites	11%

Source: Pew Research Center's Teen Relationships Survey, 2015

PROBLEM DEFINED: Despite social media's capacity to connect and support, individuals also frequently report feeling anxious, envious, and regretful when they log into these networks. Psychologists have begun referring to these uneasy feelings as the "Fear of Missing Out"—or F.O.M.O. –and theorize these emotions are triggered by the process of comparing one's current situation (or life circumstances) to the posts and images presented by members of one's social network. In this way, the fear of missing out is fueled by the underlying assumption there is something "better"—more interesting, more entertaining –going on elsewhere and you are being "left out". Researchers investigating the phenomenon of F.O.M.O. have found that 4 out of 10 young people reported they experience the fear of missing out sometimes or often in a typical month[9]. Additionally, they have found those who experience F.O.M.O are more likely to experience the sensation again in the future[10]. In this way, individuals who regularly experience the fear of missing out will likely perceive the sensation growing over time— with feelings of regret or envy becoming amplified with every viewed post and missed opportunity. To combat these sensations, many teens begin to compulsively check their phones in an effort to remain continually connected to their network's activities and potential opportunities. Other individuals report trying to overcompensate for feelings associated with F.O.M.O by distorting the image they present of themselves online to mirror that of their peer group.

BIOLOGICAL TRIGGERS: Today's desire to remain connected on social media is deeply rooted in human evolution and the creation of tools to communicate more effectively over distance and time. From this perspective, today's fear of missing out is deeply linked to the time when the survival of our species depended critically on our ancestor's ability to remain connected with their tribe. Supporting this theory, scientists have discovered evidence our brains over time have developed a specialized center—the amygdala in the limbic system –to detect when the individual is being left out and their survival is being potentially threatened[11]. When an individual's amygdala senses they are being excluded, it will activate the fight-or-flight response by releasing a flood of hormones to trigger a person's ability to defend themselves. Scientists speculate it is this sudden release of hormones that creates the strong feelings of anxiety and inadequacy triggered when individuals experience the fear of missing out[12]. These physical and psychological symptoms are often so negative and severe individuals report going to great lengths to avoid feeling that way again in the future. From this perspective, individuals who check their phone dozens of times a day— often describing it as a matter of 'life and death' –are attempting to avoid these negative emotions by remaining continually connected with their peer group and updated with the latest information.

AMPLIFIED BY TECHNOLOGY: The fear of missing out is not a new phenomenon. Researchers of adolescent development have long reported teens being highly conscious of their perceived popularity and status within their peer group. However, teens' access to rapidly changing communication technologies—like smartphones, tablets, and laptops –has transformed their daily social interactions, intertwining their online and face-to-face lives in ways that become indistinguishable. Unsurprisingly, tech-savvy adolescents have led the adoption and use of these social technologies. 95% of all teens are online, with 81% of those adolescents reporting membership to at least one social media platform[13]. These networking technologies enable approximately 22 million teens in the United States to interact with each other on a continual basis—providing them with nearly unlimited access to the minute-to-minute details of their daily lives. At the same time, these communication technologies continue to advance—becoming both smaller and more powerful –in ways that make them likely to become even further embedded in the lives of teens and adults alike. Technology researcher, Sherry Turkle, argues the pervasiveness of these communication technologies has lead to unrealistic expectations for individuals to be available around-the-clock, seven days a week—a digital culture that increasingly rewards those who multi-task, respond rapidly, and satisfies other's needs for instant gratification[14].

IMPACTS MENTAL HEALTH: Psychologists are becoming increasingly concerned about the health consequences for teens and adults who live more and more of their lives online. Social media researchers from around the world have identified the fear of missing out as being a reliable indicator for having a negative impact on one's health and sense of well-being[15]. Their studies have identified a strong relationship between the number of hours an individual spends online using social media and their reported incidence of feeling stressed, anxious, and depressed. In 2015, Australian researchers found 60% of teens reported feeling worried when they discovered their friends were having fun without them[16]. In America, 51% of teen reported feeling worried when they didn't know what their friends were doing[1]. Additionally, individuals who checked their social media accounts more than 9 times a day were 3 times more likely to report disrupted sleep and depressive episodes than someone who only checked once a day[18]. Further, these studies

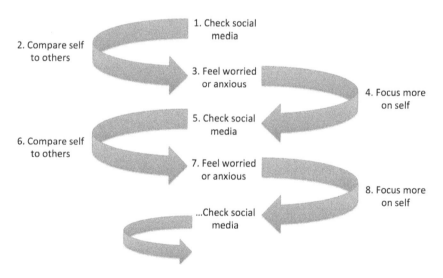

SOCIAL MEDIA DOWNWARD SPIRAL

1. Check social media
2. Compare self to others
3. Feel worried or anxious
4. Focus more on self
5. Check social media
6. Compare self to others
7. Feel worried or anxious
8. Focus more on self
...Check social media

indicate feelings with the fear of missing out do not abate with adolescence. In a recent study, young adults (from the ages of 18 to 35) reported experiencing the fear of missing out more than any other age group being studied. Health experts now speculate individuals who experience F.O.M.O. most acutely online are "opening the door" to more significant and lasting mental health problems as their symptoms and ways of coping escalate[19].

NAVIGATING TRADE-OFFS: Most individuals log onto social media platforms without considering the consequences—and perhaps for good reason. Participating within social networks allows people to maintain a sense of personal connection and immediacy in a way that would otherwise not be possible. Social media researchers have found members of online social networks report numerous advantages— like affirmation and mutual support –that provide an immediate and lasting health benefit [20]. Yet these same participants often report moments where belonging to an online community frequently made them feel inadequate about themselves and envious of their peers. Learning how to navigate these conflicting costs and benefits of belonging to social networks has become increasingly necessary for today's teens. Researchers estimate the typical teen spends 9 hours a day online consuming various types of media— playing video games, watching videos, listening to music –in which social networking platforms have become the glue connecting teens across this communal experience. For better and for worse, these new social tools are unquestionably changing human behavior and culture for the foreseeable future.

KEY CONCEPTS

Instant & Delayed Gratification: Instant gratification is the desire to experience pleasure or fulfillment without delay. Delayed gratification is the ability to use patience to place long-term goals ahead of short-term satisfaction.

Obsessive-Compulsive Behavior: Obsessive-compulsive behaviors are characterized by unreasonable thoughts and fears (obsessions) that lead to repetitive behaviors (compulsions). Attempting to ignore or stop these behaviors frequently results in feelings of extreme anxiety, worry, and depression.

Need for Inclusion: One's need for being included is based on the desire to belong to a group, a desire to be part of something greater than one's self. The need be included as part of the group—for social connection –has been found by researchers to be particularly powerful during adolescence.

Fight, Flight, or Freeze Response: This physical response is triggered in response to a perceived threat, real or imagined. These responses, triggered in $1/20^{th}$ of a second, activate the nervous system to release a flood of neurotransmitters to help your body survive imminent danger.

REAL-WORLD SITUATIONS

Study: Frequent Social Media Use May Take A Toll On Teens' Mental Health

—*Source: By Staff Writer, CBS News, Atlanta, July 28th, 2015*[21]

How much social media use is appropriate?

When can using social media become unhealthy?

"Frequent social media use could have a negative impact on young people's mental health, according to a new study. For many teens, going even an hour without checking Facebook, Instagram, or Twitter is a struggle. Twenty-four percent of teenagers go online "almost constantly," according to a recent *Pew Research Center* study.

But more alarming than the time spent is the negative consequences that young people may suffer from due to excessive screen-time. The study, from Ottawa Public Health, suggests that teens that use social media sites for two hours or more daily are at risk for poor mental health, psychological distress and suicidal thoughts, as reported by *Huffington Post*.

Researchers looked at data from 750 students in grades seven through 12 who took the 2013 Ontario Student Drug Use and Health Survey. The study found that 25 percent of students surveyed reported spending at least two hours a day on social networking sites. These same students were categorized as reporting more poor mental health issues, symptoms of anxiety and depression, and suicidal thoughts. "It could be that teens with mental health problems are seeking out interactions as they are feeling isolated and alone," Dr. Hugues Sampasa-Kayinga, the study's lead author, told The Huffington Post in an email. "Or they would like to satisfy unmet needs for face-to-face mental health support."

Sampasa-Kayinga notes that the link between social media and mental health issues is complicated, and that simple use of sites like Facebook and Twitter "cannot fully explain by itself the occurrence of mental health problems." Researchers are now investigating how this issue might be fixed, and in some cases turning the problem into the solution.

"We see social networking sites, which may be a problem for some, also being a solution," Dr. Brenda K. Wiederhold of the Interactive Media Institute in San Diego said, as reported by Huffington Post. "Since teens are on the sites, it is the perfect place for public health and service providers to reach out and connect with this vulnerable population and provide health promotion systems and supports."

Experts also suggest parents pay attention to how much time teens are spending on these sites and its possible link to mental health issues. The research was published online on July 13 in the Journal Cyberpsychology, Behavior, and Social Networking."

F.O.M.O. Linked To Stress In Teens

—*Source: By Erik Saas, The Media Post, Nov. 9, 2015*[22]

Why can social media often cause teens stress?

How do I cope with the Fear of Missing Out?

"The latest study showing a correlation (but not necessarily a causative connection) between social media and stress comes from Australia, where the Australian Psychological Society's fifth annual "Stress & Wellbeing Study" includes a special section on social media and "fear of missing out" or F.O.M.O.

The study surveyed both light and heavy social media users. The study defines heavy social media users as those who check social media five or more times a day, and light users as those who check it less. By these measures, over half of Aussie teens are heavy social media users: 25% said they check social media "constantly," while 12% check it more than ten times a day, and 19% check it about five to ten times per day. Among light social media users, 24% of the total said they check social media one to four times a day, 15% check it several times a week, and 5% said they check it once a week (unsurprisingly Aussie adults aren't as gung ho on social media, with just 23% qualifying as heavy users).

It's important to note that some of the key measures of stress in the research on F.O.M.O are self-reported, and thus open to all the vagaries of subjectivity; on the other hand, at a certain point it seems like common sense to simply ask people how they feel. Aussie teens who are heavy social media users are more likely to experience F.O.M.O, with 90% saying they are afraid they will miss something if they don't stay connected, compared to 65% of light social media users. Similarly 78% of heavy users said they feel worried or uncomfortable if they can't access their social media accounts, compared to 44% of light users, and 71% of heavy users said they feel excluded when they see pictures of an event they weren't invited to, compared to 52% for light users.

Furthermore, 70% of heavy users said they feel stressed out about how they look on social media, versus 47% of light users, and 69% said they feel "brain burnout" from constant connectivity, against 50% of light users. 64% of heavy users said they feel bad about themselves if no one comments on or "likes" their photos, versus 44% of light users."

I'm 15 And Snapchat Makes Me Feel Awful About Myself

—Source: by Ruby Clark, Mashable, Oct. 20, 2015[23]

How do I stop compulsively checking my phone?
How can my friends and family support me if I feel I'm having a problem?

"You're sitting in bed on a Saturday night, checking your phone. You go onto Snapchat to check your friends' Snapchat stories. You find that not only your best friend, but all of your friends are at a party and didn't invite you. You feel both sad and angry that you weren't informed, and experience a sense of betrayal. Welcome to the reality of missing out, and Snapchat is at the center of it.

Snapchat started out as a way to send silly or fun private photos to your friends (or people who are more than friends). Before Snapchat stories, there was just sending a picture with a caption, for 1 to 10 seconds. It was great because you could send an ugly selfie, an inappropriate photo or a new haircut to anyone you wanted. Nobody would see it ever again (unless it was screenshotted). This was the beauty of Snapchat. Then, what happened to Snapchat is what happens to most popular apps: It got an update.

The update opened up a new world. Now, there's a Snapchat "Story." This is a separate page on Snapchat, where you can post photos or videos that everyone on your contact list can view, and which disappear in 24 hours. A Story isn't sent to anyone directly, but it's there for everyone to see. In short, the effect of Snapchat Stories can be summarized with the title of Mindy Kaling's book, *Is Everyone Hanging Out Without Me?* Snapchat Stories boast about who you're with, what you're doing — and what everyone else is missing out on. And teens are obsessed with them.

Snapchat can make a person feel awful about themselves. Snapchat is the main thing that triggers teenage F.O.M.O. (fear of missing out). I can't explain how many times I've had to go upstate or been grounded, then check Snapchat to see all my friends together. I constantly check Snapchat to see what everyone is doing. Whether I'm reading or in the middle of a party, I always feel like I need to know what everyone is doing, secretly hoping it isn't better than what I'm doing.

Snapchat is worse for F.O.M.O. than other social media. Stories are posted when the party or hangout is happening, in real time, and frequent updates are encouraged. Most teens don't post exactly what they are doing, where and when on Instagram or Facebook. Most of my friends tend to do those more "artistic" and "permanent" posts when they get home. Since Snapchats can only be captured in the moment, we're privy to what happened 10 minutes ago. Almost every teen has some sense of this in them — we all want to be at the best party, or with the most people. Once, a woman in her early twenties told me when she was a teen, her dad wouldn't allow her to post a photo with more than five friends on Facebook. He didn't want any of her friends to get upset for not being invited. This rule has now been transferred to Snapchat: Almost every Story is about who you are with.

Snapchat Stories capture the very real insecurities of teenagers. This is different from direct cyberbullying. Nobody (hopefully) is doing it to make anyone feel bad, but it can make an insecure 15-year-old girl feel awful to see. Teens have this fear that people might be doing something cooler than us, so we feel like we need to make it seem like we are doing something even cooler. We don't want to seem like losers; therefore, we need to prove to people that we are still active in our "social scene." Instead of enjoying what we are doing, all we do is take pictures of what we are doing to make other teens feel bad they aren't with us.

But, those kids who are "missing out" aren't missing out on anything. Endless times have I been silently sitting next to a friend on my phone, paused what I was doing to take a cute, happy selfie with that friend, then go back into silence to check yet another app that will not help me go anywhere in life. Similarly, if I'm with a huge group of people, I'll always take a picture so people know I'm with a lot of people. I don't do this to make anyone feel bad or jealous, but deep down I know people will see it and hopefully think "I wish I were there." This doesn't give me happiness, but a sense of entitlement and makes me feel somewhat better about my social life.

Snapchat Stories give us many things, but bragging rights more than anything. We brag, again, because we all seem to need to let everyone know what we are doing every second of the day. If I'm going to the gym, there's no point unless I take a photo of how sweaty I am afterwards, with some hashtag that has no meaning in real life. We brag when we post a picture of us reading a book, showing people that we actually have minds and are smart. Snapchat makes us want to show everyone "look at what I do." Snapchat is all fun and games until you aren't featured in the big group photo everyone took while you were in the other room getting chips, or worse, when you weren't even invited. The app amplifies our fear of missing out, and turns us into whiny braggers."

LEARNING SCENARIOS

Scenario #1

It's another Friday night and you're staying at home again. Bored, you check your phone for the fifth time in the last fifteen minutes. The sensation to look at your phone feels overwhelming. You notice your friend is posting pictures from a party to which you were not invited. You can see a lot of your friends are having a great time at a birthday party for someone you know but aren't close to. What should you do? Will you post something to social media? What will you say to your friends the next time you see them?

Scenario #2

It's happened again. Your friend is in tears because they've just ended a relationship. Repeating details you've heard multiple times throughout the day, you really wish your friend would begin talking about something else. You keep checking your phone to see who's been texting. How do you think your friend feels during those moments? If you catch yourself looking at your phone, what should you say to your friend? What steps can you take in the future to avoid making the same mistake?

Scenario #3

You feel it again. The tightening sensation in your chest grows. The sense of anxiety and isolation begins to weigh you down. Checking your friends' posts to social media confirms your deepest suspicion—you feel your life is clearly inadequate compared to the lives of your friends. They're always having more fun, always doing what you'd rather be doing. What should you do in this moment? How might you cope with your feelings of anxiety and isolation? What steps can you take improve your digital health and wellbeing.

HELPFUL STRATEGIES

DOCUMENT AND VERIFY: It may be important to first track how often you're using social media to determine if you might have a problem. Social media experts recommend downloading a phone app like Checky (http://www.checkyapp.com) or Moment (https://inthemoment.io) to count how often you check your phone and measure your Internet use. Based on this data, individuals can then begin setting daily and weekly limits to regulate their online behavior.

UNPLUG AND DISCONNECT: Researchers investigating the F.O.M.O. highly recommend taking regular breaks from participating in social media, ideally before you begin to experience symptoms associated with the condition. Their advice is based on research indicating individuals need to continually interrupt the hyper-vigilant state associated with the fight-and-flight response sustained by repeatedly checking one's accounts[24]. Importantly, researchers found this method was likely to increase feelings associated with F.O.M.O in the short-run, while being ultimately necessary to decrease feelings of anxiety, worry, and depression in the long-run.

ESTABLISH ROUTINES: In addition to taking regular breaks, social media experts recommend creating strict routines regarding social media usage to decrease the likelihood of triggering emotions associated with missing out, feeling deficient, or becoming envious of another's life. First, experts recommend individuals carry their cell phone in their pocket, purse, or backpack. Second, individuals are advised to turn off the automatic 'Push notifications' within their social media applications and begin manually checking their accounts on a regular but limited basis. Finally, to promote feelings of wellbeing, individuals are urged to prohibit the use of cell phones during meal times and beside their bedside at least an hour before going to sleep.

LIVING-IN-THE-MOMENT: Individuals can become easily captivated by social media's endless procession of posts and images. After all, these social networking sites have been designed expressly to fascinate and entertain individuals during their downtimes. To counter these powerful social mechanisms, experts recommend individuals begin a number of practices to begin "living-in-the-moment". First, individuals are advised to explore reflective practices like meditation and mindfulness– learning procedures to begin using all their senses to become aware of the details of their environment and focusing on the rewards of the present situation. Second, experts recommend individuals take regular breaks to visit the outdoors and places of natural beauty to restore one's sense of natural rhythms and daily cycles. Lastly, individuals are encouraged to join clubs and organizations to provide regular social interaction, needed stimulation, and sense of belonging.

LEARNING TASKS

20-Minute Activity:

- Standards:
  - Standard 2: Students will analyze the influence of family, peers, culture, media, technology, and other factors on health behaviors.

  - *Standard 4*: Students will demonstrate the ability to use interpersonal communication skills to enhance health and avoid or reduce health risks.

- **Rationale:** Adolescents are increasingly using social media sites and applications to build and maintain relationships with their peers. Teenagers need to learn how to use these revolutionary tools in ways that don't negatively impact their developing sense of identity. Teens should come to understand how to make decisions that enable them to use social media in healthy and appropriate ways.

- **Learning Outcomes:** Students will be able to identify problems related to the Fear Of Missing Out so they may identify issues related to one's sense of wellbeing before it becomes a problem.

- **Description of Activity:** Teachers will lead students in a think-pair-share discussion of the essential question: *"When can new technologies be healthy and when can they be* *harmful?"* Students should consider as many responses as possible at this point to address these questions. Students should also be encouraged to connect their responses to personal experiences whenever possible and appropriate.

- **Supporting Resources:**
  - Teens, Social Media & Technology Overview: http://www.pewinternet.org/2015/04/09/teens-social-media-technology-2015/

  - #Being 13: Teens and Social Media Use: http://www.cnn.com/2015/10/05/health/being-13-teens-social-media-study/index.html

  - The Real Reason You Can't Stop Checking Your Phone: https://www.psychologytoday.com/blog/rewired-the-psychology-technology/201507/the-real-reason-you-cant-stop-checking-your-phone

  - Are You Happier Without Facebook: http://www.popsci.com/ are-you-happier-without-social-media

ONE-DAY ACTIVITY
- **Standards:**
  - *Standard 5*: Students will demonstrate the ability to use decision-making skills to enhance health.

  - *Standard 7*: Students will demonstrate the ability to practice health-enhancing behaviors and avoid or reduce health risks.

- **Rationale:** Adolescents are increasingly seeking validation from their peers through their participation in (and observation of) social media sites and applications. Teenagers need to learn how to use these revolutionary tools in ways that don't negatively impact their developing sense of identity. Teens should learn how to make decisions that enable them to use social media in healthy and appropriate ways.

- **Learning Outcomes:** Students will develop strategies to be mutually supportive of their peers so they can be pro-active in establishing a healthy culture and appropriate boundaries regarding social media use.

- **Description of Activity:** Teachers will help students develop a health standard for adolescents regarding the appropriate weekly usage of social media to promote adolescent health and wellness. Students should identify and investigate physical and mental symptoms associated with adolescents (and adults) that have developed a dependence on checking their social media accounts. Students should also ground their health standard on emerging guidelines and best practices regarding teenager's online behavior.

- **Supporting Resources:**
  - Teens Spend Nine Hours A Day Using Social Media: http://www.cnn.com/2015/ 11/03/health/teens-tweens-media-screen-use-report

  - How Social Media Can Induce Feelings Of 'Missing Out': http://www.nytimes.com /2011/04/10/business/10ping.html?src=recg&_r=1

  - A Clinical Psychologist Explains Why People Are Getting F.O.M.O: http://www.businessinsider.com/a-clinical-psychologist-explains-why-people-are-getting-fomo-2015-10

  - Teens On Social Media: Being Cut Off Is Awful: http://www.cnn.com/ 2015/10/02/living/being-13-teens-social-media-question-answer/index.html

ONE-WEEK ACTIVITY

- **Standard:**
  - *Standard 1:* Students will comprehend concepts related to health promotion and disease prevention to enhance health.

  - *Standard 8:* Students will demonstrate the ability to advocate for personal, family, and community health.

- **Rationale:** More and more adolescents and adults are developing an unhealthy reliance on checking and using their online devices. Teenagers need to learn how to use social media sites and applications in ways that don't lead to addictive behavior. Teens should learn how to make decisions that enable them to use social media tools in healthy and appropriate ways.

- **Learning Outcomes:** Students will be able to identify the costs and benefits of using social media so they can make more informed and responsible decisions regarding their beneficial uses of social media.

- **Description of Activity:** Teachers will help students create a support group to help teenagers who have developed an unhealthy reliance on checking their social media accounts. In developing this support group, students should identify and investigate case studies of teenagers and young adults whose professional or personal lives have been impacted by an online addiction. Students should also contact local mental health experts who specialize in helping teens and adults manage disruptive online behavior to obtain resources, materials, and validated strategies. To extend this activity, students should plan and manage the logistics of promoting, hosting, and finding a supervisor for this extra-curricular activity.

- **Supporting Resources:**
  - Teen 'Like' And 'FOMO' Anxiety: http://www.cnn.com/2014/10/16/living/teens-on-social-media-like-and-fomo-anxiety-digital-life/

  - Social Media and Friendships: http://www.pewinternet.org/2015/08/06/chapter-4-social-media-and-friendships/

  - The One Feeling That Makes You Check Social Media Incessantly: http://fortune.com/2016/01/30/social-media-fomo-sleep/

  - The Complex Link Between Social Media and Depression: http://news.health.com/2016/03/25/could-lots-of-time-spent-on-social-media-be-tied-to-depression/?xid=socialflow_facebook_health

---

[1] Some 3.2 billion people now online, but number still falls short of Internet target – UN report. (2015, November 30). Retrieved from http://www.un.org/apps/news/story.asp?NewsID=52690

[2] United States Internet Users. Retrieved May, from http://www.internetlivestats.com/internet-users/us/.

[3] Duggan, M., Ellison, N. B., Lampe, C., Lenhart, A., & Madden, M. (2015, January 09). Frequency of Social Media Use. Retrieved from http://www.pewinternet.org/2015/01/09/frequency-of-social-media-use-2/.

[4] Social Media Fact Sheet. (2017, January 12). Retrieved from http://www.pewinternet.org/fact-sheet/social-media/.

[5] Lenhart, A. (2015). *Teens, Social Media & Technology Overview 2015: Smartphones facilitate shifts in communication landscape for teens* (pp. 1-48, Report).

[6] Perrin, A. (2015, October 08). Social Media Usage: 2005-2015. Retrieved from http://www.pewinternet.org/2015/10/08/social-networking-usage-2005-2015/

[7] Lenhart, A. (2015, August 06). Teens, Technology and Friendships. Retrieved from http://www.pewinternet.org/2015/08/06/teens-technology-and-friendships/.Same Pew report on social media use citation.

[8] Hampton, K., Goulet, L. S., Rainie, L., & Purcell, K. (2011, June 15). Social networking sites and our lives. Retrieved from http://www.pewinternet.org/2011/06/16/social-networking-sites-and-our-lives/.

[9] Wallace, K. (2014, November 20). Teen 'like' and 'FOMO' anxiety. Retrieved from http://www.cnn.com/2014/10/16/living/teens-on-social-media-like-and-fomo-anxiety-digital-life/.

[10] Barker, E. (2016, June 7). How to Overcome FOMO: Fear of Missing Out. Retrieved from http://time.com/4358140/overcome-fomo/.

[11] Sanz, A. (2015, September 30). What's the Psychology Behind the Fear of Missing Out? Retrieved May 06, 2017, from http://www.slate.com/blogs/quora/2015/09/30/fomo_what_s_the_psychology_behind_the_fear_of_missing_out.html.

[12] Bloom, L. (2015, January 10). Beware the Dangers of FOMO. Retrieved from https://www.psychologytoday.com/blog/stronger-the-broken-places/201501/beware-the-dangers-fomo.

[13] Social Media Fact Sheet. (2017, January 12). Retrieved from http://www.pewinternet.org/fact-sheet/social-media/..

[14] Turkle, S. (2015). *Reclaiming conversation: the power of talk in a digital age*. New York: Penguin Press..

[15] Gold, M. (2015). *Teens suffer highest rates of FOMO* (Report). Australian Psychological Society.

[16] *Stress & wellbeing: How Australians are coping with life* (pp. 1-44, Report). (2015). Australian Psychological Society..

[17] Duggan, M., Ellison, N. B., Lampe, C., Lenhart, A., & Madden, M. (2015, January 09). Frequency of Social Media Use. Retrieved from http://www.pewinternet.org/2015/01/09/frequency-of-social-media-use-2/..

[18] Cooper, C. (2015, February 02). Too much exposure to smartphone screens ruins your sleep, study shows. Retrieved from http://www.independent.co.uk/life-style/health-and-families/health-news/too-much-exposure-to-smartphone-screens-ruins-your-sleep-study-shows-10019185.html.

[19] Vitelli, R. (2016, November 30). The FoMo Health Factor. Retrieved from https://www.psychologytoday.com/blog/media-spotlight/201611/the-fomo-health-factor.

[20] Rideout, V. (2012). *Social Media, Social Life: How Teens View Their Digital Lives* (pp. 1-46, Report). Common Sense Media..

[21] Study: Frequent Social Media Use May Take Toll On Teens' Mental Health. (2015, July 28). Retrieved from http://atlanta.cbslocal.com/2015/07/28/study-frequent-social-media-use-may-take-toll-on-teens-mental-health/

[22] Sass, E. (2015, November 9). FOMO Linked To Stress In Teens. Retrieved from https://www.mediapost.com/publications/article/262175/fomo-linked-to-stress-in-teens.html

[23] Karp, R. (2015, October 20). I'm 15 and Snapchat makes me feel awful about myself. Retrieved from http://mashable.com/2015/10/20/snapchat-teen-insecurity/#DMyUAjDSN5qY

[24] NORC at the University of Chicago. (2017, May 3). Almost 6 in 10 teens take a break from social media: Most of the breaks are voluntary and teens report feeling better for the experience. *ScienceDaily*. Retrieved from www.sciencedaily.com/releases/2017/05/170503092233.htm.

CHAPTER SEVEN

Sharing Images & Online Privacy

Why do we share (and over share)?

What does it mean to 'be yourself'?

Why is it important to "remain in the moment"?

BEHAVIORS AND THEMES

SCALE & SCOPE: Sharing and viewing photos and videos online using social media has become a highly integrated part of many people's day. Posting pictures is by far the most popular activity when using social media accounting for 43% of all participation[1]. Two of the most popular image sharing sites—Instagram and Snapchat –have over a half a billion daily users. Everyday over 3.5 billion photos are "liked" on Instagram, over 10 billion videos are viewed on Snapchat, and nearly 9,000 photos are uploaded every second[2]. Facebook alone has over 1.6 billion users every month (larger than the population of any country), with over a billion individuals viewing and posting images of their personal lives every day[3]. Combined, there are an estimated 2.5 billion people choosing to regularly document their lives online using social networking sites—sharing photos of the most special, and mundane, events in their lives[4]. In fact, researchers have found 24% of global social media users report sharing "everything" or "most things" online[5]. When asked what accounts for this desire to share, 78% of participants in a recent study stated they share images of their lives to stay connected to their friends and families[6].

PROBLEM DEFINED: This unprecedented increase in sharing of photos and videos online has been connected to a similarly unheard of increase in problems related to privacy, identity theft, and even burglary and assault. Most image-sharing sites establish user's default setting to "public" making shared photos and images readily available to anyone searching online[7]. Criminals interested in stealing your identity will frequently copy profile images to impersonate individuals and collect personal data to answer security questions commonly used to access websites or reset passwords. Additionally, when images and videos are posted online, most social networking platforms set the default setting to include geotags—data indicating one's location –automatically alongside shared photos and videos. Criminals have begun using this information to burglar homes when known to be vacant or carry out personal assaults in frequently visited locations[8]. Even if individuals are able to avoid these worst-case scenarios, they must contend with managing their "digital reputation" long after the images have been posted. Social media users need to be mindful of the impression created by the permanent trail of images they leave behind in an online world. One online recruitment website reports nearly 60% of future employers are influenced by a job candidate's online presence, with nearly 50% of employers conducting formal searches of social networking sites before offering someone a job or to terminate an existing employee[9].

BIOLOGICAL TRIGGERS: Researchers investigating why individuals choose to share images of their lives online are discovering these sharing behaviors may be deeply rooted in human evolution and psychology. Anthropologists suspect online sharing behaviors are connected to millennia of storytelling, rewarding those who told the most effective stories to gain status, convey sometime lifesaving lessons learned, and strengthen their connection with other people[10]. In addition to these evolutionary roots, sharing behaviors also appear to be intensely connected to individuals' psychological needs for belonging and approval. Many highly active "sharers" report their posting of personal images and videos online is driven by a desire and need to belong[11]. While 30% to 40% of conversations in real life consist of people talking about themselves, researchers estimate that some 80% of social-media updates are focused on the self. Taking "selfies" and posting them online has become a cultural norm for teenagers, accounting for over 30% of all photographs taken by 18 to 24 year olds[12]. Social scientists have further speculated this narcissistic need for individuals to present images of themselves is perhaps instead driven by a largely unconscious attempt to compensate for the insecurities they perceive in themselves. From this perspective, taking and posting "selfies" reflect a desire to gain approval and acceptance in the eyes of others. Posting personal images and videos provides teens with a tangible sense of validation as reflected by the number of followers or likes they receive. Supporting this theory, scientists recently discovered evidence that receiving likes and adding followers activates the brain's reward system providing social media users with regular neurochemical incentives to continue sharing images of their personal lives with their social networks[13].

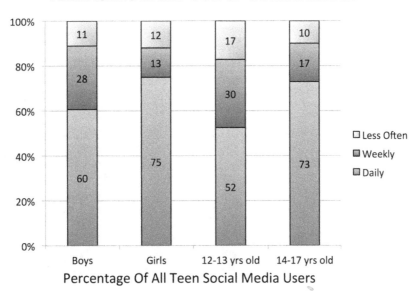

Source: *Pew Research Center Report Teens, Social Media, and Privacy (2013)*

AMPLIFIED BY CELEBRITY CULTURE: Celebrities have turned the sharing of personal photos and videos of themselves into a professional business. By endorsing a wide range of products and services, celebrities can earn millions of dollars a year by leveraging their social media followings to receive paid compensation—earning anywhere from $5,000 to $25,000 per post, with top celebrities (frequently reality stars like the Khardasians) receiving anywhere from $100,000 to

$300,000 for a sponsored post or image[14]. Of most ethical concern, celebrities most often hide this compensation and post these sponsored advertisements as if they were a natural part of their daily lives. Disturbingly this focus on celebrity appears to be influencing children and young adults as evidenced by a study that found elementary and middle school students value "fame" as the most important goal for their future[15]. Many amateur teens, emulating the practices of these celebrities, seek out large audiences of followers to gain "sponsorship" in the pursuit of advertising dollars. Thousands of teens (with at least 250,000 or more followers) can be paid huge fees as "influencers" making hundreds to thousands of dollars a day to create and share content known as "native advertising" meant to appear more authentic and natural to their peers[16]. This creates incredible economic and social incentives for teens to misrepresent their reality while attempting to create a personal brand that resonates with a large commercial audience—amplifying the dynamics of popularity seeking that are already heightened during adolescence.

IMPACTS MENTAL HEALTH: Researchers have found sharing photos and videos using social media can create a documented sense of connection, warmth, and intimacy between friends and family in ways that would otherwise not be possible. Sharing moments of one's life with others taps into nostalgic feelings associated with reminiscing that have been found to make individuals feel better about the present and more hopeful about their future[1]. Additionally, psychologists believe sharing images of our emotional lives online enables people to experiment with sharing aspects of their "true self" they might not otherwise be able to express in their face-to-face relationships[18]. Unfortunately, psychology researchers are also amassing a growing body of evidence that suggests documenting our lives online frequently detracts from the quality of the experience itself—becoming a form of "trophy hunting" that disconnects us from living in the moment[19]. This research indicates individuals tend to enjoy life less when they're focused on the act of capturing their life rather than experiencing it. 58% of respondents in a recent study reported that capturing the moment has prevented them from enjoying a life experience[20]. In the same survey, 91% of survey participants reported missing out on personal moments because they were "living through the lens of their smartphone" rather than living in the moment[21]. These studies provide a cautionary tale warning the way we use our devices may begin controlling our attention and experience of the world in ways we may not even realize.

NAVIGATING TRADE-OFFS: The rapid advance of camera technologies has forever changed how, when, and why people capture and share images. These fast emerging imaging technologies have enabled friends and family to connect and remain in each other's lives in ways that otherwise would not be possible. However, mounting evidence indicates the quest to capture and share the perfect moment interferes with one's capacity to experience life in the moment. Social media experts recommend using these amazingly accessible tools to document our lives sparingly, adopting the mindset of capturing one or two images as a "keepsake" to remember special moments in our lives rather than chronicle complete events (much less lifetimes)[22]. Increasingly musical artists (like Alicia Keyes and Jack White) are banning the use of cell phones at their concerts as a reminder to fans to remain immersed in the moment[23]. Ironically, these devices meant to commemorate life's experiences are leaving many feeling disconnected from the world right in front of them, separated by living life behind the lens of the camera. Social media experts warn users to temper their sharing of images in an endless search of praise and notice for it may come at the very expense of the memory they're trying to commemorate.

KEY CONCEPTS

External Validation: A psychological need to focus on what others think about you, seeking approval, and being liked. This need is frequently made worse by feelings of unworthiness and inadequacy.

Narcissism: A psychological problem characterized by excessive interest in oneself, one's perceived abilities, and one's need for admiration—often at the expense of focusing on the needs and feelings of others.

Impression Management: A conscious or subconscious attempt to influence people's perception of yourself, often by strategically sharing (or withholding) information about their lives.

Imposter Syndrome: A situation where individuals feel like a fake or fraud because they have tricked or deceived others about their abilities or personality.

REAL-WORLD SITUATIONS

19 Year Old Instagram Model Admits Her "Perfect Life" Was A Lie

—*Source: By Alanna Ketler, Collective Evolution, November 3, 2015*[24]

Why do people online pretend to be something they're not?

What does it take to feel genuinely confidant?

"She started a blog and a YouTube account and was posting all over social media when she was in high school. It wasn't long before this completely consumed her life. She became a widely known online sensation garnering over half a million followers on Instagram and over 250,000 YouTube subscribers. Essena O'Neil is a 19-year-old Australian Instagram star and she recently opened up and revealed the truth about her life, and the shots that made her famous on social media.

"I fell in love with this idea that I could be of value to other people," she wrote. "Let's call this my snowballing addiction to be liked by others." It wasn't too long before she was getting sponsorship opportunities and was able to completely support herself. She was also offered to model in L.A.. Many young girls completely looked up to O'Neil and were even obsessed with her. Little did they know that behind that pretty face, she was totally unhappy. "Yeah 16-year-old Essena would have been like 'you have the dream life,'" she wrote. "So why did I feel so lost, lonely and miserable?"

Very recently O'Neil decided that she had completely had enough and realized that she wasn't living an authentic life. She then decided to make a drastic change in her life and announced to her followers that she is quitting social media, and she has already begun editing all of the captions on her photos to tell the truth behind the pictures. "I was addicted to what others thought of me, simply because it was so readily available," she wrote. "I was severely addicted. I believed how many likes and followers I had correlated to how many people liked me. I didn't even see it happening, but social media had become my sole identity. I didn't even know what I was without it." Not only has she deleted her Tumblr account, but she plans to stop posting on YouTube as well. She has also deleted over 2,000 pictures from her Instagram account; she says they served no real purpose other than self-promotion.

She also went as far as to admit that her "hot body" shots were the results of unhealthy habits... "A 15 year old girl that calorie restricts and excessively exercises is not goals. Anyone addicted to social media fame like I once was, is not in a conscious state," she wrote. "...Stomach sucked in, strategic pose, pushed up boobs," O'Neill wrote. "I just want younger girls to know this isn't candid life, or cool or inspirational. Its contrived perfection made to get attention. Without realizing, I've spent the majority of my teenage life being addicted to social media, social approval, social status and my physical appearance," she wrote. "Social media, especially how I used it, isn't real."

She also opened up about how she was making money from some of her posts and was completely honest about how there were no actual "candid" photos, they were all staged and even photo-shopped. O'Neil has started up a new website to tell her full story. She hopes to encourage others to be present and live life, authentically." She is also challenging her fans to give up social media for 1 week.

The Real Reason Why So Many People Over share On Facebook
—Source: By Paul Hiebert, Slate, August 19, 2013[25]

Why do people share their lives online?
How does using social media help shape a person's sense of identity?

"When it comes to posting things on the Internet, it seems anyone and everyone is susceptible to over sharing. There's apparently something alluring about filling those empty white boxes with embarrassing anecdotes—anecdotes that *BuzzFeed* then compiles and publishes in list form for everyone else to laugh at. Plus, judging by humor sites such as Lamebook, there doesn't appear to be a scarcity of material to draw from, either. Even criminals can't resist revealing incriminating evidence about themselves sometimes, and thus examples of TMI abound online.

But why? What compels us to tell the world with our fingers what we'd hesitate to utter in a room full of loved ones?

Social scientist and author Sherry Turkle thinks we're losing a healthy sense of compartmentalization. Last year, researchers at Harvard found that the act of sharing our personal thoughts and feelings activates the brain's neurochemical reward system in a bigger way than when we merely report the attitudes and opinions of others. Meanwhile, Elizabeth Bernstein of the *Wall Street Journal* asked around and concluded that our newfound urge to disclose is partially due to not only the erosion of private life through the proliferation of reality TV and social media, but also due to our subconscious attempts at controlling anxiety. "This effort is known as 'self regulation' and here is how it works," she writes. "When having a conversation, we can use up a lot of mental energy trying to manage the other person's impression of us. We try to look smart, witty, and interesting, but the effort required doing this leaves less brain power to filter what we say and to whom."

While all these viewpoints help us better understand the over sharing epidemic, they don't exactly address how the Web itself entices us to expose information that we probably wouldn't otherwise. Some of the latest research to directly tackle this issue comes from professor Russell W. Belk, chair in marketing at York University in Toronto. In his most recent paper, "Extended Self in a Digital World," which will appear in the *Journal of Consumer Research* this October, Belk argues that our relationship with social media is gradually creating a more complex idea of who we think we are as individuals. Through Pinterest, Instagram, and YouTube, whose former slogan was "Broadcast Yourself," we construct our identities in a manner that has never before been possible.

"When we're looking at the screen we're not face-to-face with someone who can immediately respond to us, so it's easier to let it all out—it's almost like we're invisible," said Belk, of the so-called "disinhibition effect" that online sharing helps create. "The irony is that rather than just one person, there's potentially thousands or hundreds of thousands of people receiving what we put out there." As for the consequences of these actions, Belk writes: "The resulting disinhibition leads many to conclude that they are able to express their "true self" better online than they ever could in face-to-face contexts. This does not mean that there is a fixed "true self" or that the self is anything other than a work in progress, but apparently self-revelation can be therapeutic, at least with the aid of self-reflexive applications."

Just as a psychoanalyst's couch or Catholic confessional booth are settings in which we can sort out the details of who we are by divulging our innermost secrets to someone without staring directly at him, Belk believes these sorts of exchanges are migrating onto the Internet: It appears that we now do a large amount of our identity work online. For the Internet constantly asks us "Who are You?" "What do you have to share?" Coupled with new self-revealing proclivities, this incites more open self-extension than in a pre-digital world. The feedback of friends, family members, acquaintances, and strangers therefore provides continual criticism and validation. Forging a personal identity, after all, is generally considered a collaborative effort.

Of course, some might point out that the perceived increase in over sharing is nothing more than that: a perception. In other words, it's not that there's an eruption of people willing to bare everything online; it's that those who do typically post more status updates and garner more exposure on news feeds. While difficult to measure, the *Washington Post* published a survey last spring stating that only 15 percent of American social media users feel they share either "everything" or "most things" online. That's not a lot—especially considering that more than 60 percent of participants from Saudi Arabia admitted they belong in that same category. As the accompanying story implies, however, the survey doesn't account for the vastly different cultures and social norms the various participants exist within. While tweeting about your aunt's divorce might be considered taboo in one country, it might be received with a shrug in a nation inured to the antics of the Kardashians.

Another crucial ingredient encouraging online exhibitionism is, as stated by Belk, the "tension between privacy and potential celebrity." For some people, the longing to be popular far outweighs the longing to be respected, and their social media accounts can verify this. According to a 2010 study, playfully titled, "Examining Students' Intended Image on Facebook: 'What Were They Thinking?!' " Facebook users who didn't mind if strangers could view their profile, as opposed to those who did, were "significantly more likely to post inappropriate content and to portray an image that would be considered sexually appealing, wild, or offensive." In other words, they want everyone to think they're cool.

As Jen Doll notes at the *Atlantic Wire*, "No one gets criticized specifically for *under sharing*. No one says that word. People just say 'boring.'" In sum, the traditional line separating what's private from what's public is disintegrating with each and every over share, and while some offenders may not be thinking about their actions this deeply, Belk's research suggests it's our ongoing quest for identity—or as some prefer to call it, "personal brand"—that's propelling this disintegration. We want to be interesting. We want to be memorable. We want people to follow us, but we need their attention first. And if there's one thing reality TV and advertising has taught us, it's that the lowest common denominator is both the easiest and most efficient way of getting people to notice.

The High Cost Of Online Exhibitionism
—Source: By Susan Krauss Whitbourne, Ph.D., Psychology Today, April 9, 2013[26]

How do I protect my privacy and identity while online?
Why should people be concerned about sharing images online?

The Facebook world of privacy settings is a moving target. It's an endless challenge to stay one step ahead of the game and make sure that your postings, photos, videos, and liked pages are visible only to those you consider your true circle of friends. However, given the complexity of this ever-shifting online world, the chances are good that you'll slip up at least once, if not more. With luck, your Facebook slip will be a minor one, but the chances are also good that it can land you into a heap of trouble. Facebook exhibitionism in which you over-share your most personal photos and updates, can cost you plenty.

People of different ages seem to use Facebook to accomplish different goals, as shown in one international online study (McAndrew & Jeong, 2012). To no one's surprise, the most active users were found to be young-ish, female, and single. They spend more time than other users updating their status, and use the photos they post to shape the impressions that they want others to have of them. Older users tend to be more involved in family-related Facebook activities. In other words, young women want to shape the ways their followers view them, and older users (men and women) want to stay in touch with their families.

It's in the area of impression management, the one most important to these young women, in which the most acute Facebook problems can occur. According to University of Southern Indiana psychologist Joy Peluchette, who teamed up with Marshall University's Katherine Karl (2010), as many as 40% of Facebook users include comments regarding their use of alcohol, over half post photos in which they are shown drinking, one-fifth make comments about sexual activities, one-quarter post seminude or sexually provocative photos, and half use profane language. It's not unheard of for women to photograph their cleavage or their backsides in various stages of undress, from tiny tees to bikinis to short, short, shorts. Men and women take videos of themselves playing late-night drinking games or attending huge parties or concerts that are clearly getting out of control. Working adults may also litter their Facebook profiles with incriminating evidence. Peluchette and Karl reported that Facebook users also make derogatory comments about their employers (25% of those sampled), other people, and use racial slurs (10%).

PRIVACY BEHAVIORS OF TEENS ON SOCIAL MEDIA

- **92%** post their **real name** to their profile
- **91%** post **photos of themselves**
- **82%** post their **birth date**
- **71%** post their **city or town** and their **school name**
- **53%** post their **email address**

- **59%** have **deleted or edited** something they've posted
- **53%** have deleted **comments from others** on their profile
- **45%** have **removed their name** from tagged photos
- **31%** have **deleted or deactivated** their profile or account
- **19%** have **regretted posting** updates, comments, images

Source: Pew Research Center's Report on Teens, Social Media, and Privacy (2013)

In their article entitled "What Were They Thinking?" Peluchette and Karl explored the reasons for what they deemed this reckless activity, coming up with rather surprising results. People who post the most extreme tell-all Facebook photos and updates actually do so on purpose. It's not as if they forget to change their security settings or even have their photos updated by other people. They actually think they will look more popular, cool, and attractive if they reveal their wild, partying sides. And it's not just women, as men too were likely to include their share of *Animal House* images. Facebook users varied, however, in the images they wanted to portray as revealed in this study; plenty of the students that responded to the survey wanted to project a clean and wholesome persona to the outside world.

So we now know that at least some, perhaps even as many as half, of the big reveals on Facebook are deliberate attempts to project what the users believe to be a positive image to the outside world, or at least the world of their social network. Unfortunately, though they think that their postings aren't visible to non-friends, their postings may not be as protected as they think. If they fail to do their privacy settings properly, people who are not friends with them on Facebook may still be able to see at least some photos. However, even if they've fastidiously checked every single privacy setting imaginable, a potential employer may still be able to discover their indiscretions with some creative online sleuthing. The image they've worked so hard to create to build their friendship base is precisely the one that will lose them their job, or the prospect of a job, or prevent them from being accepted at the school or program of their choice.

According to a paper published by Brown and Vaughn (2011), hiring managers are increasingly utilizing sites such as Facebook and Twitter as part of their screening and selection process. Citing a study by CareerBuilder.com, they note that between 2008 and 2009, the percent of companies scrutinizing social media doubled from 22 to 45%. Companies may also be using social networking sites to terminate individuals, according to Davison and colleagues (2011). Employees don't even have to show themselves in compromising positions to receive the condemnation of their bosses. Complaining about your job on Twitter (where people are even more findable than Facebook) can cost you that job in very short order.

People may make similar mistakes in their personal lives. Using Facebook to seek revenge against a romantic partner will cause you to look less desirable to future partners in your friendship networks. Photos that put you in compromising positions can cause your friends and your friends of friends to avoid you for fear of being associated with you in status updates that they can't control. Facebook indiscretions can also ripple out to people in your extended family and community, leading if not to uncomfortable moments at family gatherings, then to actual rifts between those family members who defend you and those who are outraged at your online presence."

LEARNING SCENARIOS

Scenario #1

It's another Friday night and you're staying at home again. Bored, you check your phone for the fifth time in the last fifteen minutes. The sensation to look at your phone feels overwhelming. You notice your friend is posting pictures from a party to which you were not invited. You can see a lot of your friends are having a great time at a birthday party for someone you know but aren't close to. What should you do? Will you post something to social media? What will you say to your friends the next time you see them?

Scenario #2

It's happened again. Your friend is in tears because they've just ended a relationship. Repeating details you've heard multiple times throughout the day, you really wish your friend would begin talking about something else. You keep checking your phone to see who's been texting. How do you think your friend feels during those moments? If you catch yourself looking at your phone, what should you say to your friend? What steps can you take in the future to avoid making the same mistake?

Scenario #3

You feel it again. The tightening sensation in your chest grows. The sense of anxiety and isolation begins to weigh you down. Checking your friends' posts to social media confirms your deepest suspicion—you feel your life is clearly inadequate compared to the lives of your friends. They're always having more fun, always doing what you'd rather be doing. What should you do in this moment? How might you cope with your feelings of anxiety and isolation? What steps can you take to improve your digital health and wellbeing?

HELPFUL STRATEGIES

DOCUMENT AND VERIFY: It may be important to first track how often you're using social media to determine if you might have a problem. Social media experts recommend downloading a phone app like Checky (http://www.checkyapp.com) or Moment (https://inthemoment.io) to count how often you check your phone and measure your Internet use. Based on this data, individuals can then begin setting daily and weekly limits to regulate their online behavior.

UNPLUG AND DISCONNECT: Researchers investigating the fear of missing out highly recommend taking regular breaks from participating in social media, ideally before you begin to experience symptoms associated with the condition. Their advice is based on research indicating individuals need to continually interrupt the hyper-vigilant state associated with the fight-and-flight response sustained by repeatedly checking one's accounts[1]. Importantly, researchers found this method was likely to increase feelings associated with F.O.M.O in the short-run, while being ultimately necessary to decrease feelings of anxiety, worry, and depression in the long-run.

ESTABLISH ROUTINES: In addition to taking regular breaks, social media experts recommend creating strict routines regarding social media usage to decrease the likelihood of triggering emotions associated with missing out, feeling deficient, or becoming envious of another's life. First, experts recommend individuals carry their cell phone in their pocket, purse, or backpack. Second, individuals are advised to turn off the automatic 'Push notifications' within their social media applications and begin manually checking their accounts on a regular but limited basis. Finally, to promote feelings of wellbeing, individuals are urged to prohibit the use of cell phones during meal times and beside their bedside at least an hour before going to sleep.

LIVING-IN-THE-MOMENT: Individuals can become easily captivated by social media's endless procession of posts and images. After all, these social networking sites have been designed expressly to fascinate and entertain individuals during their downtimes. To counter these powerful social mechanisms, experts recommend individuals begin a number of practices to begin "living-in-the-moment". First, individuals are advised to explore reflective practices like meditation and mindfulness– learning procedures to begin using all their senses to become aware of the details of their environment and focusing on the rewards of the present situation. Second, experts recommend individuals take regular breaks to visit the outdoors and places of natural beauty to restore one's sense of natural rhythms and daily cycles. Lastly, individuals are encouraged to join clubs and organizations to provide regular social interaction, needed stimulation, and sense of belonging.

LEARNING TASKS

20-Minute Activity:

- **Standards**:
  - Standard 2: Students will analyze the influence of family, peers, culture, media, technology, and other factors on health behaviors.

  - *Standard 4*: Students will demonstrate the ability to use interpersonal communication skills to enhance health and avoid or reduce health risks.

- **Rationale:** Adolescents are increasingly using social media sites and applications to build and maintain relationships with their peers. Teenagers need to learn how to use these revolutionary tools in ways that don't negatively impact their developing sense of identity. Teens should come to understand how to make decisions that enable them to use social media in healthy and appropriate ways.

- **Learning Outcomes:** Students will be able to identify problems related to the Fear Of

Missing Out so they may identify issues related to one's sense of wellbeing before it becomes a problem.

- **Description of Activity:** Teachers will lead students in a think-pair-share discussion of the essential question: *"When can new technologies be healthy and when can they be harmful?"* Students should consider as many responses as possible at this point to address these questions. Students should also be encouraged to connect their responses to personal experiences whenever possible and appropriate.

- **Supporting Resources:**
  o Teens, Social Media & Technology Overview: http://www.pewinternet.org/2015/04/09/teens-social-media-technology-2015/

  o #Being 13: Teens and Social Media Use: http://www.cnn.com/2015/10/05/health/being-13-teens-social-media-study/index.html

  o The Real Reason You Can't Stop Checking Your Phone: https://www.psychology today.com/blog/rewired-the-psychology-technology/201507/the-real-reason-you-cant-stop-checking-your-phone

  o Are You Happier Without Facebook: http://www.popsci.com/are-you-happier-without-social-media

ONE-DAY ACTIVITY

- **Standards:**
  o *Standard 5*: Students will demonstrate the ability to use decision-making skills to enhance health.

  o *Standard 7*: Students will demonstrate the ability to practice health-enhancing behaviors and avoid or reduce health risks.

- **Rationale:** Adolescents are increasingly seeking validation from their peers through their participation in (and observation of) social media sites and applications. Teenagers need to learn how to use these revolutionary tools in ways that don't negatively impact their developing sense of identity. Teens should learn how to make decisions that enable them to use social media in healthy and appropriate ways.

- **Learning Outcomes:** Students will develop strategies to be mutually supportive of their peers so they can be pro-active in establishing a healthy culture and appropriate boundaries regarding social media use.

- **Description of Activity:** Teachers will help students develop a health standard for adolescents regarding the appropriate weekly usage of social media to promote adolescent health and wellness. Students should identify and investigate physical and mental symptoms associated with adolescents (and adults) that have developed a dependence on checking their social media accounts. Students should also ground their health standard on emerging guidelines and best practices regarding teenager's online behavior.

- **Supporting Resources:**
  - Teens Spend Nine Hours A Day Using Social Media: http://www.cnn.com/ 2015/11/03/health/teens-tweens-media-screen-use-report

  - How Social Media Can Induce Feelings Of 'Missing Out': http://www.nytimes .com/2011/04/10/business/10ping.html?src=recg&_r=1

  - A Clinical Psychologist Explains Why People Are Getting F.O.M.O: http://www.businessinsider.com/a-clinical-psychologist-explains-why-people-are-getting-fomo-2015-10

  - Teens On Social Media: Being Cut Off Is Awful: http://www.cnn.com/2015/ 10/02/living/being-13-teens-social-media-question-answer/index.html

ONE-WEEK ACTIVITY

- **Standard:**
  - *Standard 1:* Students will comprehend concepts related to health promotion and disease prevention to enhance health.

  - *Standard 8:* Students will demonstrate the ability to advocate for personal, family, and community health.

- **Rationale:** More and more adolescents and adults are developing an unhealthy reliance on checking and using their online devices. Teenagers need to learn how to use social media sites and applications in ways that don't lead to addictive behavior. Teens should learn how to make decisions that enable them to use social media tools in healthy and appropriate ways.

- **Learning Outcomes:** Students will be able to identify the costs and benefits of using social media so they can make more informed and responsible decisions regarding their beneficial uses of social media.

- **Description of Activity:** Teachers will help students create a support group to help teenagers who have developed an unhealthy reliance on checking their social media accounts. In developing this support group, students should identify and investigate case studies of teenagers and young adults whose professional or personal lives have been impacted by an online addiction. Students should also contact local mental health experts who specialize in helping teens and adults manage disruptive online behavior to obtain resources, materials, and validated strategies. To extend this activity, students should plan and manage the logistics of promoting, hosting, and finding a supervisor for this extra-curricular activity.

- **Supporting Resources:**
  o Teen 'Like' And 'FOMO' Anxiety: http://www.cnn.com/2014/10/16/living/teens-on-social-media-like-and-fomo-anxiety-digital-life/

  o Social Media and Friendships: http://www.pewinternet.org/2015/08/06/chapter-4-social-media-and-friendships/

  o The One Feeling That Makes You Check Social Media Incessantly: http://fortune.com/2016/01/30/social-media-fomo-sleep/

    The Complex Link Between Social Media and Depression: http://news.health.com/2016/03/25/could-lots-of-time-spent-on-social-media-be-tied-to-depression/?xid=socialflow_facebook_health

---

[1] Some 3.2 billion people now online, but number still falls short of Internet target – UN report. (2015, November 30). Retrieved from http://www.un.org/apps/news/story.asp?NewsID=52690

[2] United States Internet Users. Retrieved May, from http://www.internetlivestats.com/internet-users/us/.

[3] Duggan, M., Ellison, N. B., Lampe, C., Lenhart, A., & Madden, M. (2015, January 09). Frequency of Social Media Use. Retrieved from http://www.pewinternet.org/2015/01/09/frequency-of-social-media-use-2/.

[4] Social Media Fact Sheet. (2017, January 12). Retrieved from http://www.pewinternet.org/fact-sheet/social-media/.

5 Lenhart, A. (2015). *Teens, Social Media & Technology Overview 2015: Smartphones facilitate shifts in communication landscape for teens* (pp. 1-48, Report).

[6] Perrin, A. (2015, October 08). Social Media Usage: 2005-2015. Retrieved from http://www.pewinternet.org/2015/10/08/social-networking-usage-2005-2015/

[7] Lenhart, A. (2015, August 06). Teens, Technology and Friendships. Retrieved from http://www.pewinternet.org/2015/08/06/teens-technology-and-friendships/.Same Pew report on social media use citation.

[8] Hampton, K., Goulet, L. S., Rainie, L., & Purcell, K. (2011, June 15). Social networking sites and our lives. Retrieved from http://www.pewinternet.org/2011/06/16/social-networking-sites-and-our-lives/.

[9] Wallace, K. (2014, November 20). Teen 'like' and 'FOMO' anxiety. Retrieved from http://www.cnn.com/2014/10/16/living/teens-on-social-media-like-and-fomo-anxiety-digital-life/.

[10] Barker, E. (2016, June 7). How to Overcome FOMO: Fear of Missing Out. Retrieved from http://time.com/4358140/overcome-fomo/.

[11] Sanz, A. (2015, September 30). What's the Psychology Behind the Fear of Missing Out? Retrieved May 06, 2017, from http://www.slate.com/blogs/quora/2015/09/30/fomo_what_s_the_psychology_behind_the_fear_of_missing_out.html.

[12] Bloom, L. (2015, January 10). Beware the Dangers of FOMO. Retrieved from https://www.psychologytoday.com/blog/stronger-the-broken-places/201501/beware-the-dangers-fomo.

[13] Social Media Fact Sheet. (2017, January 12). Retrieved from http://www.pewinternet.org/fact-sheet/social-media/..

[14] Turkle, S. (2015). *Reclaiming conversation: the power of talk in a digital age*. New York: Penguin Press..

[15] Gold, M. (2015). *Teens suffer highest rates of FOMO* (Report). Australian Psychological Society.

[16] *Stress & wellbeing: How Australians are coping with life* (pp. 1-44, Report). (2015). Australian Psychological Society..

[17] Duggan, M., Ellison, N. B., Lampe, C., Lenhart, A., & Madden, M. (2015, January 09). Frequency of Social Media Use. Retrieved from http://www.pewinternet.org/2015/01/09/frequency-of-social-media-use-2/..

[18] Cooper, C. (2015, February 02). Too much exposure to smartphone screens ruins your sleep, study shows. Retrieved from http://www.independent.co.uk/life-style/health-and-families/health-news/too-much-exposure-to-smartphone-screens-ruins-your-sleep-study-shows-10019185.html.

[19] Vitelli, R. (2016, November 30). The FoMo Health Factor. Retrieved from https://www.psychologytoday.com/blog/media-spotlight/201611/the-fomo-health-factor.

[20] Rideout, V. (2012). *Social Media, Social Life: How Teens View Their Digital Lives* (pp. 1-46, Report). Common Sense Media..

[21] Study: Frequent Social Media Use May Take Toll On Teens' Mental Health. (2015, July 28). Retrieved from http://atlanta.cbslocal.com/2015/07/28/study-frequent-social-media-use-may-take-toll-on-teens-mental-health/

[22] Sass, E. (2015, November 9). FOMO Linked To Stress In Teens. Retrieved from https://www.mediapost.com/publications/article/262175/fomo-linked-to-stress-in-teens.html

[23] Karp, R. (2015, October 20). I'm 15 and Snapchat makes me feel awful about myself. Retrieved from http://mashable.com/2015/10/20/snapchat-teen-insecurity/#DMyUAjDSN5qY

[24] NORC at the University of Chicago. (2017, May 3). Almost 6 in 10 teens take a break from social media: Most of the breaks are voluntary and teens report feeling better for the experience. *ScienceDaily*. Retrieved from www.sciencedaily.com/releases/2017/05/170503092233.htm.

CHAPTER EIGHT

Texting & Driving

How has the spread of easy technology
use influenced our decision making?

Why do people feel so compelled to constantly read and send text messages?

Why do people participate in risky behavior?

BEHAVIORS AND THEMES

SCALE AND SCOPE: A survey conducted by AT&T of 1,004 adults found that 98% of cell phone owners reported awareness of the dangers of texting and driving. Despite this awareness, 75% of those individuals reported texting and driving.[1] In a more recent study conducted in 2015 close to one-third of drivers reported sending an e-mail or text message while driving a minimum of once during the past 30 days and 42% reported reading an e-mail or text message during that time frame.[2]

Clearly, there are large numbers of individuals who use their cell phones while driving. What is the consequence of this though? Are car crashes and deaths from car crashes more likely to occur when the driver is using a cell phone for texting or emailing? While clear statistics are difficult to determine, it appears the answer to both questions is yes.[3]

PROBLEM DEFINED: As the use of technology has increased over the years, we have begun to believe we are experts at multi-tasking. As a result of this thinking, the occurrence of talking on the phone, texting, and emailing while driving are increasing. According to the Virginia Tech Transportation Institute, reading and/or sending text messages while driving makes the risk of a car crash 23 times more likely than driving while fully focused on the task at hand: driving.[4]

SENDS OR READS TEXTS OR EMAILS WHILE DRIVING[5]

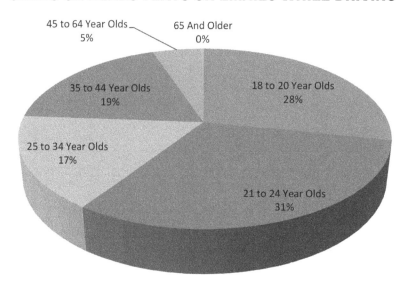

45 to 64 Year Olds 5%

65 And Older 0%

35 to 44 Year Olds 19%

18 to 20 Year Olds 28%

25 to 34 Year Olds 17%

21 to 24 Year Olds 31%

When researched and reported, texting/emailing while driving is subsumed under a category known as "distracted driving". It is important to note that using a cell phone while driving is not the only way a driver can be distracted. In addition to using a cell phone, distracted driving includes such things as eating, talking with passengers, and fiddling with the radio. The act of driving is considered the primary behavior and all other activities that drivers participate in while driving are termed, "secondary behaviors". The five most frequent activities include: holding a cell phone, talking on a hand-held cell phone, eating/drinking, talking/singing with a passenger, and manipulating a cellphone.[6] This chapter will focus on the cell phone usage, particularly texting and/or emailing while driving.

IMPACT ON HEALTH: Participating in texting while driving can have many implications for your mental and physical well-being. Clearly, the most severe implication is an accident resulting in physical injury to yourself, others or death.

Living with the aftermath of an accident in which you caused injury and/or death can impact your mental health for the rest of your of life. Nineteen-year old Reggie Shaw was driving to work one morning reading and sending text messages in 2006. Something he admits to doing frequently. He swerved across the center and hit another car head-on. The two men in the car he hit died instantly. He lives with regret every day of his life and now speaks to large groups as an advocate against texting while driving.

While regret can be utilized to make positive changes in our lives as demonstrated by the Reggie Shaw case, it can also have a lasting negative impact on our mental health. Regret can debilitate an individual and prevent one from fully engaging in life. Over time regret can lead to depression. Additionally researchers have found that regret can lead to chronic stress, which negatively impacts the bodies hormonal and immune system functioning, leading to a host of illnesses.[7]

MULTI-TASKING MYTHS: Are human beings experts at multi-tasking or are we highly skilled at making ourselves believe we are experts? According to the research, the latter is true. "People can't multitask very well, and when people say they can, they're deluding themselves," said neuroscientist Earl Miller. And, he said, "The brain is very good at deluding itself."[9] In reality, humans shift their focus from task to task exceptionally quickly making it seem like we are multitasking. When we attempt to text and drive we are focusing on only one of those at a time: driving or texting but not both simultaneously. The minimal amount of time our eyes are taken off the road when texting is 5 seconds while research suggests it takes 2 seconds for an accident to occur.[10] This results in an accident being 23 times more likely to occur when you are texting and driving.[11] The evidence is clear. Texting and driving is a dangerous activity. Given what is known about the dangers of texting and driving, why do individuals still take part in this activity?

REASONS FOR TEXTING WHILE DRIVING[8]

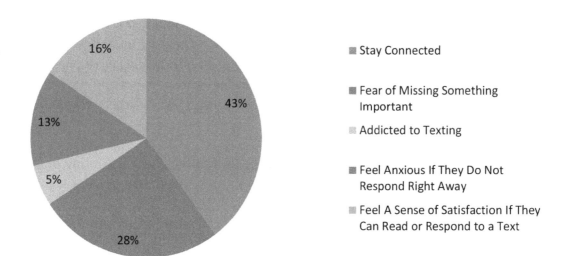

- Stay Connected
- Fear of Missing Something Important
- Addicted to Texting
- Feel Anxious If They Do Not Respond Right Away
- Feel A Sense of Satisfaction If They Can Read or Respond to a Text

Historically, data of car accidents in which the driver was texting have relied on self-reports from the drivers or eye witness reports. This data has not resulted in accurate information. In an effort to ascertain a more accurate understanding, researchers have utilized naturalist driving studies. In these studies, drivers are continuously monitored over a prolonged period of time. One such study called the Strategic Highway Research Program (SHRP2) monitored more than 3,000 drivers from 2010 – 2013.[12] Video footage of normal driving, car crashes and the moments leading up to the car crashes were captured. Of all the secondary activities in which the drivers participated, using a cell phone while driving increased the risk for a car crash the most significantly.

INTERESTING STATISTICS ABOUT TEXTING AND DRIVING

- Over half the accidents involving a car in the United States involve cell phone usage.[13]

- An on-road study examined drivers who reported frequent cell phone usage while driving. Those drivers were found to drive faster, change lanes more frequently and make more hard braking maneuvers than drivers who said they rarely used cell phones while driving…all of which are risky driving habits.[14]

- Reading a text message while driving successfully distracts a driver for a minimum of five seconds each time. This means that the chance of an accident occurring while reading a text is extremely high indeed.[15]

KEY CONCEPTS

Secondary Behaviors: Any activity or task a driver engages in while also driving a car.

Fear of Missing Out: A pervasive feeling of being left out of something fun any time you are not able to access social media.

Distracted Driving: Engaging in the act of driving while simultaneously engaging in other activities.

Multi-tasking: The belief that humans can complete two things at the same time.

REAL WORLD SITUATIONS

A Texting Drivers Education[16]

—Source: Matt Richtel, New Your Times, 9/13/2014

How does the human brain function when we engage in more than one activity?

What forces are behind our desire to constantly check our electronic devices?

On Sept. 22, 2006, Reggie Shaw, 19, climbed into his sport utility vehicle to head to a painting job. He picked up a Pepsi at the local gas station and started over the mountain pass between Tremonton, Utah, his hometown, and Logan, the big city to the east, near the Idaho border.

It was 6:30 in the morning, and freezing rain was falling. Just behind Reggie was John Kaiserman, a carrier, who was driving a truck and trailer carrying a thousand pounds of horseshoes and equipment. Mr. Kaiserman noticed Reggie swerve several times across the yellow divider and thought: This guy is going to cause us all some trouble.

Reggie came over a big crest and headed down a hill, traveling around 55 miles per hour as he hit a flat stretch. He crossed the yellow divider again. This time, he clipped a Saturn heading the other direction on the two-lane highway. Inside the Saturn were two men, Jim Furfaro and Keith O'Dell, commuting to work. The Saturn spun out of control and across the road, behind Reggie, and was hit broadside by the carrier. The Saturn slammed into a gully.

One hundred yards down the road, Reggie came to a stop, unhurt, his Chevrolet Tahoe virtually unscathed. An investigation ensued followed by a historic prosecution. The facts showed that Reggie had been texting — 11 texts sent and received in the minutes and seconds around the crash, maybe right at the moment of the crash, though for more than two years Reggie denied it.

In addition to an intense human and legal drama, something else came of this landmark case — a scientific journey by the prosecutors, including testimony from a researcher who began to answer a crucial question in the digital age: When Reggie was texting, what was going on inside his brain?

Picture a prehistoric ancestor intently starting a fire. This act of survival takes enormous focus. It uses the most advanced part of the brain, the prefrontal cortex, which sits in the front of the head. It's the nucleus of high-level decision-making, our "executive control" that is crucial in so many human endeavors from art to architecture.

And it is under constant assault from more primitive parts of the brain. Those parts alert us to acute opportunity or threat. For instance, imagine that the ancient forebear hears a noise, and that these primitive regions send a signal: Turn and look. It's a lion. Run!

There is a precious balance between these brain regions — our "top-down attention" networks that let us focus and our "bottom-up" attention networks that can co-opt focus or redirect us to more urgent stimuli. Scientists say the balance can become seriously out of whack in the digital age.

When the phone rings or a text comes in, the sound can be just as urgent as a lion in the brush — and just as tough to ignore. Is it your spouse? Your boss? A new business opportunity? Primitive brain wiring compels you to answer. But what if you're driving, like Reggie?

Much of the information that comes through is insignificant, even a nuisance, like spam. Wouldn't that cause people to learn to ignore it? Perversely, just the opposite is true. The fact that the information is of variable value actually increases its magnetism. That's because it creates a lure called intermittent reinforcement, a powerful draw that comes with uncertainty of the reward. It's the very thing that causes a rat in a cage to press a lever repeatedly when it isn't sure which press will bring the next delivery of food. It presses again and again, just as we click to open our text or email programs.

"What's happening, in essence, is that you're constantly scanning your texts and email because every once in a while you are going to get a good one and you can't predict when that is," says David Greenfield, a psychologist and an assistant professor at the University of Connecticut School of Medicine, where he teaches a class on Internet addiction. He compares the Internet to a slot machine, adding: "That's why Facebook is so popular. It's the fact that it's dynamic and novel, and constantly changing."

The idea that technology use affects the brain is supported by a growing body of neuroscience. Several studies show that when people play video games or use the Internet, they exhibit changes in the levels of dopamine, a neurochemical associated with pleasure, similar to changes in the brains of drug addicts. When you hit "send" or press a letter on the keyboard, it prompts a change on the screen, a picture pops up or an email opens, and you get a little dopamine squirt, Dr. Greenfield says, a kind of adrenaline rush. If you do it over and over, it conditions you to the rush, and in its absence you feel bored.

"It's in a sense a narcotic," he says.

That doesn't mean that electronic devices are classically addictive; instead, many researchers say that these devices have addictive properties and are habit-forming, but that more research is needed before deeming them addictive in the way that drugs can be. There is wider agreement among scientists that the risks are higher for young people, whose frontal lobes are less developed and therefore even less able to fend off the ping of the phone delivered from the more primitive part of the brain.

But even for adults, the devices appeal to such primal social urges that they can be overpowering.

"The cell phone, and other similar technology, meet a deep need for social connection with a greater ease and greater potential detriment to it in the same way that a vending machine that is right down the hall plays to our need for calories," says Dr. Nicholas A. Christakis, a physician and a professor of social and natural science at Yale; he is an expert in the use of social networks across time.

To some researchers, it feels like a process of neurological hijacking, the taking over of our decision-making process.

"When the phone rings, it triggers a whole social reward network," says David Strayer, a psychologist at the University of Utah who studies driver distraction. "And it triggers an orienting response that has been wired into us since hunter-gatherer times. You had to pay attention for survival. If you didn't attend, you got eaten by lions. We're hard-wired that way, no matter what we want to do. It's extremely difficult to turn those things off. It's in our DNA."

So maybe, on that fateful morning in September 2006, the parts of Reggie's brain were at war; his embattled prefrontal cortex was trying to focus on the road — in darkness and rain — while the reptile parts of his brain called him to the phone.

Was that an excuse?

Certainly not to Reggie. In fact, after years of prevarication and denial, he became the last person to let himself off the hook. The more he learned about the science and saw the other evidence, the more he transformed into a zealot against the use of phones behind the wheel.

"My name is Reggie Shaw."

The cavernous auditorium at Box Elder High School in Brigham City, Utah, seemed as if it could swallow Reggie, who stood alone onstage. He held a microphone in his right hand and wore a tie. It was the spring of 2013, seven years after the wreck that killed two men. "I'm going to tell you a story," he said.

He's told it dozens of times, practically anytime anyone asks, to schools and groups of professional athletes, to Oprah and to policy makers and legislators. It never gets less raw or moving. He tells how he was an ordinary kid, thought himself invincible, played football and basketball, how he got up one morning to go to a painting job. He tells about the crash. He tells about going to jail, his terror among violent offenders and about how, still, he'd have lived a lifetime there to return the lives of the Jim Furfaro and Keith O'Dell.

"I'm here for one reason. That's for you guys to look at me," Reggie choked back tears, "and say: 'I don't want to be that guy.'"

What largely caused Reggie to admit what he had done was science. In a pretrial hearing in December 2008, just weeks before he was to face negligent-homicide charges, Reggie listened to the expert testimony of Dr. Strayer. Reggie realized what he could no longer deny: that he'd been so distracted by his device that he'd not only wandered across the yellow divider but also had been unable to even perceive the situation accurately. He pleaded guilty to two counts of negligent homicide that were removed from his record after he fulfilled his sentence, including serving 18 days in jail and doing community service.

Technology distraction is an issue that scientists say is playing out in many aspects of life — not just behind the wheel, but also at work and at home. In an eye blink, the devices designed to become productivity tools can, in fact, enslave us and become decidedly counterproductive, even deadly.

Reggie shows the most extreme costs. But, on the other hand, he has made a remarkable transformation.

Don Linton, the prosecutor who brought the case against Reggie in Cache County, Utah, remarks: "I have never seen anybody try to redeem themselves as much as Reggie Shaw. Period. End of story." The judge, Thomas Willmore, says, "He's done more to effect change than anyone I've ever seen."

At the same time, Reggie is, in so many respects, ordinary. Neuroscience backs that up, too. Years after the crash, he submitted to an M.R.I. exam of his brain and to other testing to see if he was more predisposed to distraction than most others. No, the neuroscientists found, his attention networks and predisposition to distraction weren't outliers by any stretch.

In the auditorium in Brigham City, he asked the students to pledge to put their cell phones away while driving. "Keep in mind," he said, "me and you, we're not different."

Texting While Driving: Teen Shares Story[17]

—*Source: Jennifer Baileys, Fox 41 News*

What are the implications of using a cell phone or other electronic device while driving?

How can friends assist each other in making safe choices?

A Louisville high school senior goes from being a student to the teacher Thursday morning. 19-year-old Will Craig shared his story about how he nearly died because of texting while driving.

His girlfriend was at the wheel, and she was the one texting when the car crashed. "I was dead at the scene of the accident," Craig said to dozens of seniors sitting on the bleachers of the gym. "I had to be cut out of the windshield."

Craig's girlfriend walked away without even a scratch, but he said the doctors didn't believe he would be more than a vegetable the rest of his life. "The whole first month of my coma I was on life support."

He was in a coma for more than eight weeks. He struggled to learn how to speak, eat, and had many painful surgeries. "It's hard to get up every day and look at myself, because I look at my face and even when I get in the shower I look at my body and there's these scars on the side of my body from where I had chest tubes." Craig says he still has glass and pieces of wood under his skin from the accident, but he is pushing through the pain.

"I think maybe I was meant for this. I was meant for talking to large groups of people because I think maybe I'm saving lives by doing just this." Some teens listening to Craig's speech said it opened their eyes to the risky behavior related to texting while driving. Waggener senior Kadee Kimberger says, "I really don't text and drive as much, but my friends do, and the fact that he was a passenger and I'm a passenger with them that really is scary."

She says the next time she gets into a car, driving or riding, she will not put herself in danger. "My friend, I always tell her not to, but I mean she doesn't listen, but I will make sure not to."

Craig says his mother never filed charges against his former girlfriend. He will graduate this year from DuPont Manual High School. After graduation, Craig said he will continue speaking and trying to save the lives of young people like himself. "Just please don't text while driving." Will said.

Texas Church Bus Crash: Witness Accounts Highlights
Dannsgers of Texting While Driving[18]

—Source: Fox News US, 4/2/2017

What are the implications of using a cell phone or other electronic device while driving?

Why can it be so easy to make a dangerous decision?

A witness who claims the driver of a pickup truck that collided with a church minibus in rural Texas, killing 13 people on Wednesday, acknowledged he had been texting while driving — highlighting the danger of being on the phone behind the wheel.

Texas Department of Public Safety Sgt. Conrad Hein wouldn't comment Friday on whether texting might have played a role in the Wednesday collision on a two-lane road about 75 miles west of San Antonio, near the town of Concan. But officials have said the truck driver appeared to have crossed the center line.

Jennifer Morrison, the investigator in charge of the team from the National Transportation Safety Board, would only say that distracted driving will be among the issues investigated.

The witness, Jody Kuchler, a 55-year-old self-employed welder, told The Associated Press he and his girlfriend were driving back to their home in the nearby town of Leakey when he came across a truck that was driving erratically across the road.

"He kept going off the road and into oncoming traffic and he just kept doing that," said Kuchler, who first shared the account of what happened with the San Antonio Express-News.

Kuchler, who followed the truck for at least 15 minutes, said he called the sheriff's offices for both Uvalde and Real counties and told them "they needed to get him off the road before he hit somebody."

Kuchler told the AP he witnessed the crash and afterward, he checked on both the bus and the truck and was able to speak with the driver of the truck, who the Department of Public Safety has identified as 20-year-old Jack Dillon Young, of Leakey.

"He said, 'I'm sorry, I'm sorry. I was texting.' I said, 'Son, do you know what you just did?' He said, 'I'm sorry. I'm sorry,'" Kuchler recalled.

The wreck on Wednesday occurred along a curve in the road where the speed limit is 65 mph, according to Department of Public Safety officials. The bus occupants — members of First Baptist Church of New Braunfels in Texas — were returning from a three-day retreat in Leakey, about 9 miles from where the crash happened.

Twelve people on the bus died at the scene, authorities said. Another died at a hospital. One bus passenger remains hospitalized in serious but stable condition, according to the church. Young, the driver of the pickup, also remains hospitalized.

While dozens of cities across Texas prohibit the practice, there is no statewide ban on texting while driving. Local ordinances however may not have applied in the rural area where the crash occurred. Laws in 46 other states ban sending or reading email, using apps or engaging in other use of the internet while driving.

The Republican-controlled Texas Legislature approved a statewide ban in 2011 but it was vetoed by then-Gov. Rick Perry, who characterized such prohibitions as government micromanagement and said educating drivers was the key to deterrence. A similar proposal passed the Texas House a few weeks ago but has yet to make it to a Senate floor vote.

The number of motor vehicle deaths in the U.S. last year topped 40,000 for the first time since 2007, according to the National Safety Council. The number of vehicle crash deaths in Texas rose 7 percent last year to 3,464, slightly higher than the national rise. One-in-10 driving fatalities in 2015 were caused by some kind of distraction, the U.S Department of Transportation said.

One family recalled their last moments with their loved ones before the deadly wreck in an interview with FOX San Antonio.

"It was a great day. One we hadn't had in a long time," Charlotte Banks told the television station about the last day with her 83-year-old mother Avis Banks.

Banks said her mother was like her superwoman, she kept the family together.

As reality sets in, Banks told Fox San Antonio she'll forever hold the last memory she has telling her mother "I love you".

"If you forgot to tell somebody today you love them you might want to stop and pick up the phone really quick. If you are texting and you are so busy with those little thumbs, make sure the last thing you tell them when you get off is you love them," she said.

LEARNING SCENARIOS

Scenario #1

You and your friends are ready for a night out after an easy win on the football field. Your friend driving the car is texting to coordinate a place to meet up with more friends. The car is swerving over the yellow line as your friend is typing, reading and sending text messages. You are worried this is dangerous and you may crash into oncoming traffic or veer off the road and hit a tree or road sign. You want to say something but you fear looking like you are not one of the gang. What are the potential outcomes of this scenario? How do you handle this situation?

Scenario #2

You leave school late and rush off in the car to get to your job. Of course, every traffic light you come to is red, further slowing you down and making you even later for work. You cannot be late and risk getting fired. In a panic, you reach for your phone to text your co-worker. Maybe being a few minutes late will go unnoticed if your co-worker can cover for you. As you pull your phone out of your bag, it falls from your hand and lands on the floor in the passenger's side of the car. You think to yourself, "I will only need to take my eyes off the road for a few seconds to grab it." What are your options for how to handle this? How long can one safely take their eyes off the road?

Scenario #3

You arrive home from school to see police cars in the drive way. As you walk in the door, you are hugged by your crying mother and father. You listen to the words of the police who are telling you your younger brother was hit by a car and killed. It appears the driving was talking on her phone and did not notice she had swerved into the bike lane. The driver was 17 years-old and attends school with you. How do you move forward after such a tragic loss in your family? How do you react when you see your fellow classmate in school? What type of penalty should be given to this student? How might this student who hit and killed your brother be feeling and what lasting impact might this accident have on her?

HELPFUL STRATEGIES

ESTABLISH BOUNDARIES: Establish boundaries for texting by remembering there is a time and place for this activity.

SET A PHONE FREE ZONE: Do not be afraid to turn off you phone just before getting into the car. This will reduce the temptation to text and drive since you will not know if you are receiving messages. As an alternative to this, silence your phone and place it in the backseat where you cannot reach it while you are driving.

RELY ON PASSENGER: If you have a passenger in the car with you, let that person help you out. They can read and respond to text messages for you.

LEARNING TASKS

20-Minute Activity
- **Standards**
  - Standard 2: Students will analyze the influence of family, peers, culture, media, technology, and other factors on health behaviors.

- **Rationale:** Students need time and space to share and debrief the information in this chapter. This activity provides the opportunity share their experiences, perspectives, and knowledge about the need to constantly read and send text messages, which can lead to texting while driving.

- **Learning Outcomes:** Students will discuss reasons people text so they can develop a broader understanding of the impact this behavior may have on themselves and others.

- **Description of Activity:** The teachers will engage students in a think-pair-share about why people feel so compelled to text? What are the pros, cons, and implications? The students should consider current news stories and research focusing on the impact of texting and driving.

- **Supporting Resources:**
  o Impact Teen Drivers, http://impactteendrivers.org/resources/tools

  o Texting and Driving, a Dangerous Mix, http://www.pbs.org/newshour/extra/daily_videos/texting-and-driving-a-dangerous-mix/

  7 Scientific Reasons We Text & Drive and 3 Practical Solutions for Quitting, https://www.thezebra.com/insurance-news/132/7-scientific-reasons-we-text-drive/ Learn the Causes and Dangers of Distracted Driving, https://www.sadd.org/ what-we-care-about/traffic-safety/teens-distracted-driving/

ONE-DAY ACTIVITY

Take some time to research available websites for educating the public about the dangers of texting and driving. Select one and determine a way to utilize this site to teach your peers about the potential consequences of texting and driving.

BRIEF DESCRIPTION OF THE ACTIVITY

- **Standard 8:** Students will demonstrate the ability to advocate for personal, family, and community health.

- **Rationale:** Empowering students to promote healthy technology use is crucial to their development as young adults. This activity allows students to analyze the potential outcomes of texting and driving and determine meaningful ways to teach others about texting and driving

- **Learning Outcome:** Students will analyze ways to teach others about the dangers associate with texting and driving so they can make healthy decisions about their own behavior.

ONE-WEEK ACTIVITY: MARKETING CAMPAIGN

- **Project:** Develop set of marketing materials for informing the public about the issue of texting and driving.

- **Standard:** Standard 4: Students will demonstrate the ability to use interpersonal communication skills to enhance health and avoid or reduce health risks.

- **Rationale:** It is important that teenagers understand the complex issues related to texting while driving. One of the most effective ways to really learn information is to teach this information to others. This activity will allow students the opportunity to teach about ramifications of texting while driving.

- **Learning Outcome:** Students will create marketing materials to inform the public about texting and driving so they can promote safe and informed decision making.

- **Description of Activity:** Teachers will discuss marketing campaigns with students and provided necessary resources for students to research and develop marketing materials. Student should be encouraged to utilize different forms of media to create advertisements, websites, videos or public service announcements that promote awareness of the dangers of texting and driving. To extend this activity, the teacher can help students share their materials with the school community and broader community, if deemed appropriate.

- **Supporting Resources**
  http://www.wtsp.com/news/local/teaching-teenagers-the-dangers-of-texting-and-driving/346354923

  http://www.cnn.com/2015/02/17/living/feat-brutally-honest-teens-texting-driving/

  http://www.teachingmatters.org/digidocs/printable/manual/psa_manual.pdf

ADDITIONAL RESOURCES

Because Texting and Driving Kills: http://www.textinganddrivingsafety.com/texting-and-driving-stats

The Dangers of Distracted Driving: https://www.fcc.gov/consumers/guides/dangers-texting-while-driving

Distracted Driving: 7 Smart Ways to Distract Yourself from Distracted Driving: https://www.farmers.com/inner-circle/car-safety/7-tips-to-avoid-driving-distractions/

It Can Wait: How to Keep Your Scouts (and yourself) From Texting and Driving: http://blog.scoutingmagazine.org/2014/07/08/texting-and-driving/

[1] Ortutay, B. (2014, November 05). Texting And Driving Is An Even Bigger Problem Than We Realized. Retrieved May 22, 2017, from http://www.businessinsider.com/texting-and-driving-is-an-even-bigger-problem-than-realized-2014-11

[2] 2015 Traffic Safety Culture Index. (n.d.). Retrieved May 22, 2017, from https://www.aaafoundation.org/2015-traffic-safety-culture-index

[3] Distracted driving. (n.d.). Retrieved May 22, 2017, from http://www.iihs.org/iihs/topics/t/distracted-driving/topicoverview

[4] The Dangers of Distracted Driving. (2017, April 28). Retrieved May 22, 2017, from https://www.fcc.gov/consumers/guides/dangers-texting-while-driving

[5] The Impact of Michigan's Text Messaging Restriction on ... (n.d.). Retrieved May 22, 2017, from http://www.bing.com/cr?IG=673C1815C6574EDB9843FC5B0E93DCF2&CID=1B27A079FD896AC53A11AA F3FC8F6BC6&rd=1&h=ijfyAcdV5SGFwQYxw2UzutCdEWgiMv6wZLFLuqxApVw&v=1&r=http%3a%2f%2fw ww.jahonline.org%2farticle%2fS1054-139X%252814%252900007-X%2ffulltext&p=DevEx,5407.1

[6] Distracting Behaviors Are Common at Red Lights, Less So at Roundabouts. (2015, March 31). Retrieved May 22, 2017, from https://trid.trb.org/view/1359233

[7] Greenberg, M. (2012, May 16). The Psychology of Regret. Retrieved May 22, 2017, from https://www.psychologytoday.com/blog/the-mindful-self-express/201205/the-psychology-regret

[8] A. (2014, November 05). Why so many people text and drive, knowing dangers. Retrieved May 22, 2017, from http://www.cbsnews.com/news/why-so-many-people-text-and-drive-knowing-dangers/

[9] Hamilton, J. (2008, October 02). Think You're Multitasking? Think Again. Retrieved May 22, 2017, from http://www.npr.org/templates/story/story.php?storyId=95256794

[10] Bands, T. T. (n.d.). Texting and Driving Statistics. Retrieved May 22, 2017, from http://www.textinganddrivingsafety.com/texting-and-driving-stats

[11] Bands, T. T. (n.d.). DWI: Driving While Intoxicated, Because Texting and Driving Kills, Retrieved May 22, 2017 http://www.textinganddrivingsafety.com/texting-and-driving-stats

[12] SHRP 2 | Strategic Highway Research Program 2 (SHRP 2). (n.d.). Retrieved May 22, 2017, from http://www.trb.org/StrategicHighwayResearchProgram2SHRP2/Blank2.aspx

[13] The 25 Scariest Texting and Driving Accident Statistics. (2017, February 14). Retrieved May 22, 2017, from http://www.icebike.org/texting-and-driving/

[14] 2013 Publications. (n.d.). Retrieved May 22, 2017, from http://agelab.mit.edu/publications/2013

[15] The 25 Scariest Texting and Driving Accident Statistics. (2017, February 14). Retrieved May 22, 2017, from http://www.icebike.org/texting-and-driving/

[16] Richtel, M. (2014, September 13). A Texting Driver's Education. Retrieved May 22, 2017, from https://www.nytimes.com/2014/09/14/business/a-texting-drivers-education.html

[17] 2013 Publications. (n.d.). Retrieved May 22, 2017, from http://agelab.mit.edu/publications/2013

[18] Texas church bus crash: Witness account highlights dangers of texting while driving. (n.d.). Retrieved May 22, 2017, from http://www.foxnews.com/us/2017/04/02/texas-church-bus-crash-witness-account-highlights-dangers-texting-while-driving.html

CHAPTER NINE

---●---

Health Trackers

What are some key findings regarding the safety
and security of wearable devices?

How can consumers better protect their personal information?

When should consumers remove wearable devices?

What are key benefits of using wearable technology?

BEHAVIORS AND THEMES

SCALE AND SCOPE: Digital health start-up companies have experienced a boom in the past few years. In fact, the market for wearable tracking devices is expected to top $235 billion by 2020. The number one reason behind this phenomenon is the mobile health marketplace.[1] In a study conducted by organizations called Future Laboratory and Confused.com, it was revealed that roughly 60 percent of young adults between the ages of 18-34 have purchased a tracker to monitor their health. They measure physical and mental health, as well as, sleep patterns. According to a Pew Research Center report, 65 percent of adults admit to tracking such things as their weight, caloric intake and exercise regimen. The numbers are growing virtually everyday. As a matter of fact, most of us know someone who has purchased such a device or was given one as a gift.

Additionally, the report stated that about 20 percent of the apps used for fitness tracking was actually transmitting your password information to anyone with the skills to retrieve it. An astounding 52 percent of the devices tested did not even bother to develop policies surrounding privacy. Therefore, government agencies, businesses, marketers, and even the cyber criminal might find your information useful. It was also found that the apps were communicating with multiple, remote locations that included companies that specialize in analytics. Those who are interested in mining your data are driven by money. It is not outside of the realm of possibility that your information has already been sold to third party players.[2]

SHORT TERM GLOBAL MARKET DATA

Forecasted wearable device market 2018	$12,642M
Forecasted unit shipments of wearables globally 2018	$111.9M
Share of respondent interested in medical devices that transmit data	38%

SMARTWATCHES & SMARTGLASSES

Share of U.S. consumers interested in buying a smartwatch	40%
Number of Pebble smartwatches shipped to the U.S.	29,975 units
Shipment of smartwatches globally	1.23M units
Googles Glass annual sales forecast for 2018	21,148,611 units
Share of respondents who would not consider buying and wearing Google Glass	59%

HEALTHCARE & FITNESS

Remote cardiac monitoring services forecast for 2016	$867M
Shipment of healthcare wearables globally	13.45M units
Shipments of fitness gadgets globally	48.8M units
Share of Americans who own pedometers	31%

Source: Statista (2016)[4]

A report issued by the research firm ABI claims that the wearable device marketplace will explode to nearly 500 million devices moved by 2018. Quite a number of people are already wearing them as they seek to track their activities throughout the course of the work or school day.[3]

Various security companies are creating a level of security software for the wearable device. Many firms have already developed at least some type of software for mobile devices. The software, for the most part, is designed to send data to servers but it is unlikely that it will actually protect your data from being sent through the device itself.

Take for instance, your Bluetooth that is used to connect to your phone is completely unsecured. Some worry that this new technology might provide cyber criminals with easy access to pilfer your personal information. Fitness trackers, specifically, have recently been scrutinized for their lack of security and privacy. A series of security imperfections in the design, in theory, can allow outsiders to capture your private information. The apps have been known to leak login information and also be vulnerable to tampering once the device is communicating between wearable devices, smart phones and the company's servers. They have been determined to use a middle man approach to steal data that is from the app's servers.

These devices can contain vast amounts of your private information. They track your movements, the number of calories you burn, your sleep habits, heart rates and much more. They are also linked to laptops or smart phones through Bluetooth to a user profile and can send the information to the cloud. There is high probability for hackers to intercept your data during these exchanges. Once thieves enter the backdoor of an unencrypted device, they can falsify user profile information that is linked to a rewards site, for example. A hacker can also manually control results which could lead to unexpected consequences. For instance, a health provider might make adjustments to your health plan as a result of bogus data; costing you dearly.

The types of information susceptible to being hacked are where you live, your weight, sex, height, age and when you work out to start. If this information in compromised and finds its way into the wrong hands all your personal data is at risk. More than 50 percent of all devices that have been analyzed were found to be deficient and did not contain any policies regarding protecting your privacy. This appears to indicate that your data could be useful to foreign governments, marketers and cyber crooks.[5]

Those who use wearable devices, according to a Nielsen survey, are in the 18-34 age range. Also, 44 percent of adults between ages 30-39 use some form of health app. In most cases, it is critical that they do.[6] In fact, McKinsey and Company issued a report that stated that 31 percent of U.S. healthcare costs of $3 trillion can be traced to what are called behaviorally influenced chronic illnesses. The report also indicates that unless the healthcare industry finds a better solution to this behavior, costs for healthcare will continue to skyrocket. Therefore, there is a prevailing economic need for health tracking wearables.[7]

PROBLEM DEFINED: Today, your lives are becoming increasingly data driven and with each successive generation it is anticipated that our society will be even more consumed with measuring every aspect of the lives of its citizens. The mounting fascination with the counting of everything and anything, are you slowly losing track with what is really important?

It is a reasonable question in because the popularity of wearable devices jumped by 197 percent in the 4th quarter of 2015 alone. For example, the marketing group Parks and Associates has estimated that the global fitness tracker market will continue to grow at a rapid pace. These impressive sales gains suggest that an increasing number of Americans, and others, are willing exposing themselves to the aforementioned attacks and cyber threats.[8]

Key findings included:[9]

- Seven out of eight fitness trackers release a consistent and distinctive identifier. This is referred to as a Bluetooth Media Access Control address which can place the privacy and safety of users at risk. The wearer is exposed to long term tracking of all kinds of personal information even when the device is not paired or linked with a mobile device.
- Jawbone and Withings applications, for instance, have been found to be manipulated to produce false records. These bogus reports raise a number of questions about the dependability of the devices which can be subpoenaed and used in court proceedings and insurance claims.
- The Garmin Connect applications (iPhone and Android) and Withings Health Mate (Android) application has been found to contain certain security weaknesses that make it possible for a third party of access, read, write, or delete user information.
- Garmin Connect, for instance, falls short of employing the basic data exchange protections for its iOS and Android apps. Therefore, there is a consistent exposure of information vulnerable to fraudulent activity.

SECURITY: If your device is hacked the perpetrators could know:

- The mileage that you are covering
- When you usually go running
- Where you usually go running
- Where you live
- Your age, sex, height, and weight
- Your heart rate
- Your altitude
- Steps taken
- Where and when you are on vacation[10]

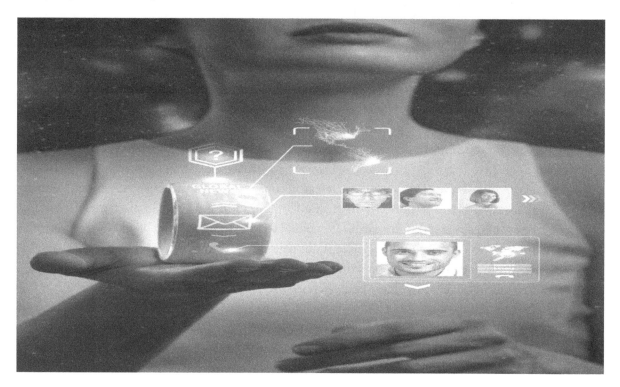

Many are concerned about the apparent lack of security of new tracking devices. As mentioned, only one of eight devices actually tested a small degree of security. It was discovered that most provided location and other personal data open to be stolen by criminals. It should be instructive for you as you consider purchasing and using a wearable device.

Among the most common brands are the Apple Watch, the Basis Peak, the Fitbit Charge HR, Garmin's Vivosmart, the Jawbone Up 2, the Mio Fuse, the Withings Pulse O2, and the Xiaomi Mi Band. Security investigators looked carefully at the devices' Bluetooth radio to determine whether user safety was at risk.[11] Again, seven of eight devices revealed identifying information which would permit devices to be traced by beacons that are typically available in local malls to profile shoppers and are widely offered for purchase. Only the Apple device contained adequate security protocols for consumer safety.[12]

The devices gather information regarding your activities, sleep patterns, and whereabouts then transmits that information to your smart phone or computer through a series of low frequency radio waves. The signal is persistent and in constant communication with your other devices. Connection with an exterior device is sustained by employing a MAC (Media Access Control) address which recognizes your individual tracker.[13] On the other hand, some of the devices are also vulnerable to being manipulated by you, its user. Fake fitness data can be developed by a motivated user and presented to dupe healthcare professionals or insurers. Nevertheless, your personal and private information should be just that—private. You must be constantly aware of where your information is being stored, where it is sent and who has access to it.[14] Your device is possibly seeping out your information to anybody who has the knowledge to access it.

WHY DO PEOPLE USE HEALTH TRACKERS

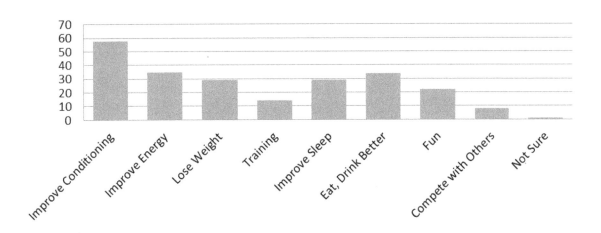

Source: GfK, 2016

IMPACT ON HEALTH: Sustained engagement with wearable devices can be habit forming. According to psychologists, habits can be defined as behaviors which are automatic and routine and are sparked by conditional cues based upon a certain situation. This is often followed by some type of emotional, mental or psychological reward. For instance, when you feel lonely, which is an internal trigger, you will feel the need to act, which serves as the external trigger. This action is manifested by strapping on a wearable device and constantly checking for results. The monitoring of progress through the device becomes the pleasure experience or reward. For several decades, the fields of psychological and neuroscience have researched habit formation. Habit formation is defined as a complex process which transpires over time. Human decision making and the other applied customs of behavior modification, setting goals, meeting objectives and perceptive neuroscience coupled with the study of health psychology provides understanding into this complicated process.

The level of social motivation that is maintained by engaging with a wearable device is largely dependent upon the skill level of the user. These social influences are an extremely powerful source of inspiration that can be utilized in a number of resourceful ways. Additionally, habits can be altered for positive results through the influence of social connections, social media and various networking outlets. This might incorporate the communication of social patterns such as posting and sharing of views, photos, and statements with one another. These represent only a few social mechanisms that sustain motivation and wider attainment of goals.

In order to achieve a level of sustained engagement, as a user, you may need to consider goal reinforcement so that you can feel that you are progressing toward your pre-determined goals. Experts at Stanford University's Persuasive Technology Lab discerned that the overall success realized by the achievement of many smaller goals lends to positive energy towards the attainment of lager ones. By setting incremental goals, you will be less likely to overestimate and ultimately fail to reach your goals. This is very helpful in maintaining momentum towards progress. Wearable devices give you a sense of making progress towards a pre-destined goal. The continuous progress and feedback helps to mark milestones and allows you to continue towards regular, sustained progress. It is not like the traditional methodologies such as getting feedback from supervisors, teachers, trainers et al. The wearable device is far more personal and provides constant feedback.

LACK OF REGULATION: These devices promise many health benefits for you. However, there is no real guarantee that they can live up to the heightened expectations. There are approximately 150,000 health and wellness apps currently in the market, yet the Food and Drug Administration (FDA) has only approved just shy of 160. It is not that the FDA has somehow failed to recognize that there are such a huge number of available apps. These devices are seen as low risk for creating health problems. They are noninvasive, they are not implants, and do not really need federal regulations to keep users from being physically injured. As far as the FDA is concerned, the devices need not require the developer to seek approval and the hope is that the creators of the apps will continue to further develop and enhance the products to promote healthy lifestyles.[15] However, the caveat is that with a lack of federal regulation comes a lack of accuracy. Therefore, while the apps might offer assertions that they provide reliable data, regardless as to how precise it might seem to you, there are no enforceable guidelines that require that whatever information supplied by these apps be correct and accurate.

However, regardless of the accuracy of these apps, researchers are using them to study movement. There are already more than 200 different studies that utilize an estimated two billion minutes of data, according to Fitbit. The use of the device allows analysts to remove data that might be biased based solely on an individual experience. In other words, participants from past research studies could unintentionally provide incorrect data or even forget to maintain accurate and complete tracking records. Fitbit does not share the systems that are used to produce the data, investigators are reluctant to rely solely on data provided by the trackers.[16]

Researchers admit that information provided by wearable tracking devices are not truly as accurate as data collected through other research methods, it is nonetheless useful. The devices are comparatively cheap and because they are becoming so popular, it is relatively simple to persuade participants to wear them around the clock. There are many current studies that track patient activity before and after surgery, for example to determine the patient's physical activity and their prospects of becoming hospitalized again as a result of sedentary habits.[17]

ISSUES: When you routinely use fitness and wellness tracking devices, you begin to develop a dependence on the technology. You begin to rely solely on the device to provide information on your health and level of fitness. There are apps that are in tandem with the more popular websites such as Healthline and WebMD that offer a great deal of information regarding the indicators of illnesses but do nothing to provide a diagnosis for a patient. And the devices are most certainly not qualified as doctors or nurses. Therefore, relying on your device alone to keep you healthy may well prove to be detrimental to your health. According to a 2015 study conducted by the Harvard University Medical School and the RAND Corporation, among the top online health checkers accurate diagnoses were recorded as first in about 34 percent of patient evaluations. In addition, the health checkers listed the right diagnosis with in the top two dozen potential diagnoses in approximately 58 percent of patient evaluations.[18]

Nevertheless, regardless of this information, health and fitness trackers are not the worst technology available in the marketplace. For example, in a 2015 study that included 726 participants, health and fitness devices users were significantly more likely to state that they engaged in physical activity regularly than those participants who did not use the devices. Further, the participants who did use the apps were found to use their spare time performing health related activities than the others. They had an overall lower BMI (Body Mass Index). So regardless of whether the apps are 100 percent accurate, they do have a positive impact and encourage users to engage in better lifestyle choices.

UNINTENDED CONSEQUENCES: Trackers are now making their way into the insurance marketplace. Presently, providers of health care are working to develop apps that are capable of working with iPhones, iPads, Apple Watches and other devices. The effort is designed to motivate consumers to change their behavior regarding health care. Specifically, physicians and clinicians are hoping to encourage the public to be more vigilant in taking meds, stay abreast of issues once diagnosed with an ailment, and even pay medical bills using Apple Wallet. The industry has even announced that it plans to subsidize the cost of some of the devices for large employers/clients looking to integrate the devices into their health and wellness programs. Therefore, it appears as though the day of ubiquitous tracking apps and devices are here to stay. For instance, Aetna is reportedly willing to pay for a significant portion of the cost of the device if consumers elect Aetna as their health carrier.

Other insurers are opting for less expensive devices but are jumping on the band wagon, nevertheless. Other devices such as Fitbit and Misfit are making their way into wellness programs; all in attempt by insurers to reduce their long term costs. They are also funding wireless scales for weight, blood pressure devices and glucose monitors. Large health insurers are now conducting studies to determine the effectiveness of the devices in helping to change patient behavior over the long term. Preliminary results suggest that the devices are having an impact. However, that does not mean that the apps are secure and able to protect the privacy of those who wear them.

Insurers are also beginning to offer financial incentives for patients who use wearables. Discounts on premiums, health care savings accounts and cash are not uncommon. The inducements are offered to workers and their spouses. The devices are free if workers meet certain criteria and maintain a certain level of health. In this way technology is being utilized to entice you to modify your behavior and lifestyles. You effectively are becoming walking targets for companies to conduct studies, extrapolate aggregate data all in the name of saving the employer money. The jury is still out as to whether employee health is actually improving. Some employers are reporting as much as 90 percent participation in their wellness programs.

The Journal of American Medicine published a clinical trial that disclosed that attaching wearables do not aid in weight loss. Approximately 475 young adults participated in the study over a two-year period and the findings indicated that they lost less weight than individuals who used traditional counseling and therapies. Those participants using the wearables lost an average of 7.7 pounds versus 13 pounds for those taking the traditional route to weight loss. This may leave many wondering whether the devices are truly effective.

RIGHTS TO PRIVACY: Although most Americans may not be quite ready for what are now being called trans-human body implants, that appears to be where we are heading. According to a study at the University of California-Berkeley, we are one step closer to developing devices that can be all but permanently embedded into the skin. Scientists and engineers at the university have created a small, sensory transplant about the size of a speck of sand that has been effectively inserted into the muscle tissue and peripheral nerves of rats. This, so-called, neural dust makes it possible to review vital signs in a real time framework. This could be the beginning of the types of tracking devices that can be designed to assist humans to neurologically scrutinize various parts of the body.[19]

Apparently, according to the developers, the sensor measures approximately three millimeters in length. It contains what is called a piezoelectric crystal that transmits ultrasound pulsations into electricity which then provides power to the implant. The sensor is powered by ultrasound pulses that provide researchers with instantaneous data. One of the major concerns with this new technology is the level of radiation that people may be exposed to over time.

So not only are wearables a reality but so are implants that are designed to track you in various ways and for a number of purposes. Not everyone is convinced that this is the best way to go. Many doctors and scientists warn that the latest must have technology might cause major health risks to those who use them. Internet connected devices such as smart watches, eye glasses and health monitoring devices places wireless technology directly on your body and may further expose you to radio waves that you are already susceptible to as a result of the technology currently in your possession.[18] And although there is no real proof of any long term harmful health affects of tracking devices, you should not assume that this lack of evidence means that they are safe over the long haul. The decision is totally yours as to how much risk you are willing to take.

Wireless trackers are known to emit non-ionizing waves much like those of cell phones. These waves have been categorized as potentially carcinogenic to humans by the International Agency for Research for Cancer which is part of the World Health Organization.[19] As a result, the National Cancer Institute has issued recommendations that include minimizing cell phone calls where the phone is placed in a head to phone position. Nevertheless, dissimilar from the cell phone, tracking devices are designed to be worn 24/7/365. Typically they are clipped onto an article of clothing around the hip or waste. This places the device near internal organs. Because users frequently sleep with the tracking device on their wrist and usually sleep with your hands near your head, there is the possibility of exposure to your brain overnight. The recommendation is to not wear devices while sleeping. The farther you maintain your device from vital areas of the body, the better and safer you'll be.

The Consumer Product Safety Commission, in a 2014 report, issued a recall of a leading device as a result of injuries sustained by nearly 10,000 people. Reportedly, the consumers experienced conditions ranging from skin rashes, blisters, and peeling of the skin if the device was worn around the clock.

In March 2014, the Consumer Product Safety Commission officially recalled a leading device due to injuries to an estimated 9,900 people.[22] These customers suffered from skin irritations such as blisters, rashes, and peeling skin after continual wearing of the device for a period of time. The company that produced the tracker admitted to the medical community that the skin irritations were probably a result of allergies to the nickel contained in the device. Nickel is an alloy embedded in the stainless steel and adhesive material used in the assembly process of the device.

It has been widely accepted that ingesting materials such as nickel will result in health issues, it is not as well known that the skin can also soak in heavy metals, as well. For instance, if you cook using acidic foods in a stainless steel pan or pot, it is widely held that the pan or pot can leek alloys like nickel in to your food. Even very small amounts of these metals absorbs by the body can result in disastrous health consequences. You should be mindful that until more concrete answers to the health dangers of wearable devices is more widely available, you should be careful of how much time you use your device.

However, if you are still doubtful as to whether you are bombarded with intense wireless radiation either from a cell phone or tracking device, there is currently a downloadable app that provides a color coded visual of waves around you with blue as indicating the strongest level of radiation and red suggesting the least amount.

KEY CONCEPTS

Data Mining--the practice of examining large databases in order to generate new information.

Data Science—a field of study designed to assess information systems and processes and to reveal specific knowledge from sets of data; whether the data is in a structured or unstructured format. This information can be derived from predictive analytics, databases, or data mining practices.

Fixation--an obsessive interest in or feeling about someone or something.

Life Hacking--refers to any trick, shortcut, skill, or novelty method that increases productivity and efficiency, in all walks of life.

Profit Motive--the motivation of firms that operate so as to maximize their profits. Mainstream microeconomic theory posits that the ultimate goal of a business is to make money. Stated differently, the reason for a business's existence is to turn a profit.

Privacy--the state or condition of being free from being observed or disturbed by other people.

REAL WORLD SITUATIONS

Privacy advocates warn of 'nightmare' scenario
as tech giants consider fitness tracking.

—Source: *Andrea Peterson* May 19, 2014 Washington Post

For what reason would consumers elect to not use wearables? Describe in detail how you might ensure that personal information remains secure?

Fitness tracking apps and devices have gone from an early adopter novelty to a staple of many users' exercise routines during the past few years -- helping users set goals and measure progress over time. Some employers even offer incentives, including insurance discounts, when workers sign up.

"There's been a tremendous amount of evolution in the app space, both generally and in the fitness app," since she joined the Federal Trade Commission six years ago, Senior Staff Attorney Cora Han acknowledges. "It's a completely different landscape."

But as several major tech companies appear poised to disrupt that landscape, privacy advocates warn that consumers aren't always aware of how sensitive the data the apps collect can be or what privacy protections exist. And changes in the privacy policy of Moves, a fitness tracking app recently acquired by Facebook, have only amplified those fears. "This is really, really a privacy nightmare," says Deborah Peel, the executive director of Patient Privacy Rights, who claims that the vast majority, if not all, of the health data collected by these types of apps have effectively "zero" protections, but is increasingly prized by online data mining and advertising firms.

Both the Food and Drug Administration and the FTC regulate some aspects of the fitness tracking device and app market, but not everyone thinks the government has kept pace with the rapidly changing fitness tracking market.

"The FTC and even the FDA have not done enough," says Jeffrey Chester, the executive director of the Center for Digital Democracy, who says the lack of concrete safeguards to protect data in this new space leaves consumers at risk. "Health information is sensitive information and it should be tightly regulated."

TECH GIANTS TURN THEIR EYES TO FITNESS TRACKING

Moves changed its privacy policy within weeks of its acquisition by Facebook. The app uses motion sensors built into smartphones and GPS information to keep a record of users' locations and activities. Algorithms developed for the app are able to tell the difference between different types of exercise—like biking, or running—and calculate distances traveled and calories burned.

The app's privacy policy went from stating the company would not "disclose an individual user's data to third parties" without consent to "we may share information, including personally identifying information, with our Affiliates (companies that are part of our corporate groups of companies, including but not limited to Facebook) to help provide, understand, and improve our Services," as first reported by the Wall Street Journal. Facebook spokesperson Jodi Seth said the company had "no plans" to connect Moves data with Facebook users. The language was changed because Facebook will be providing support and services to the app, she said.

"In order to support the provision and operation of the Moves app, Facebook will need to have access to the Moves data," she told the Post in a statement via e-mail. She further said that Moves would continue as a "standalone experience" rather than being directly integrated into the larger Facebook platform.

But a person familiar with the matter told the Post the acquisition is "about talent and tech," suggesting that Facebook may be planning to use Moves to make a bigger splash in the health and fitness space. Facebook wouldn't be the only tech giant interested in the fitness and health tracking business. Reuters recently reported that Apple is on a "medical tech hiring spree" -- possibly in anticipation of the long rumored iWatch. The company also met with FDA officials about mobile medical apps last December, as reported by the New York Times.

With its foray into wearable tech with Google Glass, Google also appears in a good position to do more work on health tracking. And elsewhere in the company's experimental lab, Google has been working on other medical related products like contacts that tell diabetics their glucose levels. (Oh, and there is that whole other company Google CEO Larry Page created to work on combating death.)

Peel says there's an obvious reason these companies are interested in having a hand in health data: "It's the most valuable information in the digital age, bar none." Chester echoed that sentiment, but also says the tech industry's pivot to health and fitness tracking "is all part of a much wider system of data collection."

"The next frontier is local, and they know that health apps and other kind of apps related to recreation and lifestyle will be an economic bonanza," he says. "They literally want to know your movements in a much more granular way and they've created business models based on this kind of intrusive hyper-local data tracking."

Data mining and advertising companies already have access to vast amounts of information related to consumer's health -- companies can glean a lot from users Web browsing behavior, or the pharmacy purchases made while using consumer loyalty cards. But fitness tracking apps have the potential to provide more direct and reliable information in greater detail. And that, Chester says, could have truly devastating consequences as the information is monetized.

"Information about consumers most intimate health conditions is going to be sold to the highest bidder," he says. "Employers might get access to it, insurers might get access to it, or mortgage lenders -- which could lead to a vast array of negative discriminatory practices."

WHAT ABOUT HIPAA?

Privacy advocates worry that regulators aren't prepared to handle the consumer privacy challenges that will come with this explosion in health data.

Part of the issue is that while fitness apps and wearable devices can create and transmit data that most consumers would consider health related, it does not have the same level of protection as data created consumers interactions with actual health care professionals.

Health Insurance Portability and Accountability Act of 1996 created a regulatory framework for digital health information and privacy protections to go along with it, but it does not apply to many casual health and fitness tracking apps because the data it collects was created by consumers themselves, rather than an entity covered by HIPAA like a doctor or a hospital.

Because of that, there may be sharing of sensitive health information that's collected by these health or fitness apps that consumers may not reasonably expect or anticipate -- particularly since they are used to sharing that information in a traditional provider context.

The FDA issued guidance on mobile medical apps last fall, choosing to focus on apps that directly transform the smartphones or tablets into devices it already regulates and exercise "enforcement discretion" on others it says pose minimal risks to consumers. Basically, that means there are a bunch of health-related apps the FDA reserves the right to regulate, but it isn't planning to actively engage with unless they see a clear and present medical danger to consumers.

A list of examples of types of apps that fall into this category on the FDA website appears to encompass features commonly found in fitness tracking apps, but a footnote includes a potential loophole -- saying that when these type of apps "are not marketed, promoted or intended for use in the diagnosis of disease or other conditions, or in the cure, mitigation, treatment, or prevention of disease, or do not otherwise meet the definition of medical device, FDA does not regulate them."

Moves describes itself as an "activity diary," but its website does use vague health related language to promote the app usage, including urging visitors to "start with small changes that can lead to healthy habits and losing weight naturally."

However, a Food and Drug Administration spokesperson said the agency could not comment on if specific apps like *Moves* fell under its jurisdiction. And the word "privacy" did not show up in its mobile medical app guidance even once.

THE (FEDERAL TRADE COMMISSION) FTC'S ROLE

But elsewhere in the government, the FTC has been working hard to figure out where they fit in that landscape -- even hosting a public conference about consumer generated health data earlier this month. Under Title V of the Federal Trade Commission Act, the agency has a pretty broad authority to engage with product creators on behalf of consumers, but only if companies are engaging in deceptive or "unfair" practices.

In the health and fitness app space, we have authority to enforce against, for example, connected device manufacturers, app developers or others that may be engaging in deceptive practices or failing to live up to their promises to users about the collection and use of their data.

But there are some additional limits to that authority: In general, the FTC doesn't have the ability to levy fines against companies who break promises to consumers on the first offense. Plus, even if consumers aren't comfortable with the way their information is shared, they may have already agreed to it.

Consumers may not always read the privacy policies of some of these apps. Even if they do some of them might be worded in legalese so consumers might not understand the choices they are making with their information. If apps say they don't sell user data, they might get around the restrictions on a technicality like trading it -- and that there's no real auditing of privacy promises beyond the FTC's investigative role.

It's worth considering the upside to the explosion in fitness tracking: There are a lot of benefits that these new technologies provide with the potential power and knowledge fitness tracking devices and apps give to consumers. But those benefits don't give developers a free pass on other consumer protection issues.

REAL WORLD SITUATIONS

My fitness band is making me fat: Users complain of weight gain with trackers.
—*Source: Jacoba Urist, TODAY Contributor, July 16, 2014*

In what ways can you limit electromagnetic spectrum exposure emitted through smart devices?

How can you ensure that your health data from tracking devices is accurate?

Suddenly, everyone from celebrities like Kelly Ripa and ultra-marathoner Dean Karnazes to my mother-in-law seems to be sporting a fitness band. The Fitbit, Jawbone Up and Nike Fuelband are part of a booming weight-loss industry, and they've helped many Americans track their steps taken and calories consumed each day to take the guess work out of losing weight.

But some wearers are experiencing fitness band frustration. They find that their Fitbit actually moves the scale in the wrong direction — making them pack on the pounds, as opposed to maintaining or shedding unwanted weight.

Watch video: Can fitness bands actually make you gain weight?

Fitness social networks and calorie-counting websites have threads asking fellow users if they're also "gaining weight on Fitbit" and what lifestyle changes or electronic tweaks they can make so their wristbands work for them. One mother posted her excitement when she got a Fitbit for Mother's Day, only to find she immediately gained three pounds when she started using her new fitness tracker. Confused, she writes, "I'm more active now than ever before."

Korie Mulholland, 24, a private SAT tutor in Chicago can relate. Last summer, she lost 40 pounds, through a healthy combination of calorie restriction and moderate exercise. But then, as dieters frequently do, Mulholland found that her weight loss plateaued. So she decided to buy a Fitbit to make it over the hump and reach her ultimate goal— especially because she planned on spending much of her summer working on a makeshift desk-treadmill with her iPad.

"Because it tracks steps and calories, I thought a Fitbit would be perfect for me as it got harder and harder to lose weight," she explained. "And since I was walking 10 to 15 miles a day at my stand-up desk, it told me I could eat 2200 to 2400 calories a day."

But Mulholland said her weight started to go up instead of down — 2 or 3 pounds here and there, as she wore the wristband and followed its calorie guidelines. "I used it for six months, until I gave up," she recalls. "It was clearly telling me to eat too much for my specific metabolism and no matter what I did, it just wasn't working right."

Now, she's back on target, without a fitness tracking device, losing weight gradually, eating the right number of calories for her specific metabolism, she says, as it varies day-to-day, even if the number of steps she takes may be consistent.

A Fitbit spokeswoman said the company makes "the most consistently accurate activity trackers on the market," even outperforming heart rate straps and treadmills that calculate calorie burn. "While there may be a small difference of a few calories or steps between tests, ultimately the success of our products comes from empowering users to accurately see their overall health and fitness trends over time," she said.

Jessica Reed, 38, a poet in Danville, Indiana, had a similar experience to Mulholland when she first got her wristband. On her blog, she called her mysterious weight gain "The Case of the Fitbit Defying Metabolism."

In the first few months she had the Fitbit, Reed was dieting and gained a few pounds, she explained, although she had been consuming fewer calories than she burned according to the device. "I speculate that my weight fluctuations correlate with my greater sense of well-being more closely than exercise habits," she emailed NBC News.

REAL WORLD SITUATIONS

The Dark Side of Your Fitbit and Fitness App: Tracking steps and inputting calories into your smart phone drown out the conversation we should be having with our bodies.

—*Source: Johnny Adamic, The Daily Beast, April 5, 2015*

How do you know when you've reached your informational limit with a tracking device?

How can trackers infringe upon your personal freedoms?

We don't trust ourselves anymore. The act of exercise is no longer a mind-to-body experience but rather a mind-to-fitness-tracker-device-to-body phenomenon. Instead of listening to our bodies—when we need a glass of water instead of food, need a nap instead of a coffee, or become suddenly hungry after processing the 42 grams of sugar from a Starbuck's classic chai tea latte (inducing a severe attack of hypoglycemia)—we turn to our Fitbit, Garmin, Nike Fuel Band, Jawbone or one of the many other fitness trackers, or MyFitnessPal.

For the record, I'm not telling you to trash your Jawbone or delete your MyFitnessPal app. As a personal trainer, your use of a fitness tracker or food app means one thing to me: you are somewhere on the spectrum of behavior change for health, you're curious about health, and if you sport the fitness tracker on your wrist in a pink coral color, you just love fitness jewelry.

Here's my problem with fitness trackers and food calorie counting apps: They all rely on very limited metrics (steps taken, movement when you sleep, calorie tracking, heart rate monitor in some, and distance traveled with the movement) giving you a very skewed analysis about your health. Your health, however, is not so black and white, just like the colors of your fitness tracker. Two hours on the row machine, like Frank Underwood does, will not cancel out the pizza you ate during your *House of Cards* binge.

Your health depends on so many factors—cultural, genetic, whether your cat lets you sleep at night—that I find it really interesting our fascination with the extraordinary simplicity of the fitness tracker and food app scene. Yet, nearly half of all smartphone users indulge in some form of health app according to the American Journal of Medicine (and half of all Americans adults have a smartphone). That's a lot of people using insufficient forms of data feedback to make big assumptions about their health.

When David Sedaris purchased his Fitbit last summer, this small piece of technology inspired him to walk after dinner instead of sitting on the couch. When his Fitbit died, however, walking became pointless without the steps being counted or measured. Sound familiar?

I equate using a fitness tracker or food calorie tracker as a marker of dishonesty with ourselves. We are missing a pivotal step: self-reflection. It's really easy to buy a Nike Fuel band and wear it. It's much harder, however, to get deep with yourself.

Fitness apps are a flawed, abbreviated version of this self-reflection process. They focus too much on the number of steps, calories, or distance traveled. Fitness tracking devices distract us from what really needs to happen: we need to look at ourselves naked in the mirror and have an honest conversation with our naked self about the status of our health. From a weight-loss standpoint, it's critical. Then let's unplug the TV, peel ourselves off the couch (if not get rid of both the TV and couch), and buy a few free weights and a yoga mat before throwing down for a fitness tracker. The cost is about the same, but the impacts couldn't be more different.

The quest to "knowing thyself" is distorted, not enhanced, when we let the fitness trackers and food calorie apps take over. Take the MyFitnessPal app, which scans and tracks calories. Here's the conundrum: Our bodies do not interpret all calories to be created equal, just like legislators in Indiana don't believe their residents are created equal, but that's another story. Point being, tracking the calories is not going to make you any healthier because the body metabolizes calories from say, one gram of sugar, differently than it does from, say, one gram of fat. Yet, our American culture wants to simplify this concept. I recommend using the time spent logging your calories by reading *Salt, Sugar, Fat* by Michael Moss and *learning* about the plotting of the food industry instead of pretending to be a nutritionist. Better yet, use the time you spend scanning your food by watching this violent salad video and getting inspired.

I have not bought a fitness tracker to be an iconoclast. Honestly, I hear the Jawbones get smelly, break after six months, and I don't believe the metrics will make me any healthier. The snap bracelet fad of the '90s is also the extent of my career wearing plastic or nickel so that I can avoid getting *the* cancer as long as possible. I also don't need a device informing me of my restless nights of sleep. I can infer that by my baggy eyes in the morning. In a way, using a fitness tracker is like going to the revered and intimate Lambeau Field and being glued to the pixels of the Jumbotron instead of watching the beauty of an Aaron Rodger's touchdown-throw from afar. The technology is eschewing the overall experience.

The battle between listening to your own body's needs versus letting technology tell you what your body needs has begun. Call me a Luddite, but I side with your inner voice. When was the last time you wrote in a journal—dear diary—how you felt physically (energy levels), what you ate and your mood two-three hours later; or what you did for exercise (walking included) and used complete sentences? It sounds cheesy, but I'm serious. You owe it to yourself. Tracking calories from your Reese's Peanut Butter Cup addiction in a food app is not going to solve your problems. Reflecting on how groggy you felt after eating the sugar bomb will.

Alas, a beacon of hope shines through with the Apple watch. Reason being, the Apple watch reportedly blends the quality of the movement (heart-rate?) paired with personalized reminders based on the S.M.A.R.T method. You set the parameters. The watch also relies on a larger variety of metrics and these data points could cultivate a better mind-to-body connection. Only time will tell, I'm still doubtful, but as my favorite Styx song suggests, "The problem's plain to see: too much technology. Machines to save our lives. Machines dehumanize."

We should be pursuing fitness activities not for the sake of pleasing the fitness app and hitting the numbers (nor to share the length of our run in Central Park) but because exercise makes us feel better, look better, and be better. Put another way, occasionally cover the treadmill screen with your towel at the gym and listen to your body, not your app.

LEARNING SCENARIOS

Scenario #1

You purchase a new wearable device because you'd like to keep track of a number of physical indicators such as blood pressure, heart rate, and how many calories you burn throughout the day. Like most consumers, you were your device while awake and asleep. After a few months, you recognize that you have been receiving tons of unsolicited advertisements. Retailers seem to intuitively know what you need and when you need it. Upon reading more closely regarding the safety and security concerns expressed by government officials in recent years, you suspect that your personal information is being leaked through your wearable device. Would this knowledge impact your use of your wearable device? How? Would you continue to use your wearable device? Why? Why Not?

Scenario #2

We live in an era where fitness has become a priority in our lives. The number of ath-leisure brands, fitness class subscriptions, and naturally, physical health trackers continue to increase and you've bought into the trend. You begin to notice an increase in the number of reports warning that health trackers are leading to a rise in mental health and psychological issues associated with the dependency on health trackers. Although researchers point to the advantages of monitoring moods, attention, heart rate, and memory, you become concerned about the long-term effects of using the devices. Will this information impact how often you use your device? Will you stop all together?

Scenario #3

There has been a rash of thefts at work. Your company says that it has no choice but to require all employees to wear tracking devices and submit to an implant tracker, along with facial recognition technology in order to make the workplace more secure. The implant will provide access to secure facilities for authorized staff and remove any need for employees to punch a time clock. Although it is not a legal condition of employment, management is applying pressure on the staff to submit to the changes. They insist that records would be kept secure but that the files will remain the property of the firm as long as the company deems necessary. Considering the high pay rate, your financial responsibilities and family obligations, would you submit to the new tracking measures? Why or Why not?

HELPFUL STRATEGIES

READ ONLINE REVIEWS: Comparison shop online to ensure you choose the right tool. Pay attention to user reviews about usability, pricing and unique features. "Make sure reviewers are commenting on the device itself, not on issues they had with customer service," adds Brown.

KNOW WHAT YOU ARE GETTING: Features differ between devices. Generally, the less expensive the device, the fewer features it will have. You don't have to spend a lot of money to get good results, just be sure to select a tool that has the features you want.

BE AWARE OF YOUR DEVICE'S LIMITATIONS: It can't track how many calories you're eating, just your activity level. Allow for a 5 percent margin of error because its readings may not always be totally accurate. Keep in mind that many devices haven't been independently reviewed for effectiveness because they are so new.

LEARNING TASKS

20-Minute Activity

- **Standard**:
  - *Standard 3:* Students will demonstrate the ability to access valid information and products and services to enhance health.

  - *Standard 7:* Students will demonstrate the ability to practice health-enhancing behaviors and avoid or reduce health risks.

- **Rationale:** This lesson will help students develop awareness of wearable technology and the potential impacts, both positive and negative, on personal health, safety and security. It will allow student to become more familiar with key terms associated with wearable technology.

- **Learning Outcomes:** Students will be able to identify the key health features of wearable technology so that they can make informed decisions regarding the use of health trackers and protect both their health and personal well-being.

- **Description of Activity**: Students will be asked to specifically address the essential question of the chapter. The teacher will design a basic formative assessment to gauge student knowledge of the key concepts of the chapter.

ONE DAY ACTIVITY

- **Standard**:
  - *Standard 6:* Students will demonstrate the ability to use goal setting skills to enhance health.

  - *Standard 8:* Students will demonstrate the ability to advocate for personal, family and community health.

- **Rationale:** This lesson is designed to help students set personal health and fitness goals through the review of various products currently in the marketplace.

- **Learning Outcome:** Students will be able to set personal fitness goals so that they can enhance their physical health.

- **Description of Activity:** Students will conduct a product review of the features of several wearable devices and how they can help keep track of a number of health indicators. Students will discuss how to use the measurement features, analytics, and optimization. They will learn to review the data at periodic intervals and adjust exercise and diet routines as a result.

ONE WEEK ACTIVITY

- **Standard**:
  - *Standard 1;* Students will comprehend concepts related to health promotion and disease prevention to enhance health.

  - *Standard 4:* Students will demonstrate the ability to use interpersonal communications skills to enhance health and avoid or reduce health risks.
- **Rationale:** For this lesson, students will present a 3-5 page research paper using one of the Real World Scenarios of this chapter. This lesson requires students research governmental concerns about tracking devices and present findings in an oral report.

- **Learning Outcomes:** Students will be able to describe wearable technology's impact upon personal safety and security so that they can ensure that their health, well-being and privacy is not negatively affected.

- **Description of Activity:** Hand out the specific requirement of the paper and its primary focus. The teacher directives should be clear and concise. Students will present a 3-5 page paper by the 5th day through an oral report of the finding from government sources involving the concerns over the safety and security of personal tracking device and the influence of big business.

ADDITIONAL RESOURCES

Can Exercise Help Relieve Teen Depression?:http://www.health.harvard.edu/blog/can-exercise-help-relieve-teen-depression-2016081010084

Payouts Of Fitness Trackers Not Just In Health Benefits — They're Monetary, Too:http://www.denverpost.com/2016/09/18/fitness-tracker-payouts-health-benefits-money/

How Fitness Trackers Can And Can't Help You Lose Weight: http://www.self.com/story/fitness-trackers-weight-loss

People Who Stop Using Their Fitbits Plagued By Guilt: http://gadgetsandwearables.com/2016/09/10/using-fitbits/

Market Size: Fitbit Extends Lead Over Apple In Wearables Sales http://gadgetsandwearables.com/2016/09/07/fitbit-extends-lead-apple/

Research Reveals The Dark Side Of Wearable Fitness Trackers: http://www.cnn.com/2016/09/01/health/dark-side-of-fitness-trackers/

The Quantified Welp: Measuring An Activity Makes It Less Enjoyable http://www.theatlantic.com/technology/archive/2016/02/the-quantified-welp/470874/

Employee Wellness Programs Use Carrots and, Increasingly, Sticks: http://www.nytimes.com/2016/01/25/business/employee-wellness-programs-use-carrots-and-increasingly-sticks.html?_r=0

Are Fitness Trackers Awesome Or Useless: http://www.zliving.com/lifestyle/beauty/fitness-tracker-wearable-tech?feed=LatestArticles

Research Reveals The Dark Side Of Wearable Fitness Trackers: http://www.cnn.com/2016/09/01/health/dark-side-of-fitness-trackers/

The Quantified Welp: Measuring An Activity Makes It Less Enjoyable http://www.theatlantic.com/technology/archive/2016/02/the-quantified-welp/470874/

Employee Wellness Programs Use Carrots and, Increasingly, Sticks: http://www.nytimes.com/2016/01/25/business/employee-wellness-programs-use-carrots-and-increasingly-sticks.html?_r=0

Are Fitness Trackers Awesome Or Useless: http://www.zliving.com/lifestyle/beauty/fitness-tracker-wearable-tech?feed=LatestArticles

---

[1] ABI Research, *Wearable and Device Sector.* https://www.abiresearch.com/market-research/practice/wearables-devices/ (see footnote 3)

[2] *Are Personal Trackers Dangerous*? http://www.drweil.com/drw/u/QAA401637/Are-Personal-Tracking-Devices-Dangerous.html

[3] (See Endnote 1)

[4] Statista, Facts and Statistics on Wearable Technology. http://www.statista.com/topics/1556/wearable-technology/

[5] Mario Ballano Barcena, Candid Wueest, Hon Lau, *How safe is your quantified self?* https://www.symantec.com/content/dam/symantec/docs/white-papers/how-safe-is-your-quantified-self-en.pdf

[6] Neilsen Survey, 70% of Consumers are Aware of Wearables and 15% of Them Currently Use One, Survey Says. (March 25, 2014).

[7] Venkat Atluri, Satya Rao and Shekhar Varanasi,*New trends in smart devices.* McKinsey and Company. (April 2014).

[8] IDC, The worldwide wearable market leaps by 127%. (February 23, 2016). http://www.idc.com/getdoc.jsp?containerId=prUS41037416

[9] http://www.wareable.com/fitness-trackers/the-best-fitness-tracker

[10]Is Your Fitness Tracker Putting Your Security At Risk? http://www.makeuseof.com/tag/fitness-tracker-putting-security-risk/

[11] (see footnote 2)

[12] Expert Answers: Is *it safe to wear my wireless fitness tracker all the time?* https://experiencelife.com/article/expert-

answers-is-it-safe-to-wear-my-wireless-fitness-tracker-all-the-time/

[13] http://www.pcmag.com/article2/0,2817,2404445,00.asp

[14] *Safety, Security And Privacy Risks Of Fitness Tracking And 'Quantified Self'.* http://www.forbes.com/forbes/welcome/?toURL=http://www.forbes.com/sites/larrymagid/2014/07/31/safety-security-and-privacy-risks-of-fitness-tracking-and-quantified-self/&refURL=https://www.google.com/&referrer=https://www.google.com/

[15] Arwa Mahdawi, *The unhealthy side of wearable fitness devices.* The Guardian. (January 3, 2014)

[16] Nick Bilton, *The Health Concerns in Wearable Tech.* New York Times. (March 18, 2015).

[17] We need to talk about the health risks of wearable technology, http://qz.com/313039/the-question-we-havent-been-asking-enough-about-wearables-will-they-make-us-sick/

[18] Hamza Shaban, *Big Doctor Is Watching, How your fitness tracker could increase your health insurance costs someday.* (FEB. 27 2015) SLATE.

[19] Is Bluetooth Radiation Dangerous? https://bengreenfieldfitness.com/2015/01/is-bluetooth-radiation-dangerous/

CHAPTER TEN

Trusting Online Information

How can online information be verified?

How can you determine whether online
information was written objectively?

Why do people produce misinformation online?

BEHAVIORS AND THEMES

SCALE AND SCOPE: Research regarding what you can and can't trust online is still pretty thin and conflicting.[1] Among many who are compiling data on this topic, the argument surrounds the electronic transactions and the consistent interactions that might become weakened as a result of diminished information modalities. Apparently, researchers insist, it becomes more troublesome to discern vital, non-verbal physical prompts and cues such as gestures, facial expressions and body language. These are the long held traditional methods used to determine whether those conveying information are being deceptive.[2]

Regardless of many years of research, there is still no authoritative data on the influence of various media such as video, audio, online, and convergent methods which include a combination of all media forms. But when it comes to trust, you need to have confidence that you can rely, without a doubt, on your online information.

On the other hand, there are those who promulgate the idea that trust can be augmented by becoming immersed in the overwhelming amount of information currently available in an increased number of forms. Social networks, artificial intelligence, automation, and virtual reality have changed the landscape forever. As a result, trust regarding the information found online has become a major question.

Many scientists in the field debate that the level of reliability of information conveyed online might be manipulated by creating a different form of social interactions and the modalities that are available in today's marketplace.[3] The various dynamics that shape your online activities tend to erase the very trust which this chapter seeks to address. It might prove to be valuable and can help you believe that what you consume online is actual and can be believed and trusted. Trust can be narrowly defined as having a certain level of faith, assurance, and confidence in the reliability of information. Much of the raw information found online, in many cases, cannot be confirmed. Therefore, the more information you consume online, the higher the level of uncertainty exists as to its accuracy.[4]

As you learn more about the internet as a user, you might begin to develop a higher degree of confidence and trust in online information. On the other hand, those individuals who work with technology as an occupation—for instance, content producers, web developers, application engineers, systems administrators and network architects—are very likely to have a greater level of trust as they have a depth and breadth of understanding of the complicated issues that surround the dependability of data and information contained online.[5] Not only does the idea of certainty challenge the linear perceptions of the association between proximity and reliance, it also brings into question what level of trust is appropriate.

A different level of trust related concerns that users of online information might be confronted with involved such matters as loss of privacy, not being able to guard personal information, scams, and paying for items that never materialize with zero options to address problems.[6] The reality is that when you go online you are placing your privacy at risk, enabling others to retrieve personal information about you. Recognize that the information is difficult or even impossible to verify and find it difficult to evaluate the quality of goods and services.

Experts suggest that there is a statistically significant negative association between internet reliability and education. In other words, those who are more educated are often quite skeptical of information found online, the services found online, and the very institution of the internet than people who possess less education.[7]

PROBLEM DEFINED: Welcome to the Internet. When the so-called information superhighway was first mentioned in the early 1990s, many had little idea of the extent to which it would alter the landscape of data availability. There is a vast amount of information on virtually any topic online. This information ranges in reliability, accuracy and usefulness. Traditional media such as books, magazines, educational materials, and documents are vetted for reliability and accuracy. However, online information does not have to be approved, analyzed, or evaluated. Therefore, it becomes your job to examine what you find and determine whether it's appropriate for your needs.

Information is ubiquitous online and in huge quantities. It is constantly being updated, created and revised. You can readily find all manner of opinions, facts, statistics, narratives and interpretations. This information has multiple purposes. It is designed and presented in order to persuade, inform, manipulate, control, sell, change belief systems, appeal to values, and present various viewpoints.[8] It's available in many forms and presented in on multiple levels of quality and dependability. It ranges from high quality information to extremely inaccurate information; and everything in between.

Today's students are "Digital Natives." You were born into a world where the internet and online activity already existed. You perhaps, in fact, do not remember a world without the internet. As a result, most students today have developed a relationship with technology and have developed a level of trust in the content found online.[9] Put simply, those exposed to the Internet gain more trust in the technology. Even past users—so called Internet dropouts—have more confidence in the Internet than do non-users, who have no experience with the technology. A similar pattern emerges with respect to perceived Net-risk, a scale combining perceptions that the Internet poses risks to privacy, the securing of personal information, and to judging the quality of products online. As in the case of Net-confidence, the gender, socioeconomic status and age variables are not significantly related to perceived risks, once other factors are controlled statistically.[10]

FAKE NEWS

The concept of fake news is not new. Since as far back as the 1st century A.D., information has been disseminated to influence public opinion. Fake news, often referred to as yellow journalism is designed to intentionally misinform the public by using eye catching headlines and sensational content. Since information online is not routinely vetted, it has become much easier to spread exaggerated claims. Technology provides so-called "click-bait" to lure readers, listeners or viewers. During the 2016 U.S. Presidential election assertions by the Trump candidacy suggested that news published by legacy media outlets such as ABC, NBC, CBS, CNN, The Washington Post and New

York Times, for instance, were false and represented fake news. In other words, these news agencies were engaging in a form of yellow journalism because the stories they published were provably false and had no basis in fact. It is a tactic used by politicians to smear news stories that they don't like. However, beyond the promulgation of the misrepresentation of false news stories, misinformation also has an impact upon today's students and the ways in which you consume and search for valid information.

STUDENT USE OF ONLINE INFORMATION: WHAT TEACHERS SAY?

According to a Pew Research Center study, approximately 75 percent of Advanced Placement and National Writing Project teachers indicate that the internet has had an overall positive effect on the research practices of their students. Nevertheless, more than 85 percent of them say that ubiquitous technology is having side effects. Students are becoming far more easily distracted with a noticeable decline in their attention spans. Nearly 65 percent of teachers think new technologies are doing more to pull students off task than aid them scholastically.

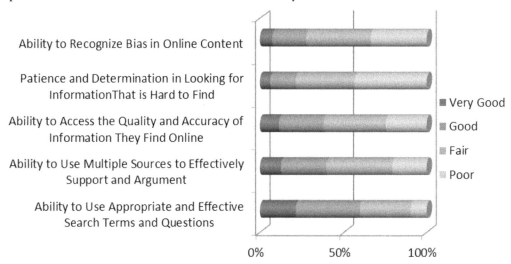

Source: Pew Research Center (2012)

The opinions may sound contradictory, but more than 2,000 secondary teachers and focus groups both online and offline reveal how teachers, in general, feel about trustworthy information online. The research took a closer look at the teachers' observations and experiences regarding how the growth of digital academic material impact how their students conduct research.

For the most part, teachers who took part in the study depict today's digital school environment as multi-faceted with a number of positives and some drawbacks. The good news is that students have instant access to a depth and breadth of information on a wide array of topics that may be of interest to them. You can avail deep, rich educational content, utilize appealing multimedia and become more independent researchers.

Yet, on the flipside, teachers are expressing some concerns. Most believe that students are becoming far too dependent on search engines and are having difficulty evaluating the quality of the information they find online. They reportedly feel that the literacy level of students has been negatively impacted. Additionally, they suggest that students are easily distracted, are developing poor time management skills and a decreased ability to think critically. Plagiarism is another major concern.

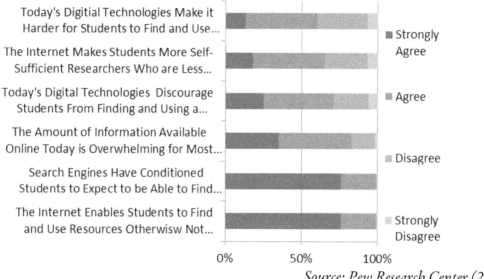

Source: Pew Research Center (2012)

The overwhelming majority of teachers say that students are failing to utilize other resources such as books, online data bases, news sources, and libraries. In fact, most feel that the number one priority today should be to teach students how to assess the trustworthiness of online information. Therefore, a great deal of class time is being spent helping students develop the skills needed to better judge what they find and pointing students in the direction of quality online resources.

This represents the primary findings of the survey that was conducted online. It was a non-probability sample of nearly 2,500 secondary teachers who are currently under contract in the U.S., Virgin Islands, and Puerto Rico. The results were compared to online and in-person focus groups. The sample met a number of diverse characteristics from ethnic, racial, geographic, gender, and subject matter. Because the sample was pulled from some of the most affluent school systems, the data is not essentially reflective of schools and all teachers. Nevertheless, their judgments and observations can be used to interpret data suggesting that students are relying too heavily on information found online.

Digital technologies and the internet are having a significant impact on how you find information. When asked to examine the total influence on student's research, more than 77 percent of teachers indicated that they felt that it was mostly positive. However, nearly all (99 percent) of teachers surveyed agreed that the internet serves as an indispensable tool in availing a greater range of resources and material than would otherwise be presented. Additionally, 65 percent say that the internet has made their students more independent researchers. The caveat, however, is that can the research and information be trusted?

Conversely, about 76 percent of those participating in the survey indicated that they "strongly agree" that search engines are creating bad habits. It is creating the expectation that all information is quickly accessible and accurate. They agree that the volume of information can be discouraging and overwhelming. Not only that, students are now refusing to even consider other methods of research outside of online information. This, they say, might make it harder for you as a student to locate additional reliable sources of data.

The internet has changed the meaning of "research."

Study habits among students have become one of the greatest concerns for classroom teachers. The very mention of research by the teachers sends students scurrying to Google. Resultantly, many teachers say that the idea of research has gone from a time consuming process where students were expected to use multiple sources that sparked academic curiosity and discovery to an instant, almost mindless, short term activity where they do just enough searching to finish the tasks assigned by the teacher. Just above 94 percent of teachers responding said their students were "extremely likely" to use Google as a primary research source. This was followed by Wikipedia and social media sites such as Youtube. Here is what the findings revealed as student preferred research tools: (Percentage of students using these modalities).

STUDENT RESEARCH TOOLS

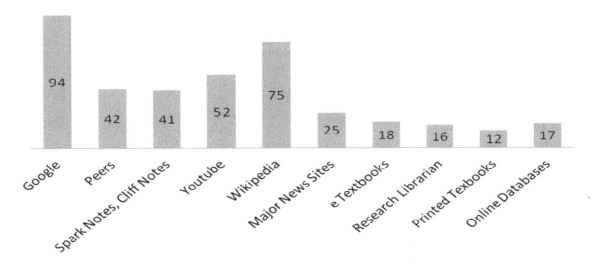

Source: Pew Research Center (2012)

IMPACT ON HEALTH: Misinformation is not just a concern for the classroom. More specifically, however, these research habits have become a concern for teachers and parents, alike. The idea that information is at your fingertips is enticing for many teens and the danger of misinformation can have potentially harmful health and wellness consequences. It is typically seen as a teenagers' process of maturing and exploring themselves and the world in which you live.[11] Health information for teens can vary dramatically based on gender, age, social status, motivation and other interests. Essentially, the wide range of data that you, as school aged students, seek provides a glimpse into your basic health concerns. The list includes searches of specific illnesses, HIV/AIDS, nutrition, sexual activities, fitness, chronic conditions like STI's (Sexually Transmitted Illnesses), mental health issues and pregnancy, among others. This research is often driven by the fear that you may have been impacted by one or more of these issues. Sexual health and drugs are among the most searched information by teens.[12] This creates behavior after the fact. You research conditions once you believe that you have been exposed; as opposed to researching so that a condition never occurs to begin with.

It is worth noting here that the majority of those seeking such information are usually females who routinely take risks and those teens who are predisposed to self-medication. Yet another example of information seeking involves contraception and or abstinence. Others tend to seek information about other teen health issues such as acne. Also, given the ever decreasing level of privacy, many students are hesitant to access LGBT (Lesbian, Gay, Bi-Sexual, Transgender) and HIV information even if they feel the need to educate themselves. The bottom line remains, can the information be trusted? Who has been charged with vetting online information for such serious health related topics?

Are you willing to trust information placed online by anyone. For many teens, mental health has become a chief focus for information seeking. More than one in three teens experience mental health struggles with more than 90 percent of you seeking online information because it lends to a higher degree of anonymity. Most teens are quite comfortable with the internet. This assistance, if it can be verified, can aid in lowering the level of embarrassment and stigma associated with health conditions. Girls are far more likely to seek help and communicate with others regarding health than boys.[13] Ideals of masculinity suggest that boys deal with their problems "like a man." Many in the health professions sound the alarm about this so-called "computerized therapy."[1]

HEALTH EFFECTS OF MISINFORMATION ONLINE

Incorrect information and stereotyping in advertising and marketing are negatively tied to consumer buying behavior and purchase intentions. Sometimes those in marketing and advertising will over exaggerate the product's benefits in such a subconscious way that you may feel psychologically pressured to try the product. The diet pill, the nutritional food lure or the new exercise program can be overwhelmingly pervasive. The psychological, sociological impacts can be devastating which in turn might lead to disappointment, unhappiness and other mental stressors. [15]

On a personal and individual level, the spread of misinformation regarding health and the maintenance of health can often create unnecessary fear and anxiety. Can you trust the information about whether to vaccinate or not? Are alternative forms of medicine effective? Will the diet program produce results as advertised? Misinformation can be harmful to your health.

KEY CONCEPTS

Bias-- prejudice in favor of or against one thing, person, or group compared with another, usually in a way considered to be unfair.

Misinformation--Incorrect information, spread intentionally (without realizing it is untrue) or unintentionally.

Reliability-- An attribute of any system that consistently produces the same results, preferably meeting or exceeding its specifications.

Trustworthiness-- worthy of confidence; specifically: being or deriving from a source worthy of belief or consideration for evidentiary purposes.

REAL WORLD SITUATIONS

The Morass of Misinformation On the Net

—Source John C. Dvorak[1]

How can misinformation impact your ability to make sound decisions?

It's becoming more and more apparent that the Internet is the biggest source of lies and bad information ever imagined.

There is nothing like it, and it has the potential to create sociological problems unlike anything we've ever seen. I'm amused that certain governments fear the power of the Internet, when they could be using it as a propaganda tool of the most powerful sort.

Here are a couple of exercises that look easy at first, then quickly turn difficult.

ERRONEOUS EXERCISES

First, try using the Internet to determine who originally said "the sky is falling." Was it Henny-penny or Chicken Little? Both characters often appear in the same story, but only one of them first uttered the famous phrase. The more you research this, the more you discover that the tale, which first surfaced in 19th-century folklore, has been rewritten so often that the contradictory information is ridiculous. And this is a situation where nobody is trying to fool anyone. The situation is just a mess.

Trying to determine the exact wording of the "bumpy ride" quote said by Betty Davis in the movie All About Eve is another amusing Internet exercise.

From my experience, the only way you can get this right is to rent the film and watch it with pen in hand. An Internet search will do you no good at all. Go to Google and search for "Betty Davis bumpy ride" or "All About Eve quotes." You'll get everything from "Hang on to your hats, we're in for a bumpy ride" to "Fasten your seatbelts, you're in for a bumpy night," and every imaginable variation. It's ridiculous.

I invite readers to join the PC Magazine forum (http://discuss.pcmag.com) and add other search suggestions that produce these kinds of discrepancies. I would like to develop a canonical list of misinformation on the Internet, although the Internet itself may be the list.

NO ONE'S SAFE FROM BEING SPOOFED

The question you have to ask is: If Internet information that should be accurate, such as a simple quote from a movie, is so often wrong, exactly what can you trust? You also have to wonder what happens if the information is a lie designed to manipulate readers. Apparently, the Nigerian scam e-mails still rope people in every year, although the number of victims is unknown.

Of course propaganda, misquotes, bad information, botches, and blatant lies are nothing new in old media, either.

The first example that comes to mind is the Wall Street Journal falling for a 2002 April Fool's gag and reporting that Harrods department store in London was going public. The store, in its phony press release, even listed the contact as Lirpa Loof to tip off anyone with a clue. That has to be the most often-used hint in these gags. Lirpa Loof, of course, is April Fool spelled backwards. I myself have used a variation (Lirpa Sloof) in at least four April Fool's gags over the years.

It gets worse with Photoshop. There is a hilarious picture of John Kerry sitting next to Jane Fonda — a beautiful Photoshop hoax that flew around the Net overnight. How many people ever discovered it was a clever hoax? And a few years ago, there was the fake picture of George W. Bush reading a fairy tale book upside down. I could not believe how many people were taken in by that one. The best photo hoaxes are designed to confirm preexisting notions.

The verbal gaffs of Dan Quayle were perfect for this sort of thing, too. During his era, all known gaffs and spoonerisms were attributed to him. And it was amazing how many people claimed they heard him say these things or they knew someone who knew someone who heard him say them.

THE HORRORS WON'T END

Anyway, this sort of thing is not new, as I've noted. What is new is the transmission medium.

When you make an error in a newspaper, for example, you can usually print a retraction before the gaffe becomes gospel. The mistake is like a pimple that doesn't spread and can be treated. With the Internet, the error is more like smallpox in an unprotected community.

Some user studies in England queried people about their concerns regarding e-mail viruses and asked how careful the subjects were to avoid clicking on weird attachments. Something like 75 percent of the respondents said they didn't care one way or the other. This in itself begs for analysis, but also tells you something about the computer-using public — it is not on the ball.

This says to me that a good propaganda campaign done right would be very successful, since the majority of users will passively receive anything. Look at how a no-name politico like Howard Dean used Internet selling techniques to cajole people out of around $50 million for a doomed campaign — a colossal waste of money, in hindsight.

In the end, people believe what they want to believe. The Internet is not a bastion of truth and freedom, it's a pit of horror and lies. It's geared up to become a mechanism of tyranny and madness. Nothing can change this. With people clicking like idiots on e-mail attachments that say "about you" or "you'll find this interesting," I see the situation as hopeless.

REAL WORLD SITUATIONS

No food is healthy. Not even kale.

—*Source: Michael Ruhlman January 17, 2016*[18]

What are the effects on personality and judgment as a result of believing that all information online is authentic?
What are the indicators that online information is inaccurate?

Not long ago, I watched a woman set a carton of Land O' Lakes Fat-Free Half-and-Half on the conveyor belt at a supermarket.

"Can I ask you why you're buying fat-free half-and-half?" I said. Half-and-half is defined by its fat content: about 10 percent, more than milk, less than cream.

"Because it's fat-free?" she responded.

"Do you know what they replace the fat with?" I asked.

"Hmm," she said, then lifted the carton and read the second ingredient on the label after skim milk: "Corn syrup." She frowned at me. Then she set the carton back on the conveyor belt to be scanned along with the rest of her groceries.

The woman apparently hadn't even thought to ask herself that question but had instead accepted the common belief that fat, an essential part of our diet, should be avoided whenever possible.

Then again, why should she question it, given that we allow food companies, advertisers and food researchers to do our thinking for us? In the 1970s, no one questioned whether eggs really were the heart-attack risk nutritionists warned us about. Now, of course, eggs have become such a cherished food that many people raise their own laying hens. Such examples of food confusion and misinformation abound.

"This country will never have a healthy food supply," said Harry Balzer, an NPD Group analyst and a gleeful cynic when it comes to the American food shopper. "Never. Because the moment something becomes popular, someone will find a reason why it's not healthy."

Here, Balzer used the most dangerous term of all: "healthy."

We are told by everyone, from doctors and nutritionists to food magazines and newspapers, to eat healthy food. We take for granted that a kale salad is healthy and that a Big Mac with fries is not.

I submit to you that our beloved kale salads are not "healthy." And we are confusing ourselves by believing that they are. They are not healthy; they are nutritious. They may be delicious when prepared well, and the kale itself, while in the ground, may have been a healthy crop. But the kale on your plate is not healthy, and to describe it as such obscures what is most important about that kale salad: that it's packed with nutrients your body needs. But this is not strictly about nomenclature. If all you ate was kale, you would become sick. Nomenclature rather shows us where to begin.

" 'Healthy' is a bankrupt word," Roxanne Sukol, preventive medicine specialist at the Cleveland Clinic, medical director of its Wellness Enterprise and a nutrition autodidact ("They didn't teach us anything about nutrition in medical school"), told me as we strolled the aisles of a grocery store. "Our food isn't healthy. We are healthy. Our food is nutritious. I'm all about the words. Words are the key to giving people the tools they need to figure out what to eat. Everyone's so confused."

Last March, the Food and Drug Administration sent the nut-bar maker Kind a letter saying their use of the word "healthy" on their packaging was a violation (too much fat in the almonds). Kind responded with a citizens' petition asking the FDA to reevaluate its definition of the word.

If I may rephrase the doctor's words: Our food is not healthy; we will be healthy if we eat nutritious food. Words matter. And those that we apply to food matter more than ever.

Kraft cheese slices cannot be called cheese but must be labeled "cheese food" or a "cheese product." Pringles cannot be called "chips" but rather "crisps." Yet packaged foods can be labeled "natural" or "all-natural" — what exactly is the difference between the two, anyway? — with little regulation.

Here is a word we think we understand: protein. Protein is good, yes? Builds strong muscles, has positive health connotations. That's why "protein shakes" are a multibillion-dollar business. Pork cracklings do not have positive health connotations because we think of them as having a high fat content. But pork cracklings are little more than strips of fried pig skin. Skin is one of the many forms of connective tissue in all animal bodies and is composed almost entirely of protein, typically undergirded by a layer of fat. When these strips of pig skin are fried, most of the fat is rendered out and the connective tissue puffs, resulting in a delectable, crunchy, salty crackling. I therefore recommend them to you as a "protein snack" during your on-the-go day.

Given the infinitely malleable language of food, it's no wonder American food shoppers are confused.

What is "mechanically separated meat," a standard ingredient in the turkey bacon and chicken sausages popularized because of our low-fat love? "Do you know what that is?" a grocery store owner asked me. "They basically put poultry carcasses in a giant salad spinner." Whatever winds up on the walls of the spinner in addition to meat — bits of cartilage (protein!), nerves (I have enough of my own, thank you), vessels, bone fragments — is scraped off and added to the mixing bowl. "Mechanically separated meat" engages our imagination only when someone attaches new words to it, such as "pink slime."

"Refined" is another critical food word. Generally, refined means elegant and cultured in appearance, manner or taste, or with impurities removed. Yet that is what food companies have been calling wheat from which the germ and bran have been removed, leaving what is in effect pure starch, devoid of the fiber, oils, iron and vitamins that make wheat nutritious.

That's not refined, Sukol said, "that's stripped." Flour stripped of the nutrition that makes it valuable to our bodies but reduces shelf life.

Because it has been stripped, we must "enrich" it. "Enriched." "Fortified." Good, yes? To make rich, to make strong. Food companies added the iron they took out during the refining process, but not enough of what we need. "Refined flour — this resulted in B vitamin and iron deficiencies," Sukol said, "so they added vitamins and iron. And what do they call that? Enriched and fortified. But they forgot to add folate, vitamin B9, until the 1990s."

What we don't know, Sukol said, is how those additions, not to mention the diglycerides and sulphates, combined with the lack of fiber, will affect our metabolism in the long run. So far, she said, "it has resulted in diabetes and metabolic syndrome."

We will be healthy if we eat nutritious food. Our food is either nutritious or not. We are healthy or we are not. If we eat nutritious food, we may enhance what health we possess.

REAL WORLD SITUATIONS

Newsweek retracts story filled with fake news about Vegas shooter's girlfriend.
—*Source: Brian Flood, Fox News, October 5, 2017*

How can you confirm the authenticity of online news?

How are news organizations policed for accuracy?

Newsweek issued another embarrassing retraction on Tuesday evening about a story that falsely detailed the life of the Las Vegas shooter's girlfriend with salacious information that turned out to be fake news.

Citing public records, the original story claimed Stephen Paddock's girlfriend, Marilou Danley, had used two social security accounts and had two husbands at the same time. The now-retracted story said that Danley is the "one person who holds the key to solving the mystery" of the deadliest mass shooting in American history. Newsweek painted her as "a shadowy figure with a convoluted life of her own," which lived "an unconventional life."

Unfortunately for Newsweek, the initial report was based on the marriage record of Danley, who was known under a different name when she married Geary Danley in Clark County, Nevada, according to the magazine.

"Newsweek mistakenly matched that record to a second public record of a different person," the publication wrote explaining the retraction. "Newsweek regrets the error."

Newsweek has now issued at least 20 corrections in 2017, including at least one per month, and even has a page on its website dedicated to its mistakes. The magazine admitted to over 50 mistakes in 2016 and even apologized for a story that praised an assault on white nationalist Richard Spencer earlier this year. Mistakes are so common at Newsweek that every digital article features a "submit correction" option beneath the text.

The latest retracted story was reported by Melina Delkic, but the correction features the byline "Newsweek staff." Delkic covers breaking news and politics for Newsweek and refers to herself a journalism school "drop-out" on her Twitter bio.

Newsweek did not immediately respond when asked whether or not she will be disciplined for the retracted story, while Delkic declined to comment.

A lot of information has emerged since Newsweek's original story falsely claimed Danley had "multiple Social Security numbers," and she has since denied any wrongdoing.

"I knew Stephen Paddock as a kind, caring, quiet man," Danley said in a statement read by her attorney outside FBI headquarters in Los Angeles on Wednesday. "I loved him and hoped for a quiet future together with him. He never said anything to me or took any action that I was aware of that I understood in any way to be a warning that something horrible like this was going to happen."

Danley was questioned by federal agents for much of the day after returning from her native Philippines, where she had been for more than two weeks. While Danley was on her way back from the Philippines, a Newsweek editor was busy praising the now-retracted story on Twitter.

As first reported by TheWrap, a Newsweek breaking news editor bragged about the "exclusive" look into the shooter's "weird" girlfriend that turned out to be fake news.

Gersh Kuntzman wrote, in a tweet that had still not been deleted at the time this article was published, "The great @MelinaDelkic shows us how it's done with this EXCLUSIVE look at LV shooter's weird girlfriend." As TheWrap pointed out, Kuntzman's Twitter feed is filled with comments referring to gun owners as "crazy" and mocking President Trump.

LEARNING SCENARIOS

Learning Scenario #1

You've always been a little overweight. After trying all manner of diets and exercise, you happen upon an advertisement online for a new "guaranteed, 100% money back, eat as much as you want" diet. Intrigued, you purchase the product. The story begins at age 4. You were extremely underweight for your height and age; and, your grandmother said you had "arms like ham" and was "getting chubby." You spent your entire childhood surrounded by weight stigma — whether it was from your grandmother constantly telling you to "go on a diet" or comparing your own body to your friends. At 12, you went on what was described as a "very strict diet." You had no clue what anorexia was. You thought it was when someone literally never ate anything due to some underlying emotional problem, when, in reality, according to your personal understanding and experience, it's a disease that manifests in the mind; an utter fear of weight gain. It does not have a specific physical appearance. It does not pick particular races or genders. It just is. How does the criticism of others impact our self worth?

Learning Scenario #2:

Bath salt usage has been associated with numerous adverse cardiac, psychiatric, neurological, gastrointestinal and pulmonary outcomes. In 2011, the use of 'bath salts' was responsible for over 20,000 emergency room visits in the United States and poisonings and deaths related to use have been occurring at large dance festivals. Increases in bizarre behavior linked to use of the 'bath salt' known as Flakka (alpha-PVP) has increasingly been appearing in headlines. 'Bath salt' use appears to be prevalent, yet, despite this, little is known about the epidemiology of this drug in the United States. You conduct online research and the information is not consistent. Your friends encourage you to try them. Knowing the above information, would you follow their advice?

Learning Scenario #3:

During a local race for mayor, a report surfaces that the incumbent mayor, a Democrat, was seen shoplifting at a high end department store. The information was reported by a member of the city council as an eye witness. The council member, a Republican, is running for office against the current mayor and asks that his identity not be revealed. The owner of the store declined to follow up or prosecute but the councilman insisted on calling the press to report what he saw. There are no other witnesses or video surveillance to prove the assertion. One local paper agrees to print the story, while others refused to print the allegation against the mayor. How can you determine if the information is true or represents "fake news?"

LEARNING TASKS

20-Minute Activity:

- **Standard:**
  - *Standard 1*: Students will comprehend concepts related to health promotion and disease prevention to enhance health.

  - *Standard 3*: Students will demonstrate the ability to access valid information and products and services to enhance health.

- **Rationale:** Students need to know that technology has changed the way in which information is consumed. This lesson is designed to familiarize students with the idea of how information can be misrepresented.

- **Learning Outcomes:** Students will be able define the concept of fake news so they can develop a better understanding of how technology has changed the ways news and information can be distorted.

- **Description of Activity:** Students will be required to research a current news story online and determine whether the information represents fact or is designed to inappropriately influence public opinion.

ONE DAY ASSIGNMENT

- **Standard**
  - *Standard 5:* Students will use interpersonal communication skills to enhance health.

  - *Standard 6:* Students will demonstrate the ability to use goal setting to enhance health.

- **Rationale:** Students must be able to discern whether the information they consume online can be verified. This lesson will help students in evaluating the accuracy of online information by using the CARS or CAFÉ Models for assessing credibility of information found on the internet as they relate to fad diets, miracle cures, instant financial success and other health claims.

- **Learning Outcomes:** Students will be able to analyze the accuracy and credibility of information online so they can make decisions based on reliable facts.

- **Description of Activity:** The teacher will discuss what makes a good website or a poor website. He/she will model web evaluation with the class using a number of pre-determined sites. Discuss fact vs. opinion & fact vs. fiction. Ask students to use CARS and CAFÉ models to check for information validity. Compare information found on the web to information found in print.

ONE WEEK ASSIGNMENT

- **Standards**:
  - *Standard 4*: Students will demonstrate to use decision making skills to enhance health and avoid or reduce health risks.

  - *Standard 8*: Students will demonstrate the ability to advocate for personal, family and community health.

- **Rationale:** For this lesson, students will develop a Public Service Announcements using the three real world situations in this lesson. This lesson requires students to serve as internet detectives and search for valid information to prove or disprove the assertions in the scenario. They will make an oral presentation of their findings.

- **Learning Outcomes:** Students will compare and contrast legitimate web resources from those that promote misinformation so they can develop an understanding for reliable sources.

- **Description of Activity:** Students will research multiple PSA models designed to provide accurate information to the public regarding an important, contemporary issue. Students will evaluate the information using either the CARS or CAFÉ Models to reach a reasonable conclusion as to the accuracy and credibility of the information. Students will then develop a Public Service Announcement regarding fake news or other misinformation found online. The students will present their PSA's to the class.

HELPFUL STRATEGIES

Getting Started: The (CARS) Checklist for Information Quality[1]

CREDIBILITY

Because people have always made important decisions based on information, evidence of authenticity and reliability--or credibility, believability--has always been important. If you read an article saying that the area where you live will experience a major earthquake in the next six months, it is important that you should know whether or not to believe the information. Some questions you might ask would include, What about this source makes it believable (or not)? How does this source know this information? Why should I believe this source over another? As you can see, the key to credibility is the question of trust.

There are several tests you can apply to a source to help you judge how credible and useful it will be:

INDICATORS OF LACK OF CREDIBILITY:

You can sometimes tell by the tone, style, or competence of the writing whether or not the information is suspect. Here are a few clues:

Anonymity:

Lack of Quality Control. Negative Meta-information. If all the reviews are critical, be careful.

- Bad grammar or misspelled words. Most educated people use grammar fairly well and check their work for spelling errors. An occasional split infinitive or comma in the wrong place is not unusual, but more than two or three spelling or grammar errors is cause for caution, at least. Whether the errors come from carelessness or ignorance, neither puts the information or the writer in a favorable light.

- Emotional earnestness accompanied by exaggeration or absolutes. Even in very controversial areas (gun control, global warming, abortion, capital punishment) and promotional contexts (product claims and evaluations) we expect reasons, data, and emotional restraint. Articles where the writer's feelings have clearly taken over from thinking make us wonder if we are reading ideology instead of information and arguments that might persuade us. Breathless, sweeping generalizations should set off your baloney detector. For example, "Did you know that none of the vitamins and supplements sold in stores work correctly with your body chemistry? Only Super Duper Vite has been formulated to blah blah blah."

- Claims of unique, secret information (which is now on the Web site) or claims of such dramatic implications that you should expect widespread discussion. For example, "The CIA was responsible for the assassination of President Kennedy." Conspiracy theories in general, because they run counter to official reports and often counter to reason, should be met with great caution.

ACCURACY

The goal of the accuracy test is to assure that the information is actually correct: up to date, factual, detailed, exact, and comprehensive. For example, even though a very credible writer said something that was correct twenty years ago, it may not be correct today. Similarly, a reputable source might be giving up-to-date information, but the information may be only partial, and not give the full story. Here are some concepts related to accuracy:

Indicators of a Lack of Accuracy:

In addition to an obvious tone or style that reveals a carelessness with detail or accuracy, there are several indicators that may mean the source is inaccurate, either in whole or in part:

- No date on the document
- Vague or sweeping generalizations
- Old date on information known to change rapidly
- Very one sided view that does not acknowledge opposing views or respond to them.

REASONABLENESS

The test of reasonableness involves examining the information for fairness, objectivity, moderateness, and consistency.

Indicators of a Lack of Reasonableness:

Writers who put themselves in the way of the argument, either emotionally or because of self interest, often reveal their lack of reasonableness. If, for example, you find a writer reviewing a book he opposes by asserting that "the entire book is completely worthless claptrap," you might suspect there is more than a reasoned disagreement at work. Here are some   clues to a lack of reasonableness:

- Intemperate tone or language ("stupid jerks," "shrill cries of my extremist opponents")
- Over-claims ("Thousands of children are murdered every day in the United States.")

- Sweeping statements of excessive significance ("This is the most important idea ever conceived!")
- Conflict of Interest ("Welcome to the Old Stogie Tobacco Company Home Page. To read our report, 'Cigarettes Make You Live Longer,' click here." or "The products our competitors make are dangerous and bad for your health.")

SUPPORT

The area of support is concerned with the source and corroboration of the information. Much information, especially statistics and claims of fact, comes from other sources. Citing sources strengthens the credibility of the information. (Remember this when you write a research paper.)

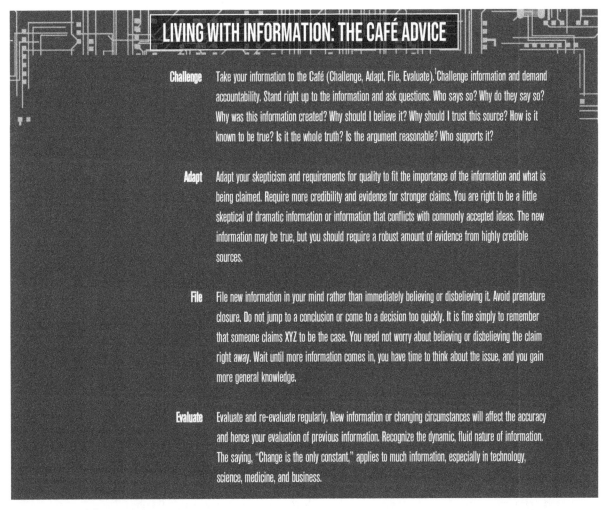

LIVING WITH INFORMATION: THE CAFÉ ADVICE

Challenge — Take your information to the Café (Challenge, Adapt, File, Evaluate). Challenge information and demand accountability. Stand right up to the information and ask questions. Who says so? Why do they say so? Why was this information created? Why should I believe it? Why should I trust this source? How is it known to be true? Is it the whole truth? Is the argument reasonable? Who supports it?

Adapt — Adapt your skepticism and requirements for quality to fit the importance of the information and what is being claimed. Require more credibility and evidence for stronger claims. You are right to be a little skeptical of dramatic information or information that conflicts with commonly accepted ideas. The new information may be true, but you should require a robust amount of evidence from highly credible sources.

File — File new information in your mind rather than immediately believing or disbelieving it. Avoid premature closure. Do not jump to a conclusion or come to a decision too quickly. It is fine simply to remember that someone claims XYZ to be the case. You need not worry about believing or disbelieving the claim right away. Wait until more information comes in, you have time to think about the issue, and you gain more general knowledge.

Evaluate — Evaluate and re-evaluate regularly. New information or changing circumstances will affect the accuracy and hence your evaluation of previous information. Recognize the dynamic, fluid nature of information. The saying, "Change is the only constant," applies to much information, especially in technology, science, medicine, and business.

Indicators of a Lack of Support:

As you can readily guess, the lack of supporting evidence provides the best indication that there is indeed no available support. Be careful, then, when a source shows problems like these:

- Numbers or statistics presented without an identified source for them.
- Absence of source documentation when the discussion clearly needs such documentation.
- You cannot find any other sources that present the same information or acknowledge that the same information exists (lack of corroboration).[1]

ADDITIONAL RESOURCES

Inside Wearables: How the Science of Human Behavior Change Offers the Secret to Long-Term Engagement:

http://endeavourpartners.net/assets/Endeavour-Partners-Wearables-and-the-Science-of-Human-Behavior-Change-Part-1-January-20141.pdf

Sherry Turkle: Always-On/Always-On-You – The Tethered Self: http://www.academia.edu/3129923/Always-on_always-on-you_The_tethered_self

Resource: Wellocracy -- Harvard's Trusted Source For Health Tracking:http://www.wellocracy.com

Electronic Tattoo Sensors Printed Directly On The Skin: https://www.technologyreview.com/s/512061/electronic-sensors-printed-directly-on-the-skin/

Sensor Can Be Implanted In Your Body And Is The Size Of A Grain of Sand. http://gizmodo.com/this-sensor-can-be-implanted-in-your-body-and-is-the-si-1784796417

Forget Wristbands, The Future Of Health Tracking Is Skin-Mounted: http://www.medicalnewstoday.com/articles/275049.php

The Advantages and Disadvantages of Health Apps: http://health-system-management.advanceweb.com/the-advantages-and-disadvantages-of-health-apps/

---

[1] Azadeh Ensha, Do you trust the internet more than other news sources? (July 9. 2009). http://lifehacker.com/5311238/do-you-trust-the-internet-more-than-other-news-sources

[2] William H. Dutton, Ginette Law, Gillian Bolsover, Soumitra Dutta, The internet trust bubble global values, beliefs and practices. (2013). World Economic Forum.

[3] Ed. Merck, Trust as a qualified reliance on information. file:///C:/Users/owner/Downloads/it-trust-part1%20(2).pdf

[4] Evaluating Internet Resources, http://www.usg.edu/galileo/skills/unit07/internet07_08.phtml

[5] F. Diane Barth, Why you shouldn't believe everything you read on the internet—even if it's true. (January 21, 2012). Psychology Today.

[6] Alfarez Abdul-Rahman & Stephen Hailes, Relying on trust to find reliable information. (N.D.). Department of Computer Science, University College. London: UK

[7] K. Sharpe, N. Di Pietro, K.J. Jacob, A dichotomy of information-seeking and information-trusting. (2016). doi:10.1007/s12015-016-9667-3

[8] Trust in the internet 'now missing,' BBC NEWS, (March 10, 2014).

[9] Harrison McKnight & Chuck Kacmar, Factors of Information Credibility for an Internet Advice Site. Michigan State University: Proceedings of the 39th Hawaii International Conference on System Sciences (2006).

[11] Kristin Sward, http://ksviudigitalcitizenshipdlf.weebly.com/uploads/1/3/9/6/13965264/rb2_trusting_internet_sources.pdf. (2014).

[12] Andrew White, Do We Trust the Internet Too Much? (April 16, 2012). http://blogs.gartner.com/andrew_white/2012/04/16/do-we-trust-the-internet-too-much/

[13] Jamie Barlett & Carl Miller, Internet Safety for kids and families: truth, lies and the internet a report into young people's digital fluency. (September, 2011). Demos: London.

[14] Kathleen Gossman, You can't trust the internet. (April 5, 2013). Enviritas Group.

[15] 14 James Salwitz, Looking up health information online: Do you really trust your doctor. (June 10, 2013). http://www.kevinmd.com/blog/2013/06/health-information-online-trust-doctor.html

[16] Pamela Hartzband & Jerome Groopman, Untangling the Web—Patients, Doctors, and the Internet. (March 10, 2010).New England Journal of Medicine. DOI: 10.1056/NEJMp0911938

[17] Robert Harris, Evaluating Internet resources using CAFÉ method. (January 21, 2015). http://www.virtualsalt.com/evalu8it.htm

[18] Dvorak, J.C. (2016).The Morass of Misinformation On the Net.

[19] Ruhlman, M. (2016). No food is healthy. Not even kale.

[20] Halper, D. (2017). Trump labels CNN as 'fake news' in fiery press conference tirade. *New York Post*.

[21] University of California Library, Organizing your social and internet realities using the CARS Model. (August 2, 2016).

[22] (see footnote 1)

CHAPTER ELEVEN

———————●———————

Video, Mobile, & Virtual Games

What role does escapism play in living a happy and healthy life?

How do you know if you have an addiction?

Should companies profit from contributing to people's health problems?

BEHAVIORS AND THEMES

SCALE & SCOPE: 1.8 billion people around the world play over 3 billion hours of video games a week.[1] More than half-a-billion gamers play at least an hour of video games a day—with 174 million daily gamers in the United States alone.[2] Surprisingly, demographers estimate 5 million gamers in the U.S. are spending the equivalent of a full time job (more than 40 hours a week) playing video games.[3] The percentage of gamers is even higher among adolescents: 99% of boys and 94% of girls under 18 play video games at least once a week, with 20% of teens reportedly playing video games more than 5 hours a week.[4] Some video game researchers estimate the average adolescent will play approximately 10,000 hours of video games by the age of 21; this is approximately the same amount of time teens spend in middle and high school combined.[5]

PROBLEM DEFINED: Excessive gameplay has been found to be associated with a number of physical and psychological health problems. Most health professionals consider the risk of becoming addicted to playing video games one of the greatest associated problems due to many games increasing realism and immersive lure. Studies on video gamers estimate that 10 to 15% of gamers exhibit symptoms the World Health Organization considers symptomatic for addiction, mirroring compulsive illnesses linked to gambling, sex, and shopping[6]. Video game addiction—while not yet recognized by the American Medical Association –has been characterized as an "impulse control disorder" that disrupts the brain's reward system[7]. Recent research suggests as many as 1 in 10 adolescents (ages 8 to 18, particularly boys) can be classified as pathological gamers addicting to video gaming[8]. Issues related to addiction can be particularly difficult for individuals who escape into virtual worlds where they are able to interact with others in ways

SYMPTOMS OF VIDEO GAME ADDICTION

PHYSICAL
- More physical illness: colds, allergies, nausea
- Feelings of restlessness, fatigue, and discomfort

CRAVINGS
- Recurring urge to return to gaming
- Only feels better when playing game

PSYCHOLOGICAL
- Feelings of emptiness and depression
- Uncontrollable feelings or fear
- Irritability or mood swings

SOCIAL
- Anger / verbal abuse
- Excessive crying
- Lack of motivation
- Procrastination and difficulty meeting obligations

OBSESSION
- Excessive sleeping
- Disruption of sleep patterns
- Fantasies and dreams about game

Source: Online Games Anonymous

they can't duplicate in real life. In addition to these psychological issues, excessive gaming has also been associated with physical symptoms related to carpal tunnel syndrome in the wrist, backaches, disrupted sleep, and chronic migraines[9].

SURPRISING BENEFITS: While many healthcare professionals remain concerned about excessive video gaming, multiple studies have found playing video games can improve people's cognition, reasoning, and hand-eye coordination[10]. Scientists have used brain-imaging scans to determine that devoted video gamers have more grey matter in their brain than non-gamers[11]. Importantly, grey matter processes information in the brain—meaning gamers with more grey matter can process information more efficiently. Counter to many negative assumptions about "lazy" video gamers, researchers have found high video game use was correlated with nearly 2 times the odds of "high intellectual functioning" (1.75 times better than non-gamers) and "high overall school performance" (1.88 times better than non-gamers)[12]. Additionally, neuroscientists have identified evidence that gamers have increased plasticity in their brain's hippocampus—responsible for regulating one's emotions, long-term memory, and spatial navigation –indicating a heightened capacity to develop new neural pathways in response to changes in one's environment and life circumstances[13]. While the overall impact of these changes is hard to characterize, there is mounting evidence playing video games regularly changes the structure of our brains and how they work.

IMPACTS MENTAL HEALTH: Many critics of video games argue these brain changes are leading to more aggressive and violent adolescent behavior. These accusations are regularly connected to reports on mass shootings, like Columbine H.S. in 1999 and Sandy Hook in 2012, linking the playing of violent video games simulating weapons-based combat to teen's subsequent violent actions[14]. Thus far, decades of research have been unable to establish a causal relationship between playing video games and increased violence or lowered empathy in the real world[15][16]. Existing research on violence and video games has been limited by researchers being unable to separate the impact of playing violent video games from the larger context of violent media consumed by teens on television, film, and the Internet. By the age of 18, American children will have seen 16,000 murders and 200,000 acts of violence depicted in video games, movies, and television[1]. However, some psychologists believe this assumption regarding video game's negative impact on adolescent behavior remains unwarranted. Several video game researchers have demonstrated boys (in particular) may be playing video games as a way to self-regulate their emotions in ways that may even be reducing violent behavior among adolescents[18]. In fact, in contrast to many stereotypes associated with video games, modern games are incredibly social activities for adolescents that require skilled collaboration, problem solving, critical thinking, and conflict resolution. A large, long-term study in the United Kingdom found video gamers were no more likely to develop mental health problems than their peers[19]. In fact, these researchers found teens that played video games reported fewer relationship problems than those who played fewer games or no games at all[20].

ONLINE GAMING BUILDS STRONGER CONNECTIONS

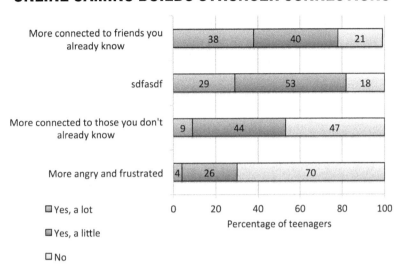

More connected to friends you already know: 38, 40, 21

sdfasdf: 29, 53, 18

More connected to those you don't already know: 9, 44, 47

More angry and frustrated: 4, 26, 70

Legend:
- Yes, a lot
- Yes, a little
- No

Percentage of teenagers (0, 20, 40, 60, 80, 100)

Source: Pew Research Center's Teens Relationships Survey, 2015

AMPLIFIED BY PROFIT: The video game industry is by far the fasting growing sector of the economy related to entertainment—generating over $80 billion in 2015, nearly 4 times as large as the music industry or almost 8 times the sales from Hollywood's box office[21]. A significant reason for this explosive growth can be attributed to the rise of mobile gaming and the emergence of "freemium" games like CandyCrush and Clash of Clans. These "free" games provide players with a free minimal experience, while creating incentives for gamers to spend hundreds, if not thousands, of real dollars to improve their gaming experience.

Game developers are increasingly hiring data scientists to analyze every click made and screen viewed by players (over 1 billion data points a day for the largest apps) to determine ways to "optimize gameplay"—programming games to maximize profits and commerce, often at the gamer player's expense[22]. In 2015 gamers spent $8 billion on virtual items and currency to be used solely within virtual worlds[23]. Game developers take advantage of algorithms designed to provide gamers with challenges that match their effort and maximize their awards— frequently employing psychological dynamics used by casinos and the gambling industry. The most popular games—like FarmVille's 70 million players –earn the game developers hundreds of thousands of dollars a day by designing experiences created to keep gamers playing—and paying –for weeks, months, even years[24].

NAVIGATING TRADE-OFFS: While the health risks associated with video gaming are real and may even necessitate treatment, a growing number of researchers have found moderate gaming (limited to around an hour a day) may lead to a number of beneficial outcomes. Playing video games increasingly provides teens with ways to participate, learn, and express themselves that are often met with disapproval in schools[25]. Video game researchers argue gaming allows for teens to immerse themselves in role-playing and fantasy, be rewarded for mistakes and repeated failure, and pursue multiple pathways to achieving a goal[26]. A growing body of evidence indicates playing video games can be a productive way to learn real-world skills like communication, leadership, teamwork, and perseverance[27]. Increasingly, corporations can be found hiring gamers off leader boards of popular video games because they believe these gamers have mastered a set of skills needed to succeed in the 21st century. Supporting this view, a number of universities and colleges have begun offering students scholarships to join competitive teams that can potentially lead to careers playing video games in professional leagues[28]. More promisingly, some video game researchers have found playing video games can improve one's perception of their quality of life and consistently produce positive emotions—feelings of optimism, curiosity, and determination –as well as stronger social connection when gaming with real-life family and friends[29].

KEY CONCEPTS

Escapism: The tendency for individuals to seek distraction and relief from unpleasant realities, most frequently by seeking diversion in entertainment or engaging in fantasy.

Impulse Control Disorder: A psychiatric disorder characterized by an inability to resist a temptation, urge or impulse that may harm oneself or others.

Self-Regulation of Emotion: The ability to respond to the minute-to-minute demands of managing one's emotional responses in a manner that is socially tolerable and viewed as appropriate for the situation.

Profit Motive: An economic theory that proposes the fundamental goal of any business is to maximize profits in order to make money for the businesses owners and investors.

Gamification: Applying game playing mechanisms and principles (competition, points, achievements) to areas of life outside of video games to help individuals modify negative habits and reward desirable behaviors.

REAL-WORLD SITUATIONS

Foldit: Gamers Succeed Where Scientists Fail
—Source: By Leila Gray, University of Washington, September 19th, 2011[30]

What could be beneficial about playing video games?

How might video games be designed to be in service of society?

"Gamers have solved the structure of a retrovirus enzyme whose configuration had stumped scientists for more than a decade. The gamers achieved their discovery by playing Foldit, an online game that allows players to collaborate and compete in predicting the structure of protein molecules. After scientists repeatedly failed to piece together the structure of a protein-cutting enzyme from an AIDS-like virus, they called in the Foldit players. The scientists challenged the gamers to produce an accurate model of the enzyme. They did it in only three weeks. "We wanted to see if human intuition could succeed where automated methods had failed," said Dr. Firas Khatib of the University of Washington Department of Biochemistry. Khatib is a researcher in the protein structure lab of Dr. David Baker, professor of biochemistry.

Remarkably, the gamers generated models good enough for the researchers to refine and, within a few days, determine the enzyme's structure. Equally amazing, surfaces on the molecule stood out as likely targets for drugs to de-active the enzyme. "These features provide exciting opportunities for the design of retroviral drugs, including AIDS drugs," wrote the authors of a paper appearing Sept. 18 in *Nature Structural & Molecular Biology*. The scientists and gamers are listed as co-authors. This is the first instance that the researchers are aware of in which gamers solved a longstanding scientific problem.

Fold-it was created by computer scientists at the University of Washington Center for Game Science in collaboration with the Baker lab. "The focus of the UW Center for Game Sciences," said director Dr. Zoran Popovic, associate professor of computer science and engineering, "is to solve hard problems in science and education that currently cannot be solved by either people or computers alone." The solution of the virus enzyme structure, the researchers said, "indicates the power of online computer games to channel human intuition and three-dimensional pattern matching skills to solve challenging scientific problems."

With names like Foldit Contenders Group and Foldit Void Crushers Group, the gamer teams were fired up for the task of real-world molecule modeling problems. The online protein folding game captivates thousands of avid players worldwide and engages the general public in scientific discovery. Players come from all walks of life. The game taps into their 3-D spatial abilities to rotate chains of amino acids in cyberspace. New players start at the basic level, "One Small Clash," proceed to "Swing it Around" and step ahead until reaching "Rubber Band Reversal." Direct manipulation tools, as well as assistance from a computer program called Rosetta, encourage participants to configure graphics into a workable protein model. Teams send in their answers, and UW researchers constantly improve the design of the game and its puzzles by analyzing the players' problem-solving strategies.

Figuring out the shape and misshape of proteins contributes to research on causes of and cures for cancer, Alzheimer's, immune deficiencies and a host of other disorders, as well as to environmental work on biofuels. Referring to this week's report of the online gamers' molecule solution opening new avenues for anti-viral drug research, Carter Kimsey, program director, National Science Foundation Division of Biological Infrastructure, observed, "After this discovery, young people might not mind doing their science homework. This is an innovative approach to getting humans and computer models to 'learn from each other' in real-time." The researchers noted that much attention has been given to the possibilities of crowd-sourcing and game playing in scientific discovery. Their results indicate the potential for integrating online video games into real-world science."

Beyond Screen Time: What Minecraft Teaches Kids
—*Source: By Rey Junco, The Atlantic, April 28, 2014*[31]

What can video games teach children?

How could schools learn from what's engaging about playing video games?

"Parents are faced with difficult choices about technology. The prevailing wisdom is that "screen time" is bad for children. But can Minecraft be lumped in with the rest of the things that kids might do on a computer or phone?

Minecraft is one of the most popular games in the United States with over 100 million registered users. It's not as flashy as typical video games—the graphics are lo-fi and 8-bit. At first glance, the game play seems incredibly simple: In creative mode, the goal is to build structures in an open 3D environment. In this way, Minecraft is different than other video games because the object is to construct, not to tear down. It's a video game, but it can also be classified as a building toy.

Minecraft offers youth the opportunity to explore an environment that is not rule-based like the rest of their lives. "On Minecraft, you can do whatever you want," a 9-year old Minecraft player told me. Not only does the open-world nature of Minecraft give children the opportunity to be more creative, it allows them to feel like they have a sense of control over themselves and their environment. It's an implicit way for them to develop self-regulation skills that then transfer to offline spaces—through having this freedom to create on Minecraft, they learn how to identify and work towards offline goals like finishing class assignments or graduating from college later in life.

Playing Minecraft teaches kids useful skills. The most clearly visible are visuospatial reasoning skills—learning how to manipulate objects in space in a way that helps them create dynamic structures. Visuospatial reasoning is the basis for more abstract forms of knowledge like the ability to evaluate whether a conclusion logically follows from its premises. Minecraft also helps youth learn how to collaborate to solve problems, and collaborative learning improves critical thinking skills that support motivation for learning. In other words, gameplay is about sharing knowledge and cooperating with your friends to build cool things.

Educators should take note and realize how they can leverage Minecraft. Some ideas include: letting kids share what they are building in the game and having them describe how they are interacting with their peers; setting up Minecraft hackathons where students who know how to mod can teach others how to do so; and devoting some class or after-school time to allowing kids to work on Minecraft-based assignments. It has been noted that Minecraft offers a way to bridge gaps between different kinds of learners, including autistic students.

Parents might be sick of their kids asking to play Minecraft, but consider what the game is teaching them. Where else are they learning some of these skills? Easily put: nowhere. Talk to them about what they are building and what they are learning. Encourage their cooperation with friends. When we encourage the enthusiasm they have for the game, we are also subtly communicating that we *like* for them to spend time creating, building, and cooperating with peers—values we want our children to develop as they work to reach their post-graduation goals."

How Analytics Are Turning Mobile Games Into Distraction Machines
—*Source: By Andrew Mayer, Digital Trends, June 20, 2016*[32]

When can playing video games become unhealthy?

How can my friends and family support me if I feel I'm having a problem?

"A few years before he passed away, Roger Ebert stirred up a lot of game fan anger when he claimed that "video games can never be art". In response, livid gamers submitted numerous examples of games that can (rightly) be used to refute that argument. But when it comes to the vast majority of games that people are playing on their mobile devices, Ebert was right. Over the last decade, we've seen the rise of mega-hits like *Farmville, Candy Crush Saga, Clash of Clans, Kim Kardashian: Hollywood, Hearthstone,* and many more of the "freemium" games that litter the mobile marketplace. They're free to play as long as you're willing to grind your way through a minimal experience. Otherwise, players are free to *spend* hundreds (or even thousands) of real dollars to buy the virtual currency needed to supercharge the experience.

Games have always been about manipulating the experience of the player, but data analytic techniques are bringing this to the next level, by focusing on profit over play. Game designers now employ the same techniques used by companies like Google and Facebook to optimize user behavior. By cleverly blending together hardcore sales tactics with the pure addictive rush of gambling gameplay, they can push players to the very brink of rage-quitting frustration without actually shoving them over into the abyss of never playing again. This isn't art. Instead these games are almost pure commerce: powerful engines of compulsion using arcane formulas derived from hardcore economics and big data designed to keep you playing (and paying) for days, weeks, or even months. And the trend has already grown to include PC and console games as well.

With hundreds of millions of players all over the world, freemium games are the first to reach a truly mass-market audience. Unlike traditional gamers, these "casual" players are looking for something that will help them to while away the hours while riding mass transit, waiting for dinner to cook, or even watching TV. They're simply looking for engaging repetitive fun, not something that will transport them to another universe, or blow their minds inside a virtual-reality experience. They're not looking to waste time or money playing something they don't like. Not long after games first appeared on the app store, it became apparent that the price most people were willing to pay for games on their mobile devices was ... nothing, or very close to it. Experiences that once sold for $60 on a console were now selling for a buck on your phone.

Developers responded to this race to the bottom by giving the games away for free. And in order to make money, they loaded them with in-app purchases that would appeal to players who were already hooked. Spending cash would allow you to speed the game up, avoid obstacles, and gain powerful abilities. Hardcore gamers have complained loud and long that these games are snake oil: addiction masquerading as entertainment. But the numbers don't lie: Freemium works. The most popular titles have millions of players delivering developers returns of hundreds of thousands of dollars every day.

The result has been that the app store for both iOS and Android devices are now jam-packed with thousands of freemium titles, and hundreds more appear daily. Each and every one of them is desperate to get noticed, and the cost of getting someone to play your game is now over $10 *per person*. That leaves desperate developers paying top dollar for celebrity marketing campaigns, getting A-list personalities such as Kate Upton and Arnold Schwarzenegger to appear in their Super Bowl commercials. With that kind of money on the line, they're forced to use every tool available to try and go after a player's accounts by going straight through their heads.

Data analytics are the most powerful tools in the box. Modern mobile games are constantly streaming data back the creators. They can (and mostly do) record every twitch and tap, from the first moment a player opens the game to (and this is particularly important) the final move they make before banishing the app back to whatever purgatory it goes to when they close it for the last time. This information gives the developers who use it effectively a great understanding of what players are likely to do, based on their similarity to other users doing similar things. By sorting their audience by *tendencies,* developers can gain deep insight into how players react, connect, and spend their time – and money.

Most players understand that they're being exposed, but don't care or understand what developers do with that data. Big data strip mines your experiences and interactions, grinding away everything except for your actions and tendencies, reducing the audience to its most basic wants and needs. And far too often, gameplay reflects this "hungry bird" mentality. Freemium games use this data to convince people to play, then push players to come back. Traditionally, games grabbed our attention by being fundamentally unique or exciting. Free-to-play games do it by becoming more addictive. The more time a player has invested, the more likely they are to spend money as a means to reap the rewards of that investment. And once they've spent, they're hooked. Players feed that addiction by converting dollars to in-game currencies that, once purchased, they can spend to minimize their effort while maximizing the rewards.

Developers have tried to resist, but if you're looking to make a profit in the mobile game space, there's little choice but to play along. The gatekeepers at Apple, Google, and Facebook get a significant percentage of every dollar spent, so they aren't fighting the tide. And besides, they were the ones who started optimizing data for profit years ago. I started doing social mobile design almost a decade ago, and during that time I've watched many developers who told me they would "never make *those* kinds of games" slowly succumb to the unending pressure of monetization. The same skills they once used to craft richer and more imaginative experiences are now used to optimize user attention experience for profit.

While freemium games may not be art, that's not to say there isn't any artistry left in their creation. Supercell, a company out of Stockholm, has managed to produce hits that are truly well designed, and precisely crafted. They understand that the key to making a great game with big data is by starting with an incredibly creative idea. Then they take the time to make sure every element is not only utterly polished, but fully tested with analytics. They combine an avalanche of user feedback with multiple iterations of development, crafting great ideas and throwing them away again and again, until every aspect of the game is honed to a gleaming finish that represents the pinnacle of development and data analysis. But the majority of developers don't have the millions of dollars it takes to devote that kind of time to craft their games. They also lack the millions more dollars needed to get acquire an audience from a pool that already has far more choices than hours to spend on their entertainment. For these developers, the tools they uses are often much more crude, and they're often coming perilously close to selling pure snake oil instead of a genuine cure for boredom.

No matter how users stumble into a freemium game, once they're hooked, almost every title is an unending staircase. They're designed so that each step up only leads to more options, and more opportunities to spend more money, and more time in the pursuit of the next goal. It's an infinite climb that, for some players, can have more in common with addiction than entertainment. When it comes to understanding freemium, the best advice may be the message that Matthew Broderick received back in the '80s when he tried to win the War Game against a machine: "The only way to win, is not to play!" But even if you know that, it doesn't mean that you still won't get hooked. I've seen the data to prove it."

LEARNING SCENARIOS

Scenario #1

It's 2:00 in the morning and you're in the middle of a marathon gaming session with your friends. This is as close as you've ever come to beating the game-- it would be an epic win! Looking at the clock, you realize you have only four and a half more hours before your alarm goes off for school. This is the third time in two weeks you've stayed up late into the night gaming. And tomorrow you have that math test. What are you going to do? How are you going to stop this cycle?

Scenario #2

Your parents are doing it again. They're always getting mad about how much time you spend playing video games. They're threatening to take away your gaming privileges. They don't understand. It's not like it used to be when they grew up. Playing video games helps you relax. You try to tell them it's better than sitting around watching television. What could you say to change their minds? What rules might you suggest as a compromise?

Scenario #3

You wish you knew what to do. Paying attention at school is so much harder than it used to be. You don't have any problem paying attention while at home. You wish school would let you learn the way you learn at home— a chance to figure things out like when you're playing a new video game. Games reward you for learning from your mistakes and sharing the answers with your friends. How could you help your teachers learn to support you more effectively at school? What would you recommend they change about their teaching?

HELPFUL STRATEGIES

ALL THINGS IN MODERATION: Researchers of video games have found both negative and positive health outcomes associated with gaming. Keep track of the number of hours you spend playing video games each week to determine if you might have a problem. Impose screen-time limits based on your overall usage to exceed no more than five hours during the school week[33].

PLAY VARIETY OF GAMES: It has been argued that not all games are created equal. Video game researchers have found evidence certain video games (particularly those that simulate combat) can increase aggressive behavior by desensitizing individuals to violent content[1]. Researchers have also found video gamers who played a range of games developed cognitive and social skills, like problem solving and collaboration, needed to succeed in the 21st century economy. Playing a variety of games (puzzle, platform, action, and sport games) helps maximize the benefits associated with playing video games while mitigating some of the problems[34]. Additionally, experts recommend playing video games, like Minecraft or World of Warcraft, that provide gamers with complex and complicated problems, encourage cooperation, reward experimentation, and promote knowledge sharing.

PLAY WITH FAMILY AND FRIENDS: Despite the stereotypes associated with lonely and isolated gamers, modern video games are frequently highly networked and incredibly social experiences. Video game researchers have found playing video games with real-world friends and family increased the sense of social connection and bonding between them. Additionally, researchers have found teens who play more socially networked games reported fewer relationship problems than those who seldom if ever played games at all[35].

WORK BEFORE PLAY: Adolescents and adults alike need to learn the basics of effective time management to experience success in life. Following this golden rule—work before play—provides gamers with a guiding principle to manage their desire to play video games with the responsibility of meeting deadlines and completing assignments. The inability to put this principle into practice is frequently a warning sign of compulsive behavior and addiction.

LEARNING TASKS

20-Minute Activity:

- **Standards**:
  - *Standard 3*: Students will demonstrate the ability to access valid information and products and services to enhance health.

  - *Standard 4*: Students will demonstrate the ability to use interpersonal communication skills to enhance health and avoid or reduce health risks.

- **Rationale**: Adolescents have access to a wider variety of video games—playable on increasingly immersive, mobile, and social platforms –than any other time in history. Teenagers need to learn how to enjoy this stimulating and engaging pastime in ways that don't come at the cost of their productivity, health and wellness. Teens should come to understand how to make decisions that enable them to play video games in appropriate and sustainable ways.

- **Learning Outcomes**: Students will be able to identify problems related to playing video games so they may identify issues related to one's sense of wellbeing before it becomes a problem.

- **Description of Activity**: Teachers will lead students in a think-pair-share discussion of the essential question: *"What role does escapism play in living a happy and healthy lifestyle?"* Students should consider as many responses as possible at this point to address this question. Students should also be encouraged to connect their responses to personal experiences whenever possible and appropriate.

- **Supporting Resources:**
  - Teens and Video Games: How Much Is Too Much? http://www.livescience.com/22281-teens-video-games-health-risks.html

  - Playing Video Games Can Help Or Hurt: http://www.npr.org/sections/health-shots/2014/08/08/338855459/playing-video-games-can-help-or-hurt-depending-on-who-you-ask

- o Study Finds Gamers Have Greater Cognitive Function:
  http://www.iflscience.com/brain/expert-gamers-show-greater-cognitive-function-their-amateur-counterparts/

- o Research Finds Video Games Boost Academics, Don't Affect Mental Health:
  http://www.gamesandlearning.org/2016/03/10/new-research-finds-video-games-may-boost-academics-dont-affect-mental-health/

- o TED Talk: Tom Chatfield, 7 Ways Games Reward The Brain:
  http://www.ted.com/talks/tom_chatfield_7_ways_games_reward_the_brain#t-922297

ONE-DAY ACTIVITY

- **Standards**:
  - o *Standard 2*: Students will analyze the influence of family, peers, culture, media, technology, and other factors on health behaviors.

  - o *Standard 5*: Students will demonstrate the ability to use decision-making skills to enhance health.

- **Rationale:** Adolescents (and adults) are spending historically unprecedented time playing video games during their free time. Teenagers need to learn how to be entertained by these technologies in ways that don't sacrifice their mental, physical, and social wellbeing. Teens should learn how to make decisions that empower them to play video games while maintaining their health and wellness.

- **Learning Outcomes:** Students will be able to identify the benefits of playing video games so they can make more informed and responsible decisions regarding their use of technology.

- **Description of Activity:** Teachers will help students write a proposal to game developers designing a new video game that promotes both mental and physical health. Students should draw on their own experience playing video games, as well as observing the behavior of friends and family. Students should also identify and investigate ways emerging technologies are being used to promote health and wellness across a growing number of situations and demographics.

- **Supporting Resources:**
  - o You Have Died Of Dysentery: How Games Will Revolutionize Education:

http://www.gamesandlearning.org/2014/01/17/you-have-died-of-dysentcry-how-games-will-revolutionize-education/

- Civic Engagement Through Video Games: http://www.edutopia.org/kurt-squire-games-civic-engagement-video

- TED Talk: Jane McGonigal, Gaming Can Make A Better World: http://www.ted.com/talks/jane_mcgonigal_gaming_can_make_a_better_world#t-1140140

- Why Girls Should Play More Video Games: http://www.businessinsider.com/why-girls-should-play-more-video-games-2013-7

- Video Games Are Key Elements in Friendships for Many Boys: http://www.pewinternet.org/2015/08/06/chapter-3-video-games-are-key-elements-in-friendships-for-many-boys/

ONE-WEEK ACTIVITY

- **Standards:**
  - *Standard 7*: Students will demonstrate the ability to practice health-enhancing behaviors and avoid or reduce health risks.

  - *Standard 8*: Students will demonstrate the ability to advocate for personal, family, and community health.

- **Rationale:** More and more adolescents and adults are playing video games as a way to cope with boredom and escape their everyday life. Teenagers need to learn how to enjoy video games in a way that takes advantages of the benefits and reduces the costs associated with these technologies. Teens should learn how to make decisions that enable them to play video games in healthy and sustainable ways.

- **Learning Outcomes:** Students will develop strategies to be mutually supportive of their peers so they can be pro-active in establishing a culture of healthy boundaries in playing video games.

- **Description of Activity:** Teachers will help students create a public service campaign to raise awareness regarding the benefits and risks associated with playing video games. Prior to developing their campaign, students should identify and investigate research related to common myths, stereotypes, and misconceptions regarding the ways teens (and adults) play video games. Students should form their campaign around emerging best practices for adolescents' daily use of technology. To extend this activity, students should plan, produce, and disseminate their campaign online coordinated across multiple social media platforms.

- **Supporting Resources:**
  - o Video Games and the Depressed Teenager: http://well.blogs.nytimes.com/2011/01/18/video-games-and-the-depressed-teenager/?_r=0

  - o Symptoms of Video Game Addiction In Teens: http://www.video-game-addiction.org/symptoms-computer-addiction-teens.html

  - o Teenagers Addicted to Video Games - 10 Important Things Parents Should Know: http://www.techaddiction.ca/teenagers-addicted-to-computer-games.html

  - o How To Help A Video Game Addict: http://www.psychguides.com/guides/how-to-find-help-treating-a-video-game-addict/

  - o Casinos Look To Video Games As A Draw For Millenials: http://www.nytimes.com/2016/07/07/technology/personaltech/casinos-look-to-video-games-as-a-draw-for-millennials.html?_r=0

---

[1] There Are 1.8 billion Gamers In The World. (2016, April 26). Retrieved from https://mygaming.co.za/news/features/89913-there-are-1-8-billion-gamers-in-the-world-and-pc-gaming-dominates-the-market.html.

[2] *Essential Facts About the Computer and Video Game Industry 2016* (pp. 1-11, Rep.). (2016). Entertainment Software Association..

[3] Frank, A. (2016, April 29). Take a look at the average American gamer in new survey findings. Retrieved from https://www.polygon.com/2016/4/29/11539102/gaming-stats-2016-esa-essential-facts.

[4] McGonigal, J. (2012). *Reality is broken: why games make us better and how they can change the world*. London: Vintage.

[5] McGonigal, J. (2010). *Gaming Can Make A Better World*. Lecture presented at TED 2010. Retrieved from https://www.ted.com/talks/jane_mcgonigal_gaming_can_make_a_better_world.

[6] Wortmann, F. (2013, January 09). OCD and Video Games. Retrieved from https://www.psychologytoday.com/blog/triggered/201301/ocd-and-video-games.

[7] Video game addiction 'not mental illnesses. (2007, June 25). Retrieved from https://www.newscientist.com/article/dn12131-video-game-addiction-not-mental-illness/.

[8] Nearly 1 In 10 Youth Gamers Addicted To Video Games. (2009, April 21). Retrieved from https://www.sciencedaily.com/releases/2009/04/090420103547.htm.

[9] Internet.Addiction.Org. (2011, April 25). Retrieved from http://internet.addictionblog.org/video-game-addiction-top-10-signs-and-symptoms-of-pathological-gaming/.

[10] Top 10 signs and symptoms of pathological gaming. (2011, April 25). Retrieved from http://internet.addictionblog.org/video-game-addiction-top-10-signs-and-symptoms-of-pathological-gaming/.

[11] Crew, B. (2015, April 28). Gamers Have More Grey Matter And Better Brain Connectivity, Study Suggests. Retrieved from https://www.sciencealert.com/gamers-have-more-grey-matter-and-better-brain-connectivity-study-suggests

[12] Bolton, D. (2016, March 09). Video games may improve children's intellectual and social skills, study finds. Retrieved from http://www.independent.co.uk/news/science/video-games-children-learning-intelligence-social-skills-study-a6920961.html.

[13] Abbott, A. (2013, September 4). Gaming improves multitasking skills. Retrieved from http://www.nature.com/news/gaming-improves-multitasking-skills-1.13674

[14] Duggan, M. (2015). *Gaming and Gamers* (pp. 1-23, Report). Washington, D.C.: Pew Research Center: Internet, Science, & Tech.

[15] Vincent, J. (2014, November 10). Long-term US study finds no links between violent video games and youth violence. Retrieved from http://www.independent.co.uk/life-style/gadgets-and-tech/gaming/long-term-us-study-finds-no-links-between-violent-video-games-and-youth-violence-9851613.html

[16] Violent video games found not to affect empathy. (2017, March 8). Retrieved from https://www.sciencedaily.com/releases/2017/03/170308081057.htm.

[17] Bushman, B. J., & Anderson, C. A. (2009). Comfortably Numb: Desensitizing Effects of Violent Media on Helping Others. *Psychological Science, 20*(3), 273-277.

[18] Kennedy-Moore, E. (2015, September 14). The Truth About Violent Video Games and Kids, Part 1-3. Retrieved from https://www.psychologytoday.com/blog/growing-friendships/201509/the-truth-about-violent-video-games-and-kids-part-1-3[19] Kovess-Masfety, V., Keyes, K., Hamilton, A., Hanson, G., Bitfoi, A., Golitz, D., . . . Pez, O. (2016). Is time spent playing video games associated with mental health, cognitive and social skills in young children? *Social Psychiatry and Psychiatric Epidemiology, 51*(3), 349-357.

[19] Kovess-Masfety, V., Keyes, K., Hamilton, A., Hanson, G., Bitfoi, A., Golitz, D., . . . Pez, O. (2016). Is time spent playing video games associated with mental health, cognitive and social skills in young children? *Social Psychiatry and Psychiatric Epidemiology, 51*(3), 349-357.

[20] Nath, T. (2016, June 13). Investing in Video Games: This Industry Pulls In More Revenue Than Movies, Music. Retrieved from http://www.nasdaq.com/article/investing-in-video-games-this-industry-pulls-in-more-revenue-than-movies-music-cm634585

[21] Parkin, S. (2015, June 15). Gaming Your Brain. Retrieved from http://www.espn.com/espn/story/_/id/13065280/video-game-data-science-profit.

[22] Alon Bonder, V. (2016, December 25). 5 lessons from the $15 billion virtual goods economy. Retrieved from https://venturebeat.com/2016/12/25/5-lessons-from-the-15-billion-virtual-goods-economy/

[23] Rigney, R. (2012, September 18). FarmVille 2 Ain't No Game, It's the Ultimate Perpetual-Motion Money Machine. Retrieved from https://www.wired.com/2012/09/farmville-2/

[24] Sohn, E. (2014, June 24). What Video Games Can Teach Us. Retrieved from https://www.sciencenewsforstudents.org/article/what-video-games-can-teach-us

[25] Lenhart, A. (2015). *Video Games Are Key Elements in Friendships for Many Boys* (pp. 41-52, Report).

[26] Miller, A. (2012, June 25). Game-Based Learning to Teach and Assess 21st-Century Skills. Retrieved from https://www.edutopia.org/blog/game-learning-21st-century-skills-andrew-miller.

[27] Szoldra, P. (2016, September 19). This California university will pay half your college tuition just for playing video games. Retrieved from http://www.businessinsider.com/uci-scholarship-for-video-games-2016-9.

[28] McGonigal, J. (2012). *Reality is broken: why games make us better and how they can change the world.* London: Vintage.

[29] Gray, L. (2011, September 19). Gamers succeed where scientists fail. Retrieved from http://www.washington.edu/news/2011/09/19/gamers-succeed-where-scientists-fail/

[30] Junco, R. (2014, April 28). Beyond 'Screen Time:' What Minecraft Teaches Kids. Retrieved from http://www.theatlantic.com/technology/archive/2014/04/beyond-screen-time-what-a-good-game-like-minecraft-teaches-kids/361261/

[31] Mayer, A. (2016, June 17). It's a numbers game! How analytics are turning games into distraction machines. Retrieved from http://www.digitaltrends.com/gaming/how-analytics-are-turning-games-into-distraction-machines/

[32] Middlebrook, H. (2016, October 21). New screen time rules for kids, by doctors. Retrieved from http://www.cnn.com/2016/10/21/health/screen-time-media-rules-children-aap/.

[33] Bergland, C. (2016, April 09). Violent Video Games Can Trigger Emotional Desensitization. Retrieved from https://www.psychologytoday.com/blog/the-athletes-way/201604/violent-video-games-can-trigger-emotional-desensitization.

[34] Needleman, S. E. (2015, September 10). Should Parents Play Videogames With Their Children? Retrieved from https://www.wsj.com/articles/should-parents-play-videogames-with-their-children-1441899567.

[35] Kovess-Masfety, V., Keyes, K., Hamilton, A., Hanson, G., Bitfoi, A., Golitz, D., . . . Pez, O. (2016). Is time spent playing video games associated with mental health, cognitive and social skills in young children? *Social Psychiatry and Psychiatric Epidemiology, 51*(3), 349-357.

CHAPTER TWELVE

Online Shopping Addiction

What are the primary symptoms of online shopping addiction?

Why do people become addicted to online shopping?

How can online addiction be addressed?

BEHAVIORS AND THEMES

SCALE AND SCOPE: According to leading researchers, denial is one of the primary factors in addictive behavior. It would be naive for you to think that those who are addicted would voluntarily admit to being uncontrollably obsessed with shopping. In a survey conducted in 2014 by CreditDonkey.com, findings suggest that a significant number of consumers exhibit, at least, some of the key signs of being a shopaholic.[1]

Essentially, the tell tale signs include shame and guilt (some 36.7 percent of participants admitted to these feelings). 20.5 percent said that they routinely hid purchases from loved ones; while 26.7 percent habitually checked credit scores at least weekly. Surprisingly, only 4.7 percent reported that they had been identified as an online shopping addict.[2]

Online shopping has exploded in the United Sates in recent years. For instance, in 1998 total online sales were $7.8 billion. By 2014, that figure had swelled to more than $347 billion, according to Statistic Brian Research Institute. The American Psychological Association found that approximately 7 percent of Americans can be labeled as having a shopping addiction; and about 70 percent go online to make purchases at least once per month. Therefore, it is reasonable to assume, based on this statistical data that the internet has contributed to an extraordinary increase in compulsive shopping behaviors.[3]

Easy access to credit doesn't help. A remarkable number of those with troublesome spending and shopping habits has some mental health professionals worried. Although it is difficult to pinpoint exactly, estimates indicate that there are nearly 15 million Americans who would qualify as shopaholics. Today, credit card has exceeded $1 trillion.[4]

PROBLEM DEFINED: Technology and the use of the internet plays a vital role in the lives of most Americans. The reality that most offline activities are now found online is not surprising. As a matter of fact, it has become increasingly difficult to differentiate offline shopping from online shopping. Many consumers comparison shop online before even stepping foot in a brick and mortar store.

AMONG THE SURVEY'S OTHER FINDINGS

- 31.7 percent of respondents said they "almost always" or "frequently" purchase things just because they're on sale.
- 18.1 percent said they often purchase items that they don't need or didn't plan to buy when they set out to shop.
- Nearly 11 percent of those polled said they frequently shop to improve their mood.
- 47.4 percent said they experience a rush of excitement when they go shopping.
- 24.4 percent admitted they have items in their closets that are still in shopping bags or have price tags.
- 18.5 percent said they have frequent arguments over money.
- 19.1 percent said their main reason for using credit cards is to pay for items when they don't have enough money.

Source: CreditDonkey.com[5]

For individuals who are addicted to shopping, the internet can be a dangerous tool. Because online shopping happens in a simulated context, some shoppers forget that they are spending real money. The indicators for both offline and online shopping addiction are similar with the only distinction being the convenience afforded shoppers by the internet.[6]

Because our online behavior is routinely being tracked by marketers, companies doing business online know exactly what you want and have begun to creatively prod consumers to their shopping cart. It really does not matter whether you are online to shop or simply browsing the net. Therefore, that dress that you looked at last month mysteriously and magically appears in a pop up on your screen while you're online.

Advertisers and marketers have become highly proficient in exploiting shoppers by focusing on a concept psychologists call "cue-reactivity." This term refers to the excitement and stimulation you receive from shopping. You are cleverly lured towards hitting the "buy" button as a result of the company catching and holding your attention just long enough to get you to click.[7]

However, this strategy only works if the company succeeds in creating a "craving," an almost overpowering yearning to buy when you see their product.

These two theories—"cue-reactivity" and "craving"--derive from behavioral addiction. It can also include issues such as becoming hooked on cybersex and gambling.

Shopping addiction is called many things; for instance, *pathological buying, compulsive buying, buying addiction,* and *oniomania.*[8]

Mental health professionals continue to grapple with how to classify online shopping addiction. They question whether it is an impulse control disorder, an obsessive-compulsive disorder or simply an addiction

IMPACT ON HEALTH

MENTAL AND EMOTONAL: Being addicted to online shopping can prove detrimental to your personal relationships, emotional health and social lives.

Online shopping addiction is a part of shopping addiction, in general. It is an extension of one of five distinctive categories of internet addiction disorder. Therefore, those addicted to online shopping is by default hooked on the internet. These impulse behaviors have no limits and overtime become uncontrollable. Just like all other addictions, there are deleterious outcomes that manifest from the overwhelming need to chronically shop. As time passes, the intense pleasure of online shopping takes precedence over other life priorities such as relationships, financial prudence and, in some cases, your employment.

Because the internet provides virtual experiences, the lack of an actual transfer of money exacerbates the online shopping condition. Therefore, an addicted shopper might be compelled to make even more purchases while continuing to chase a "shopper's high." The detachment between buying an item and your wallet serves as further encouragement to spend. The rush of endorphins only bolsters the "shopper's high." It is very much like the feelings that drug addicts and compulsive gamblers experience.[9]

Much like with drugs and gambling, the addict makes every effort to conceal the addiction. If you begin to routinely hide bills, receipts, statements, shopping bags, boxes and bank documents, you are very likely a shopaholic. You might notice that you begin to cherry pick your lies. For example, you may admit that you went online to shop but fail to disclose how much you actually spent.

Additional emotional signs that you are a shopaholic include the following:

- Spending more than you can afford
- Shopping as a reaction to feeling angry or depressed
- Shopping as a way to feel less guilty about a previous shopping spree
- Harming relationships due to spending or shopping too much
- Losing control of the shopping behavior

PHYSICAL: Unlike that vast majority of addictions, online shopping addiction does not come with noticeable physical symptoms. However, those with a shopping addiction will exhibit emotional signs. If one could point to a physical manifestation of online shopping  addiction it may well be a deterioration of personal financial health. In the short term, the symptoms of online shopping addiction might feel good. You could experience a sense of euphoria once a transaction has been completed but this feeling is extremely short lived. Additionally, online shopping addiction may come with profound feelings of guilt and anxiety that might result in you going back to shop again in order to experience the shoppers high again and again. The need for immediate gratification and the desire for control can be compared to other addictions like gambling, eating disorders and sexual addictions. The goal is to free yourself from feelings of anxiety, stress and depressive episodes.

In the long term, the effects of online shopping addiction differ in scale and scope. Initially, online shopping addicts will encounter a range of financial issues and become plagued with crushing debt. Not only is there a risk of exceeding credit card limits, but some even go as far as to mortgage homes or inappropriately use a company expense account for personal purchases; which could lead to criminal charges for fraud. Further, online shopping addiction has a negative effect on personal relationships leading to break up and even divorce. Therefore, physical symptoms may also include distancing yourself form family members.

For the online shopping addict, going on one or even two shopping binges does not satisfy your craving to continue to needlessly buy. Regardless of the myriad of negative consequences, you continue to engage in the same online shopping behaviors. Most of the time, you spend simply to make a purchase. You don't need that pair of shoes and may never even wear that article of clothing. You hide price tags, receipts, and lie consistently about money. Some of the behavior patterns you might exhibit are:

- Having a sense of euphoria when spending money
- Commonly spending more than you can afford
- Spending unusual amounts of time and/or money buying on the Internet, in catalogues, or on shopping channels
- Frequently spending time shopping that could be spent with family, friends or on work
- Feeling guilty, ashamed, embarrassed or confused after shopping or spending
- Hiding purchases and receipts and lying about purchases
- Feeling lost without credit cards or a check book
- Feeling on edge, agitated, or irritable when you have not been able to shop.

CREATES DEPRESSION, ADDICTION AND COMPULSION: For the online shopping addict, depression and anxiety are almost a given. Attempting to treat your addiction to shopping, you will need to address other mental health issues. While seeking to address online shopping addiction and other associated problems, you must find a program that addresses, not only the shopping addiction, but the other problems simultaneously.

Online shopping addiction is defined as excessive, out of control and inappropriate spending. The impulsive nature of this behavior leaves you vulnerable to a further decline into the abyss of uncontrollable shopping. In the United States, going to the mall and shopping is engrained in our collective psyche. It is not difficult to engage in excessive shopping and not realize that you have entered into a dangerous pattern. Often called shopaholism, online shopping addiction can destroy your life, your family relationships, and your family's financial health.

Just like compulsive shopping, your online shopping addiction can potentially harm your social, personal, and emotional health. In many ways, it is even more harmful than shopping at brick and mortar stores. One of the biggest issues is that shopping with credit cards online gives the false impression that you are not spending real money. Just like shopping at stores, online shopping provides a thrill from the purchase and the acquisition of the goods. It represents a false connection between emotional, physical, psychological and financial consequences.

Perhaps the greatest factor in online shopping addiction is the fact that you don't leave with merchandise in hand. This leads to a need to make a greater number of purchases until you reach the shopper's high. Auctions online are even more dangerous to the online shopping addict. The bidding process serves as enticement, providing a way to strategize and win against other shoppers. Ultimately it becomes less about the merchandise and more about winning.

The volume of available goods is another lure. You can head to Amazon or eBay, for instance, to buy a single item and end up buying several things that you don't need simply because of the sheer amount of items available. The feeling that you are somehow part of a community that shares a commonality creates a comfort level that is very appealing. The experience with the auction, for example, builds a certain level of self assurance because you may become dependent upon the flattering comments that may be posted on your profile page. The fact that virtually every American home or school provides internet access, impulse shopping online has become a serious issue. The 24/7/365 access can also serve as a trigger with the addiction literally at your fingertips. This truth makes it nearly impossible to refrain from addictive behavior[1]

- Addicts neglect their families.
- When you're not online shopping, you're often thinking about it.
- You overspend and regularly buy things you don't need just to get a buzz.
- You lie about your purchases.
- You rack up major bills.

For many people, online shopping addiction develops as a result of the brain experiencing a rush of endorphins while shopping. As you continue to shop, the flood of dopamine and endorphins are discharged and the feeling turns into an addiction. It is estimated that between 10 and 15 percent of the American populous is currently vulnerable and inclined to these feelings.

In the vast majority of cases, it is hard to discern whether you, a friend, or family member has become an online shopaholic. We often hear others talk about the idea of "retail therapy." This is when certain stressors overwhelm you and you begin to feel as though you need to do something to reward yourself. This alone is not a serious issue. However, you must be mindful that the need for "retail therapy" can also develop into online shopping addiction. Be aware of the signs and symptoms that online shopping addicts exhibit so that you have an idea of what to look for. If you are suffering from online shopping addiction, you are very likely to not really care about the price of items—you'll pay any price. The sense of power and control can be captivating.

Additionally, a spending addiction serves as a way to avoid negative feelings. Online shopping can become a crutch in an attempt to deaden these feelings—at least in the interim. Beware of episodes when you are feeling lonely, angry, bored, insecure, or empty because these thoughts can lead to compulsive behavior; resulting in over spending and shopping addiction. While shopping might alleviate these negative feelings, it is only temporary. However, attempting to deal with the addiction may very well cause the same negative feelings to resurface. The short-lived pleasure creates the impression of power and control. The result is that you begin to ignore, diminish or fail to see the long-term injurious effects of the addictive conduct.[10]

There are five elements for depression and online shopping addiction as illustrated in the graph below. Additionally, there are three other factors that can make you susceptible to online shopping addiction especially vulnerable to an online shopping addiction. Some may overlap; for instance, pathological buying and anxiety—social anxiety specifically. Some people don't like the idea of going into a congested shopping environment. Therefore, online shopping is ideal. The danger is that this isolation only serves to enhance avoidance behaviors.

1. Pathological shopping often produces shame and regret about shopping. You want to hide your habit. The anonymity of online shopping makes it worse.

2. Online shopping addicts enjoy a wide variety of goods and the constant availability of items. Online shopping nurtures pleasure in those who love many options. On top of this, the online stores never close. This can spark habitual cravings for shopping.

3. Online shopping appeals to those who like instant gratification.

Empirical data continues to illustrate that the typical online shopping addict experiences depression and other maladies like substance abuse, or eating disorders. Like all other forms of addiction, spending by the online shopper spins out of control.[11] Our materialistic society so immersed in conspicuous consumption tends to promote an atmosphere of where you are encouraged to accrue possessions today and not deal with the cost until later.

The truth is, our culture places a great deal of weight on material possessions like clothing. Many retailers utilize celebrities to endorse and pitch their products. This subconscious advertising encourages you to spend in order to buy in order to fit in, and accomplish a certain look or style. It's everywhere. Shopping channels are now broadcast 24 hours a day. The online shopping behavior is designed to induce feelings of satisfaction and happiness that comes from the power associated with achieving instant gratification. Nevertheless, the high you feel from the buying, ordering, and charging does not last. The side effects of guilt and regret sends you right back to the online shopping venue because you need to get the emotional high back.

HOW OFTEN DO YOU PURCHASE ITEMS YOU DON'T NEED OR PLAN TO BUY?

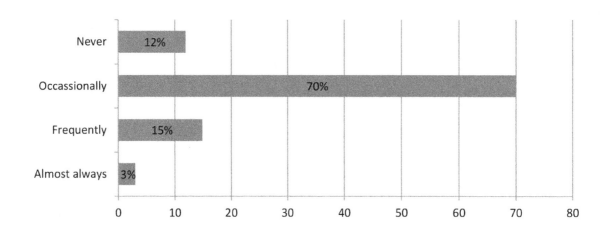

HOW OFTEN DO YOU PURCHASE THINGS JUST BECAUSE THEY ARE ON SALE?

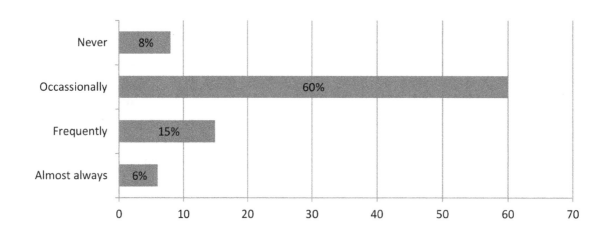

HOW OFTEN DO YOU SHOP TO IMPROVE YOUR MOOD?

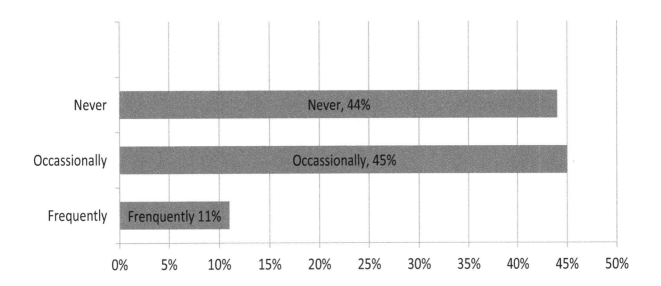

Source: CreditDonkey.com, 2013[12]

Habitual and addictive online shopping has been shown to cause interpersonal, job related, financial and family issues.[13] The resulting consequences are essentially the same as that of other addictive behavior.

The destruction of relationships will occur when you engage in over spending; particularly when you begin to attempt to hide purchases and lie about spending. Because you become so engrossed with the addictive behavior, you begin to spend far less time with important people in your life. Additionally, it is an almost certainty that school performance will suffer greatly.

The financial consequences that arise from addictive spending have far reaching and damaging results. Too often the harm is not discovered until such huge amounts have been spent leaving you with debts that are almost impossible to pay off. The debt then forces a change in lifestyle choices. [14] If not, the consequences will prove disastrous. It is estimated that online sales account for more than $2.2 trillion in retail sales annually.

The term compulsive buying refers to your intent to purchase a certain item and the actual item purchased; and they are completely different. For instance, you sign on to an online store to buy one pair of shoes. If it turns into a 20 pair purchase, you are a compulsive buyer. The compulsion to buy is so pervasive that cost and budget restrictions no longer factor into the decision making process. It should not come as a surprise, therefore, that your emotional state will oscillate from delight to disappointment almost instantly after having made the purchase and logging off the website.

For the vast majority of us shopping is an ordinary experience. Most of the time very little thought goes into the purchases. Online shopping has become just as normal as walking through the mall. However, the internet has ushered in a greatly increased capability for shopping anywhere and at anytime. You can shop as long as you want without interruption from pushy sales staff chasing a commission. Online shopping is a seamless endeavor.

With the escalation of e-commerce and online auctions, spending money has never been so easy. Online shopping can produce compulsivity. When you shop online, you are often caught in the fantasy that you aren't really spending money, it's more like a game where the things you want materialize out of thin air without the exchange of currency. As a result, you keep going back again, and again, and yet again. You are now possibly an online shopping addict.

KEY CONCEPTS

Compulsion-- An abnormal impulse to buy things, or a condition characterized by such impulses. Includes compulsive buying, pathological buying, and buying addiction.

Shopper's High—A rush shoppers experience upon making impulse purchases that is quickly abated shortly after the purchase is made.

e-Commerce--Commercial transactions conducted electronically on the Internet.

Cue-Reactivity--Excitement from online ads that attempt to capitalize on emotional purchasing.

Craving--An intense desire for some particular thing.

Pathological Buying--Feeling preoccupied with shopping and feeling powerless to control the need to buy.

REAL WORLD SITUATIONS

My Life: "I spent online until my credit cards were maxed out and my bank accounts were overdrawn, and then I spent more."

—*Source: Britni De La Cretaz, January 5, 2016*

What are some key causes and effects of online shopping addiction?

What are the early symptoms of online shopping addiction?

I've always really loved *things*.

It's never mattered much what *kind* of things, as long as they were new to me. From the time I was small, I would turn to my mother while watching commercials and say, "Mom, I *need* that." It was never a want; it was always a need.

I was incapable of going into a store without buying something — I always found a reason for needing whatever thing it was, even if I couldn't really afford it. When I was bored, I'd go to the mall. I'd wander the long concourses lined with shops, see something I wanted in a store window, and tell myself, "If I'm still thinking about it in three days, I'll go back and get it." And I was *always* thinking about that thing three days later, because once I saw something I wanted, I couldn't get it out of my head. It became an obsession.

When I was a teenager, I'd beg my parents to buy me things and, eventually, they'd give in. They spoiled me rotten and I took advantage of it. If I couldn't get my mom to buy me what I wanted, I'd bat my eyes at my father. I became an expert at manipulation. Obviously, I was lucky to have been born into a family with the resources to spoil me, but because I'd always been able to have almost anything I wanted, I never really learned the value of money.

When I went away to college, I realized quickly that if I wanted to keep buying things, I'd need a strategy. So I opened several credit cards — the perfect solution to my problem. I figured I'd pay my monthly minimums and I could continue to spend the way I wanted to.

At first, I was in heaven. I spent most of my money on clothes and shoes. I was sure that these things would make me happier and cooler. I thought they'd get me the attention and validation I craved. I thought I wouldn't be okay without them.

I maxed out every single one of my credit cards in a matter of months. I couldn't even pay my minimums, and I panicked. Ashamed, I didn't tell anyone about my financial situation. I began throwing away the unopened bills. Then the debt companies started calling, sometimes up to 20 times a day.

I changed my number.

Despite my lack of cash, I didn't stop acquiring things. I couldn't just *stop* when I ran out of money. My bank account was always overdrawn, and more than one bank closed my account when I couldn't pay my hefty overdraft fees. I didn't tell anyone how empty I felt inside.

Eventually, I ended up in rehab for another one of my addictions — alcohol. It was there that I was forced to recognize my shopping addiction for what it was. Both addictions came from the same place: the feeling of emptiness.

Getting clean was the hardest thing I've ever done. Not only did I have to stop drinking and using drugs, but I had to stop spending money in destructive ways. I had to learn to live within my means and confront the damage I'd done to my life.

The first step was opening all the bills that had piled up at my house while I was in treatment. It was the only way to know what I owed and to make a plan to deal with my debt. I had a combination of credit card bills and medical bills, some of which I'd been ignoring for years. One by one, I opened each and every envelope--simply doing that was incredibly freeing.

The next thing I had to do was figure out what I could afford to pay. Because I had to make so many different payments, I couldn't afford to pay more than $10 per month on any one bill. So I called the creditors up and explained my situation. I told them I wanted to start to pay them back, but I couldn't afford to make my minimum payments. I started small, and eventually, when I began to make more money, I increased my payments.

It's been four years, and my life is drastically different today. I've paid off most of my debt, and I was lucky enough to have some help from my parents. My grandparents helped with some of the payments, too, and I've paid them back over a couple of years. But that doesn't mean that my shopping addiction is a thing of the past — I still struggle with spending money and buying things I don't need.

That's why I now adhere to a very strict budget to make sure that I stay within my means: My husband and I sit down every week and go over our budget and note how much money was spent and on what.

I'm still living with the repercussions of my disease: I don't have a single credit card — my credit is terrible, and I'm working to rebuild it. I've tried to get a single credit card so that I can begin to build back the credit I destroyed, but I can't get approved for any of them. I've also been denied bank loans for home improvements.

My shopping addiction nearly destroyed my life. Trying desperately to medicate my self-loathing with *stuff* left me financially and spiritually bankrupt. But hitting rock bottom taught me a crucial lesson: No gorgeous pair of shoes or one-of-a-kind dress will ever be a substitute for the self-love I've found through recovery.

REAL WORLD SITUATIONS

My Online Shopping Addiction Was Costing Me Hundreds a Month
—*Source: Natasha Burton, Grow Magazine, May 2016*

How does online shopping addiction impact mental, emotional and physical health?

What are the biological triggers for online shopping addiction?

I am an admitted Amazon addict. As a freelance writer who works from home, I enjoy the convenience of not having to leave my desk, or get out of my sweats, to buy both essentials (toilet paper and dog food) and non-essentials (the Shonda Rhimes memoir). The mega online retailer has everything *and* the kitchen sink. I know this because I bought mine via "1-Click," that handy little feature that saves your payment and shipping information, and makes procuring almost anything as easy as, well, one click.

But earlier this year, my shopping was getting out of my hand. My Amazon Visa is linked to my account—to take advantage of points that can be redeemed for more Amazon credit, of course—and my monthly balance was sometimes topping $1,000. My spending went from mostly needs with a fun purchase here and there to using 1-Click on the mobile app whenever the mood struck. A particularly persuasive beauty commercial prompted me to buy an expensive night cream, while reading an article about new ways to de-stress compelled me to order an adult coloring book. When you shoot the breeze with both the UPS and USPS guy daily as they deliver packages, you've got a problem.

So when the Grow editors asked if I wanted to participate in a new series focused on identifying and cutting down the bulge in our budgets—in other words, the area where we know we're consistently overspending—I signed up. Then I embarked on a two-week break from my favorite online retailer to change my impulse-spending habits and give my bank account a break.

Here are the most valuable lessons I learned.

1. The wish list provides a happy medium. Each time I felt the urge to click, I instead added the item in question to my Amazon wish list to revisit later. Not only did this ensure I stuck to my no-spending goal, it also showed me when prices dropped, providing unexpected discounts when I eventually ordered a couple (necessary!) things post-fast. Even better, the break allowed me a cooling-off period to evaluate whether I *really* needed items like that retro bread box for my kitchen. (Turns out, I could live without it.)

Two months later, the wish list is still helping me save money—I've found that prices tend to fall between 2 to 10 percent if I wait a little while to pull the trigger—and avoid emotional buys I don't care about a day later.

A lot of retail sites offer wish list features. But if they don't, you can simply screenshot the item or write down the info and give yourself some time to think about whether you really need it. There are also services like Slick deals Price Tracker and CamelCamelCamel that will alert you when an item's price has dropped.

2. Time is money. When I was in full-blown 1-Click-happy mode, I'd sometimes buy without thinking, knowing I could return whatever I didn't like later. But this meant I spent time printing out labels, re-packing boxes and making trips to UPS to drop off returns. Now, I'm not wasting precious time keeping track of which labels I've already printed or habitually buying packing tape because I'm more thoughtful before I click "buy." And that means I no longer see the folks at UPS multiple times a week.

3. It pays to shop around. I'd always assumed Amazon's prices were lower than brick-and-mortar stores, not to mention other online retailers—but the fast forced me to test my theory. Many items were cheaper at Amazon. But using the barcode-scan feature on Amazon's app, I was surprised to learn that my body lotion is actually cheaper at CVS and paper towels cost less when purchased with my grocery store's rewards card. When our bathroom faucet stopped working mid-way through the two weeks, I thought I'd have to cheat to buy a new one—but I found the one I wanted on Amazon was actually less expensive on Jet.com.

Overall, my Amazon fast kept me from making impulse purchases or buying items I liked but didn't really need, potentially saving me hundreds of dollars. While I'm back to being an Amazon shopper, I'm much wiser in my approach now, which has allowed me to maintain that decreased spending rate. Moving forward, I'm planning to focus on necessities only and fill my wish list with splurge-worthy items I can buy one or two at a time once I've stuck to my plan for several months in a row.

REAL WORLD SITUATIONS

I have a shopping addiction: Am I a Compulsive Shopper?

—*Source: http://www.experienceproject.com/stories/Have-A-Shopping-Addiction/818537,*

December 8, 2009

How does online shopping addiction contribute to anxiety? Can compulsivity be overcome without professional intervention?

Hi, my name is Serafina, and I'm a shopaholic.

I want to write about how I overcame (well, how I am *overcoming*) my addictions. An addicted person must reach "rock bottom" to become aware of the fact that they have a problem, but once they can acknowledge their problem, the only place to go is up. As Tyler Durden would say, "It's only after you've lost everything that you're free to do anything." I don't know how I overcame my compulsive addiction to spend money. There were no "Debtors Anonymous" meetings or counseling sessions with the purpose of uncovering a traumatizing childhood experience while laying on a couch. There were, however, appointments with my mother and a psychiatrist, as well as prescriptions for antidepressants and amphetamines, which, in retrospect, seem to have fixed nothing.

I have attributed my addiction to symptoms of anxiety and OCD, which I was diagnosed with in 4th grade. I was also diagnosed with ADD in 4th grade, but when no medicine was found to effectively relieve my symptoms, I stopped taking them altogether. Their negative effects outweighed the potential positive benefits. At 16, I was diagnosed again and put on a new medication. Since then, I have been switching back and forth from methylphenidate to amphetamine salts for periods of a few months to a year to keep them from losing their effectiveness. To my family, 16 also seems to be the age I was when my compulsive "need to spend" manifested itself.

I am now nearly19 years old and $10,000 in debt. And no, I did not buy a car or a college education with that money. Actually, I still cannot account for many of the things I bought. I received two credit cards in March, 2009. One had a $1,500.00 credit limit and the other a $4,000.00 credit limit. Now, it seems necessary to mention that these cards were issued to me two months after eighteenth birthday with no proof of income. How many 18 year-olds do you know who fill out credit applications by answering "student" to the employment question that are capable of paying a bill for a credit card that has a $4,000 limit? During the summer, in an attempt to help me better deal with my debt, my mother consolidated my credit card debt into a loan. She had the intention of helping me, however, I was only able to see this as an opportunity pay off my credit card with the loan, continue making purchases with the card, and go into more debt. Finally, last month, I reached the limit on both cards. This left me with no choice but to cancel the accounts.

During the summer, I had a boyfriend who acknowledged my behavior but never did anything to change it. Besides myself, he was the only person who did not make me feel bad about how much money I was spending, so I appreciated having him around. We broke up a week before school started. School became a huge struggle for me, because I was dealing with a situation in which I had to meet completely new people while taking new classes and struggling with addiction and social anxiety. At the time, I was unaware that I had a problem with spending money and even at times when I didn't go out, I would do things like purchase "virtual" money for Facebook applications such as Farmville and order take-out. I would purchase music on itunes, even though I knew I already had it somewhere on CD. I had so much stuff that I could never find anything. (Hoarding is another symptom of OCD.)

I knew I had a problem, but I attributed it to my recent break-up and lack of a job rather than the real issue. I became depressed and even failed my first class. I also would frequently get into arguments with my family. I'm normally very close to my Mom, but I would find myself lying to her about anything that had anything to do with spending money – even to the extent of lying about where I was, just in case I might possibly be in a place where money could be spent. I would lie to my sisters or ask them to lie for me, just to hide the fact that I was spending money. I knew it would upset my mother. It began to construct a divide between my family, and though I know they'll always be there for me, it was a struggle to get past the point where I was afraid of being disconnected from them forever because of my addiction.

Finally, one month, my mother asked to see my credit card bills after I received a speeding ticket (my first and hopefully only, ever.) I'm considering this my breaking point because after that week, I haven't had a relapse. I cancelled the cards (which had both just reached their limit.) It has been about a month and a half since this occurrence, and I'd like to talk more about the recovery process as well as some of the ways I've been able to change the way I think about things, but I'm new to this website, and I'd like to see if I can get some feedback first. I obviously haven't completely recovered, I've still got a long way to go. People who struggle with addictions usually do so even after treatment and recovery, but eventually I'd like to think I'll be able to deal with my addiction without having to think so hard about it.

Like I said, I'm new to this website, and this is something I haven't really been able to talk about with people before. So, if you're struggling with a similar situation or have any feedback to give me, I would love to hear from you!

LEARNING SCENARIOS

Scenario #1

You are a popular student, and recently celebrated your 17th birthday. Your family is a first generation middle class family who lives is an upper-middle class suburban community in Chicago where most residents own spacious homes, drive late model, expensive cars, and who appear to live the American dream. Your neighbors have legacies of wealth dating back for generations. It is a forgone conclusion that children from these families will inherit positions and power and influence. Many families have servants, gardeners, nannies, or other caretakers.

However, your family hides a dark secret. Although both your parents are professionals in their respective fields, they struggle to "keep up with the Joneses." Their living expenses exhaust their combined incomes each month. Nevertheless, in an attempt to keep up appearances they gave you a credit card in your name. There was no indication of a "limit" or any discussion about spending.

Your friends are from more prominent families and routinely exhibit out of control spending. However, their families can afford it. Having learned the "masking" behavior from your parents, you began engaging in the same reckless spending behavior as your friends.

Upon receiving the first statement, your parents were shocked to discover that you had charged more than $10,000 online within the first few days of receiving the card. Upon learning this, they cancelled your charging privileges immediately. However, the damage was already done. They began to notice that you have suddenly become withdrawn and started isolating yourself from friends and other social activities. Your mental, emotional and social well being has clearly changed. You have become irritable and often agitated easily. You are showing classic signs of depression as a result of the loss of your ability to make impulse purchases. Your out of control spending also had a negative impact upon your family dynamics. In order to pay your debt, your parents were forced to forego other pressing financial obligations that severely strained their marriage. Soon, the loud arguments and fights could be heard by neighbors. Still, you continued to insist that you are not to blame and that your purchases were not a problem. That next night, you stole a credit card from your dad's wallet, went on-line and binge and spent another $6,000. How should your parents address your issues with online shopping? Is there a correlation between revoking your shopping privileges and the signs of depression you've begun to exhibit?

Scenario #2

You and your best friend, Malik love Nike Air Jordan's. You spent countless hours comparing the various brands, styles, colors and customized sneakers online. Suddenly, you notice that he has begun to appear at school with a new pair of Jordan's for every day of the week. He does not have a job and his family lives in one of the poorer areas of the community. What started as a hobby has become an obsession for him. You notice that Malik has become judgmental, to the point of embarrassing other fiends because they do not have the latest Nikes. He appears to be willing do anything to secure more shoes. During class he spends all his time online looking at new styles. He is failing classes and skipping others. You wonder where he is getting the money for these expensive items. He avoids answering your questions. However, you notice that he is now hanging around a new group of friends who appear to have items beyond what a teenager can afford. He is showing signs of being physically, emotionally, and psychologically addicted to compulsive online buying. Would you approach Malik about your concerns? Would you approach adults close to Malik about this issue? If so, who would you approach first, and why?

Scenario #3

Your sister, 17, just landed her first job. She is a clerk in a high end department store in the center of town. She does not make much money but she does receive a 40 percent discount on purchases with the chain; for online purchases only. She told you that she is paid every Friday but is constantly asking you for money. Nevertheless, you begin to notice that her choice in clothing has changed dramatically. She has applied for, and received, several credit cards which have all reached their limit. She has shown you her credit card bills totaling more than $1,000 per month. Her before tax -part-time income is $750 per month. Each month she increases her debt while falling further behind in making payments on her cards. Soon, collection notices and legal documents begin to appear in the mail demanding payment. Her behavior has shifted from that of a carefree teen to a person exhibiting stress, anxiety, and desperation. As her brother and closest friend, what would you say/do to begin a conversation with her to about her spending habits and how they may contribute to her change in character? How might she address her online shopping addiction?

LEARNING TASKS

20-Minute Activity

- **Standard**:
  - *Standard 3*: Students will demonstrate the ability to access valid information and products and services to enhance health.

  - *Standard 7*: Students will demonstrate the ability to practice health enhancing behaviors and avoid or reduce health risks.

- **Rationale:** This lesson will help students develop an awareness of on-line shopping and the potential for addictive behaviors, as well as, the social, mental and physical effects on personal health.

- **Learning Outcome:** Students will be able to compare and contrast compulsive buying and shopping addiction so they can determine whether they are at-risk of addiction.

- **Description of Activity:** E-malls provide consumers with convenience and almost unlimited choices. However, because there is no brick and mortar store to go to, or salesperson to consult, it is important to follow a few safe and smart online shopping practices. Distribute vocabulary worksheet of key terms. Discuss and define vocabulary with students. Listen or view Youtube video: Top 5 Tips: How to Shop Online.

ONE DAY ASSIGNMENT

- **Standards**:
  - *Standard 5*: Students will demonstrate the ability to use decision making skills to enhance health.

  - *Standard 6:* Students will demonstrate the ability to use goal setting skills to enhance health.
- **Rationale:** This lesson is designed to assist in creating awareness of the potential addicting characteristics of on-line shopping.

- **Learning Outcomes:** Students will be able to describe how online shopping contributes to an increase or decrease in customer satisfaction so that they can develop a heightened awareness of emotions associated with shopping.

- **Description of Activity**: To set lesson context and engage students in the beginning of a lesson, the students are given 3 questions about shopping: When was the last time you went shopping online? What did you buy? Did you like what you bought? The students work in pairs and ask each other and then give their answers. This is done to create their interest into the topic, and asking the students about their shopping experience is an example of personalization.

ONE WEEK ASSIGNMENT

- **Standard**:
  - *Standard 4*: Students will demonstrate the ability to use interpersonal communication skills to enhance health and avoid or reduce health risks.

- **Rationale:** This lesson will aid student comprehension in developing critical skills required to avoid risky behaviors associated with online shopping and impulse purchases.

- **Learning Outcome:** Students will be able to analyze how pathological buying leads to online shopping addiction so they can make more informed purchasing decisions.

- **Description of Activity:** Allow students to go shopping on a typical online site. Half the class will have shopping lists and the other half be partners in an online shop. There are five shops: (1) a computer/tech shop, (2) a gaming store, (3) a shoe retailer, (4) an athletic/sports shop, (5) a jewelry store. Students will be given a strict budget in which to select an item from each store. All students MUST work within their allotted budget. The teacher will determine the budget limits. As shoppers, you are in competition with other shoppers to purchase the most items given the teachers determined budget. As shop owners, you notice that students are spending an extraordinary amount of money in your shop. While this is good for your bottom line; you are concerned that they are addicted to shopping. Shop owners should determine if they should say something. If so, what should they say and to whom? Pre-teach vocabulary that is essential for the understanding in this part of a lesson, we will work on some vocabulary. I chose: 1. On-line browsing; 2. Compulsion; 3. Cue-Reactivity; 4. Craving; 5. Addiction 6. Frustration; 7. Pathological Buying; try to elicit some words from them first, i.e. the term shopaholic and Buyer's remorse.

HELPFUL STRATEGIES

IDENTIFY THE SHOPPING TRIGGER: What activates a person's urge to shop -- boredom, guilt, shame, anger? Keep a written journal or electronic record and document what leads to the shopping.

DISCOVER THE NEED SHOPPING FULFILLS: Excessive shopping doesn't serve a functional purpose -- you probably don't need 15 purses -- it serves a psychological purpose by meeting an unfilled or under-filled need

REPLACE SHOPPING WITH SOMETHING HEALTHIER: The shopaholic needs to find a healthier alternative to filling the need. Brainstorm how you could fill this need in other ways.

CHANGE YOUR ENVIRONMENT: Our environment plays a huge role in our behavior. If you keep a bowl of jellybeans on your desk, it's clear what you will snack on throughout the day.

UNSUBSCRIBE FROM ALL PROMOTIONAL EMAILS: When you get a promotional email, do not click on "display the images." Instead, go straight to the unsubscribe link within the message. Do not mark these emails as "spam" or "trash" – that won't stop them.

BLOCK INTERNET ACCESS TO YOUR FAVORITE SITES: You can restrict your computer from accessing certain sites by blocking them on your preferred browser. You can go through the entire operating system or network router, or you can use web-filtering software to automatically block them for you.

DELETE SHOPPING APPS FROM MOBILE DEVICES: Shopping apps are particularly dangerous for all consumers – not just addicts. Just visit a site like appcrawlr.com and read the reviews on the most popular shopping apps.

RETRAIN YOUR BRAIN: Identify the negative feeling, and look for an alternative solution. Retail therapy is very real. The Huffington Post found that 1 in 3 people shop to deal with stress. Instead of relying on retail therapy to lift your mood, teach your brain to seek out a different experience.

SUPPORTING RESOURCES

Internet May Be Fueling Shopping Addiction: http://newyork.cbslocal.com/2010/
09/24/seen-at-11-internet-may-be-fueling-shopping-addiction/

How Does Peer Pressure Influence Teen Purchasing Choices?: http://motherhood
.modernmom.com/peer-pressure-influence-teen-purchasing-choices-8191.html

Peer Pressure: Its Influence On Teens And Decision-Making: http://headsup.scholastic.com/
students/peer-pressure-its-influence-on-teens-and-decision-making

Peer Pressure: Keeping Up With The Joneses' Teenagers: http://www.forbes.com/
sites/nealegodfrey/2016/07/10/peer-pressure-keeping-up-with-the-joneses-
teenagers/#7b3500a96db7

How To Hype-Proof Your Tween: http://www.goodhousekeeping.com/
life/parenting/tips/a18210/tween-shopping-peer-pressure/

OnGuard Online.gov Video-*Online Shopping Tips:* http://www.onguardonline.gov/
media/video-0082-online-shopping-tips

Shop Online? Many Teens Do It, But More Prefer The Store: http://www.pewresearch.org/
fact-tank/2013/06/10/teens-shop-with-clicks-but-prefer-bricks/

Online sales will reach $523 billion by 2020 in the U.S.: https://www.internetretailer.com/
2016/01/29/online-sales-will-reach-523-billion-2020-us

E-Commerce and Internet Facts for 2016: https://hostingfacts.com/internet-facts-stats-2016/

How Teens Are Shopping Today: http://www.refinery29.com/teen-clothing-shopping-trends.

---

[1] Charles Tran, Survey: Shopping Addiction Statistics. Survey Finds a Significant Number of Americans Who Show Signs of a Problem. (November 13, 2013). https://www.creditdonkey.com/shopping-addiction.html

[2] And the Shopping Addiction Continues (N.D.) http://www.hungrymeetshealthy.com/and-the-online-shopping-addiction-continues-with/

[3] Katherine Todd,. Online Shopping Addiction. E-commerce. (N.D.) http://www.psychalive.org/online-shopping-addiction/

[4] Donald W. Black, The Dark Side of Shopping. A Special to CNN. (April 2, 2013) http://www.cnn.com/2013/04/01/opinion/black-shopping-addiction/

[5] Jesse Fearon, How to Overcome Online Shopping Addiction. (February 27, 2015) http://thebudgetmama.com/2015/02/overcome-online-shopping-addiction.html

[6] Robin Smith and Nicole Lapin, How to Overcome Your Online Shopping Addiction. Dr. Oz Special: CBS Television Network. (January 14, 2016). http://www.doctoroz.com/episode/secrets-high-functioning-alcoholic?video_id=4703722812001

[7] Renee Jacques, Online Shopping Addiction: 15 Signs that You May be Addicted to Online Shopping. The Huffington Post. (January 23, 2014). http://www.huffingtonpost.com/news/online-shopping-addiction/

[8] An Exploratory Study of Indicators of Online Shopping Addiction Article in Journal of Behavioral Addictions (2:12-13). (January 2013). https://www.researchgate.net/publication/296406043_An_exploratory_study_of_the_indicators_of_online_shopping_addiction

[9] (J.D. Wei,). 10 Signs You're Addicted to Online Shopping: Could Your Shopping Habits be a Problem. Psychology Today (November 4, 2015). https://www.psychologytoday.com/blog/urban-survival/201511/10-signs-you-re-addicted-online-shopping

[10] The Web Listers, Confessions of an Online Shopping Addict. (April 19, 2016). http://theweblisters.com/blog/2016/04/19/confessions-online-shopping-addict/

[11] Kara Durst, 15 Ridiculously Stylish Fictional Females to Fuel Your Online Shopping Addiction. (N.D.) http://bust.com/style/15826-10-ridiculously-stylish-fictional-females-to-fuel-your-online-shopping-addiction.html

[12] Amazon's New Installment Loan: Another Way to Feed Your Online Shopping Addiction. (February 16, 2016). http://www.brittandthebenjamins.com/home/amazons-new-installment-loan-another-way-to-feed-yo

[13] Are Teens Giving Up the Mall?http://www.emarketer.com/Article/Teens-Giving-Up-Mall/1013423

[14] Tran, C. (2013). Credit Donkey. (2013). Survey: Shopping Addiction Statistics. https//www.creditdonkey.com/shopping-addiction.html

CHAPTER THIRTEEN

---•---

Inappropriate Online Content

What makes it so difficult to identify inappropriate material?

How do you respond to uncomfortable, offensive,
or potentially harmful experiences or interactions?

How do our experiences shape how we treat and perceive others?

BEHAVIORS AND THEMES

SCALE AND SCOPE: Much has changed in recent years when it comes to teens and their technology use. One issue typically examined related to this use is the types of content teenagers access when online. When considering teenagers' content viewing patterns, it is important to pay attention to their social media usage and preferences, as this is a primary method for teens to view, create, and share online content. Researchers at the Pew Research Center found that teenagers prefer social media because they desire their own space that they can define, create, and shape for themselves.[1] While Facebook remains a dominant force as one of the most used social media platforms among American teens ages 13 to 17, the popularity of Instagram, Snapchat, Twitter, Tumblr, Vine, Pheed, and other applications are quickly trending upwards. It is common for teenagers to use links discovered on social media as launching off points to access online content.

While teenagers spend a considerable amount of time each day consuming online content via social media, they also spend time just surfing the web. This browsing activity, which typically involves the use of Google, Bing, and Yahoo as they are still by far the most used Internet search engines, includes time spent completing school assignments as well as casual surfing based on personal interest. Browsing interests often include reading up on current events, tracking sporting events and athletic teams, perusing online shopping retailers, and checking out recommendations from friends. Because the Internet is a gigantic library that is constantly growing, there is also plenty of inappropriate content that teenagers view while online. In a 2012 survey, researchers at Mcafee, an online security software designer, found that it is common for teenagers to view a variety of inappropriate online content and while parents are not always aware of this behavior and frequently disapprove, a large percentage of teens consistently hide their online behavior from their parents or guardians.[2] This reality is significant because many teens spend great deal of time online with little

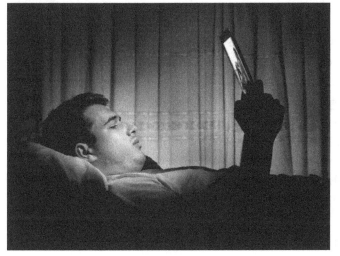

supervision over the types of content they are viewing or sharing or the activities in which they are engaging.

Pornographic and other sexually explicit material, which are readily available, comprise the majority of inappropriate content that is viewed, especially by teenagers. It is not uncommon for teenagers to come across this explicit content, whether they seek it out our not, and exposure to this content, which includes pictures, video, and even live chatting, is starting at increasingly earlier ages. Personal arousal, boredom, curiosity, and learning are all popular reasons why teens view online pornography. Also, while many assume online pornography is a male dominated activity, females now comprise a rapidly growing viewing audience. In addition to sexual explicit content, it is not difficult for teenagers to locate and browse websites that sell illicit materials and glorify violence and other risky and illegal behaviors. For example, some of these sites offer step-by-step text or video instruction on anything from making bombs to learning how to play drinking games to making homemade explosives. There are also many places online where kids can play video games that celebrate and simulate killing and other forms of violence. Some websites even explain and encourage harmful behaviors such as cutting, suicide, drug use, and anorexia. It is also not difficult to identify websites that allow, and even encourage, teenagers to gamble and purchase prescription and other illegal drugs.

PROBLEM DEFINED: The ability and opportunity to always "be connected" to the Internet has fundamentally changed how people function day-to-day, communicate and engage with others and experience the world. One way this impact can directly be seen is through the unlimited access to a constantly expanding repository of digital content that, for the most part, is freely available anytime to anyone with an electronic device. For all the opportunities this access to content provides, there are also many potential hazards and threats. These can include, for example, unmonitored content on social networking platforms, adult-themed web sites, trolling predators, identity thieves, and an excess of violent and sexually explicit content. This reality, that anyone can go online to view, share, and download what ever is desired, demands critically examining the types of digital content teenagers access and view and discussing what makes content inappropriate.

In addition to the never-ending buffet of online digital content, two other dynamics highlight the need for pointed conversations about inappropriate online content. First, when online, teenagers typically have a tremendous amount of autonomy and typically receive little guidance about the potentially harmful elements of Internet content. This independence means teenagers are responsible for making thoughtful, informed decisions about the content they access and view when online. While content filters aimed at protecting privacy and monitoring online activity do exist, they are far from perfect and can create tension between kids and parents. Online activity can be difficult to effectively monitor, and many parents acknowledge that what young people do and view online is often unclear, misunderstood, or unfamiliar to them. Researchers at the Family Online Safety Institute found that parents admit varying levels of knowledge about what their children are looking at when online and ultimately, have a hard time keeping up with what kids are doing online.[3] The reality of this autonomy makes it extremely difficult for adults to educate and protect their kids from the unexpected and unintended things that can happen online.

Second, while some parents report a high level of confidence in the ability to keep up with their child's technology use[4], teenagers tend to be more familiar with newly developing applications and technologies and are proficient in hiding online behavior from adults. A 2012 survey conducted by McAfee revealed 70% of teens consistently hide online surfing behavior from their parents.[5] Some of the ways they do this include clearing browser history, closing/minimizing browser when parents are present, hiding or deleting content they view, lying or omitting details about online activities, and using privacy settings or private browsing modes to make certain content only accessible by friends. In a 2015 survey of 1,000 teens/pre-teens, researchers at Intel Security found 42% of teens use anonymous names or aliases for social media profiles, with one in three reporting they do so because they simply do not want others to know what they are looking at or posting.[6]

SEXUALLY EXPLICIT MATERIAL: Accessibility to sexually explicit material, which includes  pornographic images, video, and chatting, are pervasive elements in teenagers' lives. In 2008, a survey of 1,400 British youth ages 14-17 found that 58% of respondents said they have seen pornography, 71% of sexually active teenagers have viewed pornography, 42% of sexually active teenagers view pornography regularly, and more than a quarter of boys use porn at least once a week (5% of them every day).[7] In a study examining exposure to Internet pornography before the age of 18, researchers found ninety-three percent of boys and 62% of girls were exposed to online pornography during adolescence.[1] Moreover, a survey of children's Internet behavior revealed that "sex" and "porn" are among the most-searched terms.[8] If participants in any of these studies are truly characteristic of teenagers' habits and behaviors, exposure to Internet pornography can be described as a normative experience.

While teens viewing pornographic material might consider it a form of entertainment and exploration, research has demonstrated that it can, for teenagers, serve as a form of sex education and create misguided ideas about healthy relationships, body image, sexual expectations, and even romance, intimacy, and love. Additionally, there is, unfortunately, a large amount of sexually explicit material on the Internet that wrongly portrays violence and abuse against women as both a desired and socially acceptable behavior. Pornography disorients teens during an important developmental phase of their lives when they are learning about sexuality and are most uncertain about both their identity and sexual beliefs. It is also worth noting that a significant relationship also exists among teenagers between repetitive pornography use and feelings of isolation, loneliness and depression; teens exposed to high levels of pornography have shown lower levels of sexual self-esteem.[9] [10] [11] Because sexually explicit material is both prevalent and accessible to pretty much any teenager with an electronic device, it makes sense to foster intentional conversations about this issue to help teens make informed and responsible decisions about Internet use, and to draw attention to the litany of consequences associated with online pornography.

ONLINE VICTIMIZATION: Online victimization is a real issue that must be taken seriously – it happens! In a study conducted by the National Center for Missing and Exploited Children research found that in the past year, more than one-third of teenage Internet users (34%) saw sexual material online they did not want to see, 1 in 7 (13%) reported receiving unwanted sexual solicitations, 34% stated they communicated online with people they did not know, and 11% said they formed close online relationships with people they met online.[12]

The anonymity of the Internet combined with the large amount of autonomy teenagers have when online provides an ideal situation for predators to easily misrepresent themselves, hide their identity, troll for victims and take advantage of unsuspecting individuals. An online relationship that leads to face-to-face interaction can easily turn into an extremely dangerous situation that can lead to physical and psychological harm, sexual abuse, and even death. It is not uncommon for teens to receive unwanted sexual solicitations when online. Internet chat rooms are one of the most common venues for first encounters with sexual predators. These realities demand teenagers take an active role in closely monitoring online activities and pay close attention to unsolicited, unwanted, or inappropriate messages and advances they receive from unknown online users, and report any online activity that makes them uncomfortable or feel like a target.

INAPPROPRIATE ONLINE CONTENT

Directly harms or targets an individual. Teenagers spend a tremendous amount of time online everyday. While this time provides opportunities to learn new things, interact with family and friends, share experiences, and stay abreast of current events, it also opens the door to a number of potentially harmful experiences. These can include adult-focused marketing, being a target for cyberbullies, identity thieves, or sexual predators, and exposure to unsettling, disturbing, embarrassing, and offensive information that is difficult to process or understand.

Facilitates or encourages unlawful, unsafe, or harmful behavior. Teenagers have the ability to view digital content that can lead to dangerous situations. These situations can include, for example, the use of adult-themed dating and networking platforms, websites aimed at promoting violent or pornographic content, and even e-commerce websites targeting teenagers for financial scams, gambling, or the purchase of illicit drugs, products, and materials.

Intentionally misrepresents topics, situations, or ideas with malintentions. Internet content in unending and new material appears on a continuous basis. One of the most challenging tasks for teenagers to do when online is deciding what to believe and how to identify credible sources that do not purposely skew information. Our perspectives and beliefs are highly influenced by the information that we receive and seek out. For this reason, it is critical to be thoughtful consumers of online content. Our understandings need to be shaped by multiple perspectives and sources. It is not difficult to find examples online of individuals and groups spreading ideas that are intentionally harmful, dangerous, and incorrect. It is important to be an informed, critical, and thoughtful consumer of online content.

Specifically targets adult audiences. The web is full of material designed specifically for adult audiences. Unfortunately, much of this information is also accessible to anyone with an electronic device and Internet connection. It is also important to realize that in some cases adult content is purposely marketed to younger audiences as a way to create a consumer base and to spread ideas and influence. While the impact of this material may not cause immediate harm, the consequences can come later and manifest themselves in many different and unexpected ways.

KEY CONCEPTS

- **Inappropriate Online Content**: Any digital content encountered online that negatively impacts one's social, emotional, psychological, and/or physical safety or wellness.

- **Cyber Safety:** The safe, responsible, and thoughtful use of electronic communication technologies.

- **Cyber Accountability:** The ability to act in a safe and responsible manner when online to minimize potential threats and situations that could negatively impact health and wellness.

- **Victimization:** An individual threatened, harmed, injured, or killed as a result of an act by another person.

REAL-WORLD SITUATIONS

"Sextortion" is an Online Epidemic Against Children

—Source: By Marisol Bello, USA Today, July 2nd, 2014[13]

Why can it be so easy to trust people that are encountered online?

When encountering inappropriate advances online, what actions need to be taken to protect yourself?

Unemployed high school dropout Tremain Hutchinson spent a lot of time talking to young girls on Tagged.com, a teen chat site. Sometimes he was "Mario," sometimes "Quan" or "Money," but Hutchinson, 28, always pretended to be a cute 16-year-old Georgia boy. He used a photo of a younger cousin in the profiles. He was interested in girls 11 to 17. Race or economic background didn't matter. His opening line was always the same: " What's up? You be my freak once a month. I will spoil you, buy you a cell phone, keep your bill paid. Hair, nails done. Buy you shoes, clothes, whatever you want." Dozens of girls responded. One of them was a 15-year-old girl in the Atlanta area who has regretted it ever since, her father says. Hutchinson enticed the girl to send naked photos. Then he turned vicious. For weeks, he pressed her for more images. He threatened to post her nude photos online. He threatened to kill her and her parents and blow up her house. Every time she begged him to leave her alone, he told her he would if she did one more thing. Then came the day he ordered her to do something so unthinkable, it led federal investigators to his door.

A CRIME OF THE DIGITAL AGE

It's called "Sextortion," a crime exclusive to the digital age. Predators pretend to be teens on social media and gaming sites. They befriend young people, gain their trust and entice them to send lewd photos of themselves. Then they use the photos to extort more and more illicit images. The number of complaints of online enticement of children is climbing. The Internet Crimes Against Children Task Force, which helps state and local law enforcement agencies fight online child pornography, reports that the number of complaints to its 61 offices nationwide has grown from 5,300 in 2010 to 7,000 in 2013.

The crime has serious, even deadly, ramifications for children, say the parents of some who were victims. Canadian Amanda Todd was one of the earliest and ultimately most prominent victims. When she was 13, in 2010, the Vancouver-area girl used video chats to meet other teens. She became friends with someone who talked her into showing her breasts during a webcam chat. She did. It was a fleeting moment, something she did on impulse. She didn't know he had taken a photo. Shortly after, the person messaged her via Facebook and said if she didn't show him more, he'd post her photo for others to see. He messaged her several times. When she didn't do it, the photo went to all her Facebook friends. She was ridiculed and so embarrassed that she changed schools. She became anxious and depressed. She was teased by schoolmates and harassed online.

In a cry for help, Amanda told her story in a poignant nine-minute video in September 2012. "I have nobody," she said on the video. "I need someone." A month later, she committed suicide. The video has gone viral with more than 30 million views. Six months ago, Dutch police arrested Aydin Coban, 35, and accused him of extorting Amanda and dozens of other girls, as well as adult men, in Canada, the United States, Britain and the Netherlands. "In the back of my mind, I never thought of a predator," says her mother, Carol Todd. "I thought the person who wanted the pictures was an older teen. I was never thinking it was a 35-year-old man on the other end." I've learned about the whole dark world that's out there on the Internet."

She tells her daughter's story as a cautionary tale, urging parents to talk often with their teens about how they lead their virtual lives. The increase in sextortion cases has led authorities to go beyond law enforcement to also educate parents and teens about online safety. Homeland Security Investigations, the investigative arm of Immigration and Customs Enforcement, has started a program called iGuardian in which agents visit elementary, middle and high schools. They use real-life examples to warn kids never to send nude photos of themselves electronically or share identifying information such as their school or address. "Predators used to stalk playgrounds. This is the new playground," says Brock Nicholson, HSI special agent in charge in Atlanta. "I would argue that this is an epidemic and people have no idea." What sets this crime apart is that one suspect can victimize hundreds of children anywhere in the world, says Patrick Redling, head of the child exploitation unit at HSI's Cyber Crimes Center.

VICTIMS SUFFER EMOTIONALLY

Tremain Hutchinson was arrested in April 2012 for what a federal judge called at his sentencing "a six-month reign of terror" online against young girls. From his mother's apartment in suburban Atlanta, Hutchinson was targeting dozens of victims, most in Georgia, says HSI special agent Tony Scott, who investigated the case in the spring of 2012. After his arrest, Scott says, Hutchinson admitted to raping four girls, several of whom he met on online while pretending to be a teenage boy. The youngest rape victim was 11. Authorities had no idea until the family of the 15-year-old girl came forward.

Usa Today does not name victims of sexual abuse. To protect the identity of the victim, her name and her father's name are being withheld. The girl met someone who told her he was 15 on Tagged.com, her father says. They talked for a week or so before the boy asked for a partially nude photo. The girl sent it. When Hutchinson demanded more explicit photos, she balked, her father says. Hutchinson threatened to have her beaten up in school and said vaguely at one point, "You don't want to end up like the other girl" who didn't give in to his demands.

Then he ordered her to do the unthinkable: Perform oral sex on her 13-year-old brother and send a photo. She panicked and told her brother. They staged a photo, pretending to do what he ordered, her father says, and sent it to Hutchinson. "She felt that if she sent the picture, he would leave her alone," her father says. "It's easy to ask why she didn't go to her parents, but you aren't in that situation. You are not in the mind of a 15-year-old girl. "She was genuinely afraid," he says. "She thought she could handle it, and it got out of control."

Amy Allen, a forensics interview specialist at Homeland Security Investigations who talks with victims, says preteens and teenagers are targets of predators because they are at an age where they experiment sexually and take risks, but their brains are still developing and they can make bad decisions. The girl's pretense didn't work. Hutchinson became angry that the photo was not graphic enough, the girl's father says, and sent the photo back. She wasn't using her own phone, because it couldn't send pictures — and he knew it. The photo went to her aunt, who ran to the girl's mother. Thinking her daughter was molesting her son, the mother called the police. The truth soon came out. Hutchinson was charged with extorting 16 child victims, including the four rape victims and three sets of siblings that he ordered to engage in sexual activities. "The guy was a terrorist," Scott says. "He terrorized these children. That's the only term for this."

Hutchinson pleaded guilty in December to several charges and was sentenced to life in prison for what the judge called "a reign of terror. "The crime has taken an emotional toll, the girl's father says. His son, who never had direct contact with Hutchinson, was angry but has been able to move on. His daughter, though, talked about suicide, began cutting herself and went into therapy. Her grades plummeted. Her relationship with her parents and brother, once close, fractured. She has gone to live with relatives in another state. "She just wanted to get away," her father says. At Hutchinson's sentencing in December, her father and parents of the other victims told heartbreaking tales of suicidal girls who barely went out, no longer had friends and in one case refused to bathe, thinking that would make her less attractive to men. The father of the 15-year-old spoke for all of them when he told the defendant, "You have left a permanent scar on my family."

Pornography "Desensitizing Young People"
—Source: By Katherine Sellgren, BBC, June 15, 2016[14]

Why are websites showcasing violent and sexually explicit content so popular?

What are potential consequences associated with viewing violent and sexually explicit content online?

Most children are exposed to online pornography by their early teenage years, a study warns. About 53% of 11- to 16-year-olds have seen explicit material online, nearly all of whom (94%) had seen it by 14, the Middlesex University study says. The research, commissioned by the NSPCC and the children's commissioner for England, said many teenagers were at risk of becoming desensitized to porn. The government said keeping children safe online was a key priority.

NAKED IMAGES

The researchers questioned 1,001 children aged 11 to 16 and found 65% of 15- to 16-year-olds reported seeing pornography, as did 28% of 11- to 12-year-olds. They also discovered that it was more likely for the youngsters to find material accidentally (28%), for example via a pop-up advertisement, than to specifically seek it out (19%). More than three-quarters of the children surveyed - 87% of the boys and 77% of the girls - felt pornography failed to help them understand consent, but most of the boys (53%) and 39% of girls saw it as a realistic depiction of sex. Some of the children's approach to sex was also informed by pornographic scenes, with more than a third (39%) of the 13- to 14-year-olds and a fifth of the 11- to 12-year-olds boys saying they wanted to copy the behavior they had seen.

The report also found:
- More boys than girls had viewed online pornography through choice

- 135 (14%) of the young people who responded had taken naked and/or semi-naked images of themselves, and just over half of these (7% overall) had shared these images

- Of those children who reported seeing online pornography, the greatest proportion (38%) had first seen it on a portable laptop, 33% through a mobile phone and just under a quarter (24%) on a desktop computer

- Nearly 60% of the children and young people surveyed who had seen online pornography reported seeing it for the first time at home, followed by 29% who reported doing so at a friend's house

The report is published a week after expert witnesses told the Women and Equalities Committee that girls were wearing shorts under their school skirts to avoid sexual harassment and warned that online pornography was giving children unacceptable messages about sex and intimacy.

YOUNG PEOPLE'S CONCERNS

One 11-year-old girl told researchers: "I didn't like it because it came on by accident and I don't want my parents to find out and the man looked like he was hurting her. He was holding her down and she was screaming and swearing." A 13-year-old boy said. "One of my friends has started treating women like he sees on the videos - not major - just a slap here or there. It can make a boy not look for love, just look for sex, and it can pressure us girls to act and look and behave in a certain way before we might be ready for it," said one 13-year-old girl. Another 13-year-old girl said, "A few of my friends have used it for guidance about sex and are getting the wrong image of relationships." Dr. Elena Martellozzo, who co-led the research, said. "Although many children did not report seeing online pornography, it is worrying that some children came across it accidentally and could be sent it without seeking it. If boys believe that online pornography provides a realistic view of sexual relationships, then this may lead to inappropriate expectations of girls and women. Girls too may feel pressured to live up to these unrealistic, and perhaps non-consensual, interpretations of sex. There is a huge task ahead for parents, teachers and policymakers. We found that children and young people need safe spaces where they can freely discuss the full range of issues related to sex, relationships and the accessibility of online porn in the digital age.

Anne Longfield, Children's Commissioner for England, said it was worrying that many children were exposed to pornography. "Only now are we beginning to understand its impact on 'smartphone kids' - the first generation to have been raised with technology that's taken the Internet from the front room, where parents can monitor use, to their bedrooms or the playground, where they can't," she said. "We know from the research that very many children are shocked, confused or disgusted by what they see, and it is our duty to help them to question, challenge and make sense of it."

NSPCC chief executive Peter Wanless said: "A generation of children are in danger of being stripped of their childhoods at a young age by stumbling across extreme and violent porn online.

"Industry and government need to take more responsibility to ensure that young people are protected. "Some companies have taken the initiative when it comes to online safety, and we will continue to put pressure on those that have not yet done so. "Age-appropriate sex and relationship education in schools, dealing with issues such as online pornography and children sending indecent images, are crucial." A Department for Culture, Media and Sport spokeswoman said: "Keeping children safe online is one of government's key priorities. "Just as we do offline, we want to make sure children are prevented from accessing pornographic content online, which should only be viewed by adults. "In the forthcoming Digital Economy Bill, we will bring in legislation that will require companies providing pornographic material online to make sure they have a robust age-verification system in place, so that those accessing their websites are over 18."

Survey: 70% of Teens Hide Online Behavior from Parents
—Source: By John D. Sutter, CNN, June 25th, 2012[15]

Why is it so common for teenagers to hide online behavior and activities?

What are the potential dangers with hiding online behavior and activities?

Here's a real shocker: Teens are better than their parents at using the Internet, and are likely to hide some of their online behaviors from them. That news comes from a 2,017-person survey funded by the online security software maker McAfee, which is pushing a product that helps parents monitor their kids online.

Seventy percent of teens "hide their online behavior" from parents, according to the report, which was released Monday. That's up from 45% in 2010, the group says.

These hidden behaviors include some things you might expect -- such as accessing violent (43%) or pornographic (32%) content online -- but also a few surprises. Fifteen percent of teens have hacked into social networks; 9% have hacked into e-mail accounts; 12% have met face to face with a person he or she met on the Internet; and 16% of teens surveyed said they had used their phones to cheat on tests at school. McAfee said parents are often unaware of these behaviors.

"Parents, you must stay in-the-know," McAfee's Robert Siciliano wrote in a blog post. "Since your teens have grown up in an online world, they may be more online savvy than their parents, but you can't give up. You must challenge yourselves to become familiar with the complexities of the teen online universe and stay educated on the various devices your teens are using to go online."

"As a parent of two young girls, I proactively participate in their online activities and talk to them about the 'rules of the road' for the Internet. I'm hoping that this report opens the eyes of parents to become more involved and also consider using technology such as McAfee Safe Eyes to protect their kids online. McAfee Safe Eyes, like similar products from other security companies, lets parents spy on their kids' online behaviors and block certain websites. According to an online description of the product, Safe Eyes lets parents log the social-media posts and instant message conversations of their children.

Nearly half of parents install some sort of online controls, the survey said. Forty-four percent know their teens' passwords, and one in 10 uses a location-monitoring device. Not everyone advocates that approach to teen online security, however."We don't think it's a good idea for parents to spy on their kids surreptitiously, because eventually they're going to find something they have to confront them about, and it's going to destroy the other lines of communication," Justin Patchin, a criminal justice professor and co-director of the Cyberbullying Research Center, told CNN in 2010.

In the report, McAfee also encourages parents to be upfront with their children if they decide to monitor their behaviors. "Half of teens say they would think twice about their online activities if they knew parents were watching," the report said.

The McAfee-funded report, which was carried out by the research company TRU, surveyed 1,013 parents and 1,004 teens between the ages of 13 and 17. The interviews were conducted online in May.

The report, titled "The digital divide: How the online behavior of teens is getting past parents", also includes a list of the "top 10 ways teens are fooling their parents."

Here's the list, with the percentage of teens who said they engaged in these behaviors, according to the survey results:

1. Clear browser history (53%)

2. Close/minimize browser when parent walk in (46%)

3. Hide or delete IMs or videos (34%)

4. Lie or omit details about online activities (23%)

5. Use a computer your parents don't check (23%)

6. Use an Internet-enabled mobile device (21%)

7. Use privacy settings to make certain content viewable only by friends (20%)

8. Use private browsing modes (20%)

9. Create private e-mail address unknown to parents (15%)

10. Create duplicate/fake social network profiles (9%)

LEARNING SCENARIOS

Scenario #1

Over the past few weeks, one of your closest friends has been regularly hanging out in an online chat room exchanging funny memes, videos, and web links with someone named, 'looking4fun'. Your friend has told you about a number of these interactions and has even told you that 'looking4fun' is really easy to chat with, they get along well, and have engaged in a number of helpful chats about life and the challenges of being a teenager. Your friend says 'looking4fun' likes the same music, watches the same movies and TV shows, and has really similar interests. Your friend also says 'looking4fun' understands him/her more than most other people in their life, including family members. Last night, your friend was online and 'looking4fun' asked for a phone number, address, and other personal information. Your friend also told you that 'looking4fun' wants to set-up a time to meet so they can get to know each other better. What concerns do you have about this situation? What actions can you take? What types of advice and warnings would you give to your friend? If your friend does not listen, what should you do?

Scenario #2

As part of a class project you are assigned by your teacher to work in a group with a few classmates. While none of the group members are close friends, you have been in school with them your entire life and know them all fairly well. The project requires the use of the Internet to conduct research on a topic that the group selects. While doing research one day in the school library one of your group members shows you a few pornographic images he recently downloaded. What has made this situation even worse is this individual emailed you and the other members of the group a few pornographic pictures and links to a few pornographic websites. Initially, you are concerned about telling anyone because you are worried about the potential consequences. What actions can you take? How do you respond to group members?

Scenario #3

In the past few months, there have been a number of after school fights between a few different groups of students. These altercations have led to multiple arrests and injuries that have required hospital visits. On a few of these occasions, a number of your classmates recorded the fights with their smartphones. One of these videos, which is both graphic and violent, has been posted online to one of your close friends social networking profiles. Additionally, this friend shared the video with others and texted out a web link for the video to a large number of the kids in school. As of today, the video has over 6500 views and 50+comments, some of which are disturbing and highly concerning. What concerns you about this situation? What is the motivation behind sharing and watching this video? Why is it so easy for us to watch, share, and be entertained by violent content?

HELPFUL STRATEGIES

1. *ENGAGE IN CONVERSATION:* Navigating the online world is a complex process and many times, there are just not always clear answers. It is useful to engage in conversation with family members, friends, and even teachers about both positive and negative online experiences.

2. *CYBER-ACCOUNTABILITY:* Take responsibility for online behavior. Be aware that online behavior will leave a digital trail and can have consequences, some of which might be difficult to reverse. It is imperative to think carefully about both the people met online and the types of content that is viewed.

3. *USE AN INTERNET FILTER:* While Internet filters are by no means perfect, they can help enhance online experiences, protect identify, and keep violent, offensive, and graphic material out of sight. Typically, these filters can be modified by users and can be easily updated as preferences and needs change.

4. *BE RESPONSIBLE WITH PERSONAL INFORMATION:* Never share personal information with anyone. This includes passwords, phone number and address, or location on applications such as Snapchat or Instagram.

5. *REPORT CONCERNING MATERIAL:* If you come across online material that is inappropriate and may be harmful, report the content immediately to an adult or website administrator. If it is believed that the content may result in immediate danger to anyone, inform a trusted adult and contact the local police department.

LEARNING TASKS

20-Minute Activity:

- **Standard:**
  - *Standard 1:* Students will comprehend concepts related to health promotion and disease prevention to enhance health.

  - *Standard 5:* Students will demonstrate the ability to use decision-making skills to enhance health.

- **Rationale:** Many teenagers access and view online content out of view of adult supervision. Learning how to self-regulate and make distinctions between inappropriate and appropriate content when online is an important life skill that has to be taught, practiced, and developed over time. Ultimately, when teenagers come across online content they identify as inappropriate, we want them to understand why they should close their browser, surf elsewhere, and if necessary, communicate this information to a trusted adult.

- **Learning Outcomes:** Students will be able to make distinctions between inappropriate and appropriate digital content so they can make more informed decisions about the content they view when online.

- **Description of Activity:** Teacher will facilitate class discussion focusing on the differences between inappropriate and appropriate online content. Students can start in small groups before sharing ideas in a large group. Additionally, examples of online content can be shared as a way to start discussion, challenge students, or to play devil's advocate.

- **Supporting Resources:**
  o Handbook for Facilitating Difficult Conversations in the Classroom, Queens College – CUNY, http://www.qc.cuny.edu/Academics/Centers/Democratic

  o Teaching Your Students How to Have a Conversation, Edutopia, http://www.edutopia.org/blog/teaching-your-students-conversation-allen-mendler

ONE-DAY ACTIVITY

Develop a set of descriptive criteria to evaluate and better understand what can be considered inappropriate and appropriate online content.

- **Standard:**
  o *Standard 4:* Students will demonstrate the ability to use interpersonal communication skills to enhance health and avoid or reduce health risks.

  o *Standard 8:* Students will demonstrate the ability to advocate for personal, family, and community health.

- **Rationale:** To support more informed online decisions, it is useful to help teens develop a concrete framework for evaluating online content to establish whether it should be considered inappropriate or appropriate. Having a set of criteria to utilize when online will support teenagers in making more informed decisions.

- **Learning Outcome:** Students will work in groups to develop a set of descriptive criteria that can be used to critically evaluate online content so they can make informed distinctions between inappropriate and appropriate online content.

- **Description of Activity:** Teachers will lead students in a process of identifying the types of criteria can be utilized to decide whether online content should be considered appropriate and inappropriate. In addition to developing a set of criteria, groups will need to identify different examples of these criteria and provide clear rational for their decision-making. Each group will share this information with class. As a final task, the class should work to synthesize the variety if criteria to develop a class set that can shared with others.

- **Supporting Resources:**
  o Evaluating Internet Resources, Georgetown University Library, http://www.library.georgetown.edu/tutorials/research-guides/evaluating-internet-content

  o Evaluating Web Sources, Harvard University, http://isites.harvard.edu/icb/icb.do?keyword=k70847&tabgroupid=icb.tabgroup1077866

ONE-WEEK ACTIVITY
- **Standard:**
  o *Standard 2:* Students will analyze the influence of family, peers, culture, media, technology, and other factors on health behaviors.

  o *Standard 3:* Students will demonstrate the ability to access valid information and products and services to enhance health.

- **Rationale:** It can be hard to promote change if there is not a clear understanding about the extent or dynamics shaping problems. This activity will help students create awareness about the issues and dangers related to inappropriate online content. These artifacts, which can be posted around the school and even disseminated to local media, can help students foster meaningful conversations about the challenges of growing up in a digital world that facilitates opportunities for constant and consistent access to inappropriate online content.

- **Learning Outcome:** Students will develop artifacts that can be used in a media campaign so they can inform others about the existence and dangers and consequences of inappropriate online content.

- **Description of Activity:** Students will work in "marketing" teams to develop materials that can be used to inform others about the issues related to inappropriate online content. These materials can include paper-based advertisements, video commercials, social media, webinars, blogs, graphic art, etc. Students are encouraged to be as creative as possible and to consider how they might reach the broadest audience. Ultimately, these materials can be displayed within the school and/or places within the community. It will be important for teachers and students to work with school administrators and other relevant school staff to identify a plan for how these materials might be integrated within the school.

- **Supporting Resources:**
  - ○ Strategies for developing a health promotion campaign, The American International Heath Alliance, http://www.aiha.com/wp-content/uploads/2015/07/24-Strategies-for-Developing-a-Health-Promotion-Campaign.pdf

  - ○ Best practices for a healthcare social media campaign, Modern Healthcare, http://www.modernhealthcare.com/article/20140923/INFO/309239990

  - ○ 5 tips for running your best social media campaign ever, Entrepreneur, https://www.entrepreneur.com/article/272231

ADDITIONAL RESOURCES

*American Girls: Social Media and the Secret Lives of Teenagers, Nancy Jo Sales*It's Complicated: The Social Lives of Networked Teens, Danah Boyd

Teaching for Critical Thinking: Tools and Techniques to Help Students Question Their Assumptions, Steven D. Brookfield

National Criminal Justice Reference Service, Internet Safety - Online Safety for Youthhttps://www.ncjrs.gov/internetsafety/children.html

Teens & Technology, PEW Research Center, http://www.pewresearch.org/topics/teens-and-technology/

---

[1] Wexler, E., & Taylor, C. (2014, February 18). What Are Teens Doing Online? Retrieved from http://www.pbs.org/wgbh/frontline/article/what-are-teens-doing-online/

[2] Sutter, J. D. (2012, June 25). Survey: 70% of teens hide online behavior from parents. Retrieved from http://www.cnn.com/2012/06/25/tech/web/mcafee-teen-online-survey/index.html

[3] Family Online Safety Intitute. (2015, November 17). Parents, Privacy and Technology Use. Retrieved from https://www.fosi.org/policy-research/parents-privacy-technology-use/

[4] Family Online Safety Intitute. (2015, November 17). Parents, Privacy and Technology Use. Retrieved from https://www.fosi.org/policy-research/parents-privacy-technology-use/

[5] Sutter, J. D. (2012, June 25). Survey: 70% of teens hide online behavior from parents. Retrieved from http://www.cnn.com/2012/06/25/tech/web/mcafee-teen-online-survey/index.html

[6] Family Online Safety Institute. (2015, June). The Realities of Cyber Parenting: What Pre-teens and Teens Are Up To Online. Retrieved from https://www.fosi.org/policy-research/realities-cyber-parenting/

[7] CovenantEyes. (2013). Pornography Statistics: 250+ Facts, Quotes, and Statistics About Pornography. Retrieved from http://blog.clinicalcareconsultants.com/wpcontent/uploads/2013/12/porn_stats_2013_covenant_eyes.pdf

[8] Sabina, C., Wolak, J., & Finkelhor, D. (2008). The nature and dynamics of Internet pornography exposure for youth. *CyberPsychology & Behavior*, *11*(6), 691-693.

[9] Goldsmith, B. (2009, August 12). Children use Web to watch videos, look up "sex". Retrieved from http://www.reuters.com/article/us-internet-children-tech-idUSTRE57B0P520090812

[10] Ybarra, M. L., & Mitchell, K. J. (2005). Exposure to Internet pornography among children and adolescents: A national survey. *Cyberpsychology & behavior*, *8*(5), 473-486.

[11] Yoder, V. C., Virden III, T. B., & Amin, K. (2005). Internet pornography and loneliness: An association? *Sexual addiction & compulsivity*, *12*(1), 19-44.

[12] Morrison, T. G., Ellis, S. R., Morrison, M. A., Bearden, A., & Harriman, R. L. (2007). Exposure to sexually explicit material and variations in body esteem, genital attitudes, and sexual esteem among a sample of Canadian men. *The Journal of Men's Studies*, *14*(2), 209-222.

[13] Finkelhor, D., Mitchell, K., Wolak, J. (2006) Online Victimization of Youth: Five Years Later. Retrieved from http://www.unh.edu/ccrc/pdf/CV138.pdf

[14] Bello, M. (2014, July 02). 'Sextortion' is an online 'epidemic' against children. Retrieved from http://www.usatoday.com/story/news/nation/2014/07/01/sextortion-teens-online/11580633/

[15] Sellgren, K. (2016, June 15). Pornography 'desensitizing young people' Retrieved from http://www.bbc.com/news/education-36527681

[16] Sutter, J. D. (2012, June 25). Survey: 70% of teens hide online behavior from parents. Retrieved from http://www.cnn.com/2012/06/25/tech/web/mcafee-teen-online-survey/index.html

GLOSSARY

———————●———————

And Key Concepts

Addiction: A state of physical or psychological dependence on a behavior or substance, particularly compulsive dependence, to the extent that this dependence leads to harm to oneself and/or those around them.

Bias: Prejudice in favor of or against one thing, person, or group compared with another, usually in a way considered to be unfair.

Binging: A period of habitual, excessive, and often uncontrolled indulgence.

Bullying: An unwanted, aggressive behavior that involves a real or perceived power and control imbalance, unwanted, negative actions, and a pattern of behavior that is repeated over time.

Bystander: A person who witnesses or has knowledge of an event, action, or correspondence but does not directly participate and does not engage in direct action to stop or prevent a bully's harmful actions and behaviors.

Consent: Giving permission to another individual so that individual can do something or see something personal.

Craving: An intense desire for some particular thing.

Cue-Reactivity: Excitement from online ads that attempt to capitalize on emotional purchasing.

Cyber Accountability: The ability to act in a safe and responsible manner when online to minimize potential threats and situations that could negatively impacts health and wellness.

Cyber Safety: The safe, responsible, and thoughtful use of electronic communication technologies.

Data Mining: The practice of examining large databases in order to generate new information.

Data Science: A field of study dedicated to the systems that retrieve information from data through a number of different sources, whether structured or unstructured. This data is an extension of other endeavors like statistics, data mining and predictive analysis. The discovery of knowledge is central to this interdisciplinary field.

Distracted Driving: Engaging in the act of driving while simultaneously engaging in other activities.

Doxxing: Having your personal information shared on the Internet as a way of coercing you to refrain from stating your opinion or as retaliation for stating your opinion. Doxxing is most often used against specific groups based on sexual orientation, disability, gender, race, religion, or ethnic origin.

e-Commerce: Commercial transactions conducted electronically on the Internet.

Escapism: Actions and behaviors that seek to distract, avoid, and provide relief from the unpleasant realities of daily life, especially through entertainment, recreation, or fantasy.

External Validation: A psychological need to focus on what others think about you, seeking approval, and being liked. This need is frequently made worse by feelings of unworthiness and inadequacy.

Fear of Missing Out: A pervasive feeling of being left out of something fun any time you are not able to access social media or access others via an electronic device.

Fight, Flight, or Freeze Response: This physical response is triggered in response to a perceived threat, real or imagined. These responses, triggered in 1/20th of a second, activate the nervous system to release a flood of neurotransmitters to help your body survive imminent danger.

Fixation: An obsessive interest in or feeling about someone or something.

Gamification: Applying game playing mechanisms and principles (competition, points, achievements) to areas of life outside of video games to help individuals modify negative habits and reward desirable behaviors.

Harassment: Applying aggressive pressure or intimidation to another individual.

Hate Speech: Any form of speech (oral or written) that attacks a person or group on the basis of characteristic such as sexual orientation, disability, gender, race, religion, or ethnic origin.

Imposter Syndrome: A situation where individuals feel like a fake or fraud because they have tricked or deceived others about their abilities or personality.

Impression Management: A conscious or subconscious attempt to influence people's perception of yourself, often by strategically sharing (or withholding) information about their lives.

Impulse Control Disorder: A psychiatric disorder characterized by an inability to resist a temptation, urge or impulse that may harm oneself or others.

Inappropriate Online Content: Any digital content encountered online that negatively impacts one's social, emotional, psychological, and/or physical safety or wellness.

Instant & Delayed Gratification: Instant gratification is the desire to experience pleasure or fulfillment without delay. Delayed gratification is the ability to use patience to place long-term goals ahead of short-term satisfaction.

Life Hacking: Any trick, shortcut, skill, or novelty method that increases productivity and efficiency, in all walks of life.

Misinformation: Incorrect information, spread intentionally (without realizing it is untrue) or unintentionally.

Multi-tasking: The belief that humans can complete two things at the same time.

Narcissism: A psychological problem characterized by excessive interest in oneself, one's perceived abilities, and one's need for admiration—often at the expense of focusing on the needs and feelings of others.

Need for Inclusion: One's need for being included is based on the desire to belong to a group, a desire to be part of something greater than one's self. The need be included as part of the group—for social connection –has been found by researchers to be particularly powerful during adolescence.

Obsessive-Compulsive Behavior: Obsessive-compulsive behaviors are characterized by unreasonable thoughts and fears (obsessions) that lead to repetitive behaviors (compulsions). Attempting to ignore or stop these behaviors frequently results in feelings of extreme anxiety, worry, and depression.

Oniomania (Compulsive Buying Disorder): An abnormal impulse to buy things, or a condition characterized by such impulses. Includes compulsive buying, pathological buying, and buying addiction.

Passive Consumption: Behaviors revolving around watching, listening, and reading rather than engagement in interactive activities like online gaming, social networking, or developing content through coding or creating digital art or music.

Pathological Buying: Feeling preoccupied with shopping and feeling powerless to control the need to buy.

Profit Motive: The motivation of firms that operate so as to maximize their profits. Mainstream microeconomic theory posits that the ultimate goal of a business is to make money. Stated differently, the reason for a business's existence is to turn a profit.

Privacy: The state or condition of being free from being observed or disturbed by other people.

Reliability: An attribute of any system that consistently produces the same results, preferably meeting or exceeding its specifications.

Secondary Behaviors: Any activity or task a driver engages in while also driving a car.

Self-Regulation of Emotion: The ability to respond to the minute-to-minute demands of managing one's emotional responses in a manner that is socially tolerable and viewed as appropriate for the situation.

Sexting: The sending and receiving of sexually provocative messages and/or photographs via electronic devices.

Sextortion: The combination of sex and extortion. This is a form of sexual exploitation that includes using force to obtain money or sexual favors from someone in exchange for keeping their sexting material private.

Shopper's High: A rush shoppers experience upon making impulse purchases that is quickly abated shortly after the purchase is made.

Social Learning Theory: The premise that individuals learn by observing the behavior and actions of others.

Trustworthiness: Worthy of confidence; specifically: being or deriving from a source worthy of belief or consideration for evidentiary purposes.

Upstander: Actively engaging in behavior to combat hate speech or other inappropriate activity. Courageous, powerful individuals who take direct action that prevents or reduces the bullying they observe. An upstander stands up for a victim when they are being bullied.

Victimization: The singling out of an individual or group for subjection to harassment, violence, sexual solicitation and approaches; or unwanted exposure to sexual material.

CPSIA information can be obtained
at www.ICGtesting.com
Printed in the USA
BVHW07s0931140818
524202BV00001B/2/P

9 781640 073579